Sin, the Savior, and Salvation

Robert P. Lightner, Th.D.

Sin

THE

Savior

AND

Salvation

The Theology
of Everlasting Life

Robert P. Lightner, Th.D.

THOMAS NELSON PUBLISHERS
Nashville

SIN, THE SAVIOR, AND SALVATION

Copyright © 1991 by Robert P. Lightner

Published in Nashville, Tennessee, by Thomas Nelson, Inc., and distributed in Canada by Lawson Falle, Ltd., Cambridge, Ontario.

Library of Congress Cataloging-in-Publication Data

Lightner, Robert Paul.
  Sin, the Savior, and salvation : the theology of everlasting life
/ Robert P. Lightner.
    p.   cm.
  Includes bibliographical references.
  ISBN 0-8407-7498-2
  1. Salvation.   2. Sin.   3. Jesus Christ—Person and offices.
4. Immortality.   I. Title.
BT751.2.L47   1991
236'.22—dc20   91-7419
                                                            CIP

Printed in the United States of America
1 2 3 4 5 6 7 — 96 95 94 93 92 91

To Pearl
the one of great price
in my life

CONTENTS

SECTION III—SALVATION

ACKNOWLEDGMENTS

Portions of this book were adapted from the following by the author: *Foundations of Faith*, 1969; *The Death Christ Died*, 1983; *Heaven For Those Who Can't Believe*, 1981, Regular Baptist Press, Schaumburg, Illinois; *Prophecy in the Ring*, 1976, Accent Books, Denver, Colorado; *Evangelical Theology: A Survey and Review*, 1986, Baker Book House, Grand Rapids; "The Savior's Sufferings in Life," *Bibliotheca Sacra*, January-March, 1970. All used by permission from the publishers.

PREFACE

This book explains how to evaluate one's beliefs in the light of important theological considerations. The three doctrines studied in this volume, sin, the Savior, and salvation, belong together. Whatever one thinks about any one of these will affect what he thinks about the other two.

My emphasis is on salvation. Sin and the Savior are studied as they affect and relate to salvation. The reader will not find, therefore, a full orbed presentation of these two doctrines but only what is crucial to salvation.

I am convinced that one of the primary reasons for so much confusion among evangelicals today over major aspects of the biblical teaching of salvation stems from a failure to see the relation of it to sin and the Savior. Just as in all other areas of theology, so here—these doctrines must not be seen in isolation from each other. They are intricately related in Scripture and therefore must be in our thinking also.

I have explained the biblical teaching and the major problems and areas of difference among evangelicals. The book gives practical help in decision making concerning today's burning issues surrounding these three doctrines. Your understanding of sin, the Savior, and salvation affects the way you live your life for Jesus.

Sin, the Savior, and Salvation

Robert P. Lightner, Th.D.

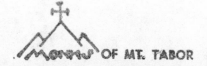

MONKS OF MT. TABOR

SECTION I

Sin

1

DEFINING SIN

Whatever happened to sin? We seldom hear it mentioned anymore. Even in many Christian circles the word is about as common today as is *haystack* among farmers or *Model T* among car manufacturers.

This scarcity prompted American psychiatrist Karl Menninger to write his book *Whatever Became of Sin*. It's a good question and a good book too. Both Menninger and I agree that sin dropped from our common vocabulary at the same time that society became permeated with the philosophy of secular humanism.[1] Secular humanism makes man himself the measure of all things.[2] This contradicts the biblical teaching that man is measured against *God's* standards. From the perspective of the Bible our culture has replaced the relationship between God and man with man's love for himself.

In this short chapter we define sin from a biblically defensible perspective. Later in this study we will explore the question, "Where did sin come from?" along with the age-old question, "Why evil?"

WHAT IS SIN?

There are eight principle words used for sin in the Greek New Testament and twelve in the Hebrew Old Testament. It is from the meanings of these that we arrive at our definition of sin. Taken together, these terms stress the dynamic nature of sin. Sin is not only a failure to measure up to the divine standard, sin is primarily disobedience to God. It has a dynamic side. Sin is far more than missing the right mark. It is hitting the wrong mark! Or to put it another way, sin involves more than the passive omission of what is good and right. It is a positive commission of what is bad and ought not be done.

Based on 1 John 3:4, where sin is described as lawlessness, the Westminster Shorter Catechism defines sin this way: "Sin is any want of conformity unto or transgression of the law of God." This is a good definition as far as it goes. Sin is more than failure to do what is right; it is also doing what is wrong.

This follows from the Bible's appeal to the holiness of God Himself as the basis of His law and criterion of judgment. Illustration of this is in Leviticus 19:2, where God's appeal to His people to be holy was to Himself as the standard: "You shall be holy, for I the LORD your God am holy." Another example of God as the divine standard is when the Prophet Isaiah recognized his own sinfulness; in his vision he saw the holy character of God (Isa. 6:1–6).

GOD'S HOLINESS

In the New Testament God's holiness is still the standard. To sin is to come short of God's glory (Rom. 3:23). Everything the believer does is to be done for God's glory, and therefore whatever does not bring glory to Him is sin (1 Cor. 10:31). James presented sin as siding against God. How terrible! Friendship with the world, he wrote, is "enmity with God" (James 4:4). He who is a friend of the world "makes himself an enemy of God." Peter, the apostle, appealed to what Moses wrote in Leviticus 19:2 in his challenge to saints of his day to live holy lives (1 Peter 1:16). Personal holiness on the part of the people of God in any age is based upon the holiness of God, their heavenly Father.

An illustration will help to clarify how the Bible defines sin by God's character. My wife keeps a detailed diary. She has done this for years. Her diary is a revelation of herself. You do not have to read very far to discover what she likes and dislikes in life. Her true self is revealed in her diary. Even though my wife does not state in specific detail what she likes and dislikes in life you could soon discover this by reading her diary (but you had better not try). The diary reveals her character. The Bible is like God's diary to us and for us. He does not need to pronounce a right or wrong on every specific action. His holy character is revealed in Scripture. When we know Him, we know what conforms to His character and what violates it. He Himself is the divine standard. James Oliver Buswell's definition and description of sin expresses my thoughts well.

> Thus sin is not only violation of the divine law which is an expression of God's will; more profoundly, it is violation of the expression of God's holy character. It is corruption of the goodness which God originally imparted to His creatures; especially it is the corruption of the godliness with which God originally endowed man when He created him in His own image . . . sin may then be defined ultimately as anything in the creature which does not express or which is contrary to the holy character of the Creator.[3]

CHAPTER 1 DISCUSSION QUESTIONS

1. Why do you think many people do not talk about sin anymore?

2. What are some of the idols people today have chosen to worship instead of God?

3. Write a good definition of "sin" based on your reading of this chapter.

4. Give an example from your own life of "dynamic sin."

5. Explain what you think the "passive aspect of sin" means.

2

SIN IN THE ANGELIC WORLD

Who committed the first sin? We usually think of the biblical account of the sin of Adam and Eve in the garden, but when we look more carefully we see that it was not really the first sin after all. Our parents were not the first intelligent creatures to violate the law and character of God. In Genesis 3 we are told of one called the serpent who was already God's enemy, and who tempted the first humans to eat of the forbidden fruit, thereby disobeying God's clear command not to eat of it. So before we discuss the origin of sin in the world of human beings, we must understand sin's beginning among the angels.

By the time Eve was tempted sin had already been committed. The first woman in the world was challenged to disobey the clear command of God by a sly creature called "the serpent" (Gen. 3:1).

SATAN THE SERPENT

The identification of the serpent of Genesis 3 with Satan or the devil is explicit in two passages in the Book of Revelation. The first of these is Revelation 12:9: "The great dragon was cast out, that serpent of old, called the Devil and Satan, who deceives the whole world." The second passage is Reve-

21

lation 20:2: "He [the angel] laid hold of the dragon, that serpent of old, who is the Devil and Satan, and bound him for a thousand years."

> We must therefore understand the serpent in Genesis 3 as an actual serpent who really talked (through the malicious power of the devil) but who was an instrument of Satan. Satan, in other words, used the serpent as his tool in leading our first parents to sin against God.[1]

When did Satan sin? What was his sin? Was he the only one who sinned? Before asking these questions, we should ask, was Satan created evil, or did he initiate his sin by his own free will? Clear biblical theology answers that Satan's free choice, not God, was the source of his sin. He was not created wicked. God is the Creator, and all He created was pronounced "very good" (Gen. 1:31).

SATAN'S SIN

The Bible does not state specifically when Satan sinned. It clearly presents him as wicked in the worst possible sense, but it does not tell us exactly when he became wicked. He is seen in Scripture as the chief opponent of God, leader of other fallen angels or demons. Jesus Himself identified Satan with Beelzebub, the prince of demons (cf. Matt. 12:22–32). The biblical writers present Satan as the chief of the wicked angels who sinned before Adam and Eve (1 John 3:8).

Satan's fall, his sin, must have come before his appearance in the Garden of Eden. That much we know for sure. Several passages of Scripture show us this, and give us some indication of the nature of his sin. The two most important texts are Isaiah 14:12–17 and Ezekiel 28:11–19.[2] Before considering these texts, three other passages will be looked at which describe Satan's sin in a general way.

Pride was the sin of Satan. This is clear from 1 Timothy

22

3:6. Here Paul was giving qualifications for elders in the local church. Such a one must not be a novice or recent convert, the apostle said, "lest being puffed up with pride he fall into the same condemnation as the devil." It appears from this that the devil was not content with the status or position God had given him. He desires at some point a higher authority. The most basic aspect of his sin was pride.

FALLEN ANGELS

Jude 6 and 2 Peter 2:4 might be helpful in determining the nature of Satan's sin. Jude tells us of angels who did not keep their positions but abandoned them to strive for a higher one. Their sin resulted in their confinement in darkness until their day of final judgment. But when did this happen? We are not told. Further, it is uncertain that Jude is describing the plight of all the wicked angels. From passages like Ephesians 6 it appears that some wicked angels are free to roam, to inflict the saints. Not all are in chains until the judgment.

Peter condemns the angels that sinned and were confined "into chains of darkness, to be reserved for judgment" (2 Peter 2:4). Peter does not say what their sin was. It was of such a serious nature as to merit their restriction and ultimate judgment, however. This passage probably does not refer to *all* the wicked angels, especially in view of the reference to Noah's day and to Sodom and Gomorrah (vv. 5–6).

Satan is not mentioned specifically in either Jude 6 or 2 Peter 2:4. It may be inferred, though, that his sin was of the same nature as that of all the other wicked angels.

THE SIN OF PRIDE

What about Ezekiel 28:11–19 and Isaiah 14:12–17? Do these describe Satan's creation and sin? Charles Ryrie said regarding the Ezekiel passage:

23

Many debate whether or not Ezekiel 28:11–19 has Satan in view, but if it does, then it provides us with a number of descriptive details as to the characteristics of Satan's original condition, that is, creation. All agree that the subject of verses 1–19 is judgment on Tyre and its leader. The question is, do verses 11–19 go beyond the human leader to reveal things about something or someone else?[3]

It seems clear that the Spirit of God working through Ezekiel had in mind an historical leader of Tyre in the denunciations. It is just as certain that there is reference here also to one greater than this historical human leader, namely to Satan. There are simply too many superlatives and figures— "seal of perfection," "perfect in beauty," "in Eden, the Garden of God," "anointed cherub," "perfect"—to be literally true of any human leader. The human leader is in view in verses 1–10 and Satan, the superhuman leader of the wicked angels, seems to be primarily in view in verses 11–19.[4]

Assuming Satan's sin is described in Ezekiel 28:11–19, it is found in verse 15. This would be the Bible's answer to the question of where sin originated.[5] This interpretation fits with our Lord's description of Satan before His critics. The devil, He said, "was a murderer from the beginning" (John 8:44). His sin came from himself.

What of Isaiah 14:12–17 with its five "I wills"? Does this text refer to Satan and his sin, or simply to the king of Babylon mentioned in verse 4?[6] Ryrie claims, "the fall of the king of Babylon is an antitype of the previous fall of Satan and a type of the future fall of Antichrist."[7] This is the view of the Hebrew scholar Franz Delitzsch.[8] I agree, primarily because there is too much in the passage which is impossible to apply to any human king.

SIN'S ORIGIN

Where did sin originate? Where was it first expressed in opposition to all that is holy and good and not only as a hypothetical possibility? Sin first found expression in the angelic world. Lucifer sinned first. His sin was pride, a desire to be like the most high God. When he sinned, many angels, who also were created holy, joined Lucifer in sin. They followed in his rebellion against God. Sin entered the universe. God's plan allowed for its entrance through free will.

CHAPTER 2 DISCUSSION QUESTIONS

1. What do you think motivated Satan to sin?

2. How do you think Satan's sin of pride is imitated in our world today?

3. Why do you think God is just in making Adam and Eve responsible for their sin when they were tempted by Satan?

4. Make your own list of five "I wills" from your own experience that interfere with your Christian walk.

5. What do you think makes Satan and the other angels' sins different from Adam and Eve's (and your own)?

3

THE SIN OF ADAM AND EVE

The origin of sin in the human race began with our first parents, Adam and Eve. This teaching is contrary to many who deny the history of Adam and Eve and the fall as recorded in Genesis 3.[1] Evangelicals affirm the natural biblical interpretation of the actual existence of Adam and Eve and their fall as historical fact. They were people who lived in a real place called Eden and committed a particular sin at a particular time. The literal interpretation of Genesis 1–3 harmonizes perfectly with other portions of Scripture (i.e., 1. Chron. 1:1; Matt. 19:46; Luke 3:38; Rom. 5:12–21; 1 Cor. 15:21–47; 1 Tim. 2:13).

In this chapter we are concerned with man's sin, for which God provided salvation. The devil succeeded in getting our first parents to do on earth what he had done previously in heaven—act contrary to the will of God. That, of course, is what he continues to encourage God's people to do.

THE SETTING

Both the privileges and the prohibition of Eden were made very clear to man (Gen. 2:15, 20). The privileges were many, summarized as fulfilling the will of God for man. Doing the will of God is always a privilege. There was only one prohibition placed on our first parents. The restriction and consequent punishment are stated in Genesis 2:17: "but of the tree of the knowledge of good and evil you shall not eat, for in the day that you eat of it you shall surely die." God promised that disobedience to this command would result in death.

We do not know what kind of fruit the tree bore (nor is that important). What is important to observe is that by God's decree a certain tree in the garden, the tree of the knowledge of good and evil, was forbidden to Adam and Eve. Later, after they sinned, they were barred from another tree, the tree of life. The issue confronting them was their continuing relationship to the expressly revealed plan and will of God: to obey it or not to obey it, that was the decision.

The environment surrounding our first parents was perfect. Adam was lord in the garden. There was no external stimulus for coveting. Adam was married to the only woman in the world. No other woman existed to tempt him to sin. Everything was Adam and Eve's to enjoy except the fruit from the forbidden tree. Eve could not be jealous of any other woman. There wasn't any. The only area for possible sin was a repudiation of God and that, of course, was the area in which Satan tempted and the sin into which the first two fell. They were tempted by evil outside themselves.

THE SERPENT

Satan, then as now, did not appear as he really was to the first pair. Instead he spoke through an animal, one with which Eve must have been very familiar.

From Genesis 3 it is easy to discover the approach "the angel of light" used. First he encouraged Eve to doubt concerning the goodness, justice, and love of God. He succeeded through his question, "Has God indeed said?"

There lurked the hint that God had no right to place a restriction upon humans. Satan convinced Eve to doubt both the justice and the goodness of God. Accomplishing his first goal, the devil proceeded to deny the threat of God: "and the serpent said to the woman, You will not surely die" (Gen. 3:4).

THE SIN

Eve disregarded and disobeyed God's command and will when she followed Satan's suggestion in candid denial of God's Word. As soon as she had eaten the forbidden fruit, she gave it to Adam and he ate also. Their sin was unique. It can never be repeated. It was particular disobedience to a particular command of God without a propensity to sin already in them. The first two became sinners only by sinning. We not only choose to sin, we sin because we are sinners. Before the fall, Adam and Eve possessed creature perfection. They were not only innocent but belonged to what God said was "very good." Adam and Eve did not have a sin nature before they sinned. They received one when they disobeyed God. "Sin nature" refers to a propensity to sin. It is more than an ability or desire to sin; it is an irresistible urge. This is a theological designation of what Adam and Eve received when they sinned and what they passed on to their offspring. Since all of humanity is descended from them, the result is that everyone since, except Christ, was born with this bent toward sin.

THE SEQUEL

The moment Adam and Eve broke God's command and acted independently of His will, three forms of death became operative. This was in fulfillment of the Creator's clear statement, "For in the day that you eat of it you shall surely die" (Gen. 2:17). *Spiritual death* was immediate: they were separated from God. They hid themselves from the presence of the Lord God. Adam and Eve revealed their newly sinful hearts as they accused each other for their own sin. The fact that man was expelled from the garden "lest he put out his hand and take also of the tree of life, and eat, and live forever" (Gen. 3:22) substantiates the reality of *physical death* for him. The repetition of the phrase "and he died" in chapter 5 affirms the presence of physical death. In addition to these two forms of death, man became subject to *eternal death*. Eternal death is the final result of spiritual death. It was the potential fate of Adam and Eve and is the potential fate of all their posterity, apart from the acceptance of redemption provided by God in Christ. Without salvation in Christ all would be eternally separated from God.

Specific penalties for sin are spelled out in Genesis 3:14–20. There are penalties to the serpent (v. 14), to Satan (v. 15), to Eve (v. 16), to Adam (vv. 17, 19), and to nature (vv. 17–19). The curse upon nature encompasses all the others and needs special attention.

Earthly Lordship

Originally man was given lordship over the earth as the crowning act of God's creation. God said, "Let Us make man in Our image according to Our likeness; let them have dominion over the fish of the sea, over the birds of the air, and over the cattle, over all the earth and over every creeping thing that creeps on the earth" (Gen. 1:26). After God created male and female in His image, He blessed them and said to them and all mankind to come from them, "Be fruitful and multiply; fill the earth and subdue it; have dominion over the fish of the sea, over the birds of the air, and over every living thing that moves on the earth" (v. 28).

Some today refer to this as a "cultural" or "dominion" mandate, still dictating to the believer that he is to bring all

human government under the authority of God and in subjection to the law of God as expressed in Mosaic legislation.[2]
This becomes the driving force for the church. However, Mosaic legislation as a rule of daily life has been done away with
by Christ and is not the economy by which God governs
today.[3] Ryrie comments:

> Observe that the phrase "subdue the earth" is not part of
> the mandate given to Noah and his descendants (which we
> are) after the flood (9:1). Further observe that the word "sub-
> due" in 1:28 comes from a root that means "to knead" or "to
> tread" and refers to bringing the earth under cultivation so that
> the race could multiply. Adam was to administer the earth and
> its creatures so that it would sustain the people who would fill
> it. This was the context in which Adam was commanded to
> cultivate and keep the Garden of Eden (2:15).[4]

The Curse on Nature

But then the fall came. Our first parents disobeyed God's
command and sin entered God's perfect world. Fallen man's
sin had a devastating effect on the created world over which
he originally had been given authority. God said to Adam,
"Cursed is the ground for your sake; in toil you shall eat of it
all the days of your life" (Gen. 3:17). All of creation became
"subjected to futility, not willingly, but because of Him who
subjected it in hope; because creation itself also will be delivered from the bondage of corruption into the glorious liberty
of the children of God" (Rom. 8:20–21). The penalty placed
on nature because of man's sin remains to this day. It has far-
reaching consequences for all mankind. Both sinner and
saint must cope with it. The curse upon the ground will remain in effect until God lifts it in the future millennial age.
Every form of human suffering and deprivation results from
this curse. We all live under the effects of it. The whole creation "groans and labors with birth pangs" (Rom. 8:22) until
the curse is lifted. It will be lifted when the Lord Jesus Christ

returns to Jerusalem and establishes the messianic kingdom on earth (Zech. 14:11).

THE SALVATION

God's grace is manifested abundantly in His dealing with fallen man. To begin, He sought after the sinner. To the sinful, erring, guilty, hidden Adam He called, "Where are you?" It is that way all through the Bible. From beginning to end God searches for man. Liberal theology has always seen the Bible as a record of *man's* search for *God*. It has man groping after God, hoping somehow to find Him. Such a concept does not fit the context of Scripture, however. It's the other way around completely. The Bible is the inspired record of God's search for and securing of salvation for sinful man.

God's search for man also reveals His justice. Sin must be judged. The righteousness of God is likewise apparent. Adam's feeble attempt to justify himself to God was totally unacceptable to the holy and offended God. A life must be given, a substitution made; blood must be shed to make atonement for sin. Only God's intervention, symbolized by the coats of skin provided by the righteous, offended God, could rescue the first humans who sinned. God has never accepted any contribution from the sinner as payment in part or in whole for his sin. He didn't then, He doesn't now, and He never will.

Before the animals were slain, however, God gave Adam and Eve the promise of the coming Seed of the woman. He was to bruise the head of Satan (Gen. 3:15). This prophetic preview indicated there would be enmity between the serpent and the woman, between Satanic hosts and mankind, and between the Seed of the woman (Christ) and Satan. At Calvary Satan bruised Christ. The Savior died. But the wound was not fatal. Christ arose victorious on the third day. There on the cross, Christ inflicted the mortal wound to

Satan—He bruised his head. The Savior said, in preview of the cross, "the ruler of this world is judged" (John 16:11). The devil is a defeated foe. His sentence of judgment has been issued. In a day yet future that verdict of judgment will be executed and he will be cast in the lake of fire where he will remain forever. The lake was prepared for him and his angels.

CHAPTER 3 DISCUSSION QUESTIONS

1. What are some scriptural reasons we believe Adam and Eve's fall was historical?

2. How do you think you would have reacted to Satan's temptation? Why?

3. What are the three forms of death Adam and Eve incurred by sinning?

4. How has sin affected your own life?

5. Think of some examples of the effect of sin in the natural world.

4
MANKIND'S SIN

A brief review of the ground we have covered so far in our study of sin is in order. Sin is a violation of the holy character of God. It is an affront against Him in thought, word, or deed. The first concrete act of sin in the universe was committed by Satan. He acted contrary to God. Adam and Eve sinned when they disobeyed God's command not to eat of the forbidden fruit.

We now want to know what effect, if any, the sin of the first humans had upon the race which came from them.

IMPUTED SIN

The term "imputation" means putting to someone's account what may or may not be his. It's an accounting term. Lewis Sperry Chafer gave this helpful explanation of the theological meaning of imputation:

> In the matter of man's relation to God, the Bible presents three major imputations: (a) imputation of Adam's sin to the human race, (b) imputation of the sin of man to the substitute, Christ, and (c) an imputation of the righteousness of God to the believer. Imputation may be *real* or *judicial*. That which is real is the reckoning to one of that which is antecedently his, while judicial imputation is the reckoning to one of that which is not antecedently his.[1]

What is the relationship between Adam and the race of mankind? Does his sin affect the rest of the human race? The Bible's answer is "yes." Adam is viewed by God as the representative head as well as the natural head of the human race. The apostle Paul put it this way: "Therefore just as through one man sin entered the world, and death through sin, and thus death spread to all men, because all sinned" (Rom. 5:12). Sin entered the world by one man who committed one sin. The result was death not only upon the one man who committed the sin, but upon all he represented and who were to come from him. Paul explained why the penalty of death was imposed upon all. It is because "all sinned." The Greek is very emphatic here.

Erickson's explanation of the "all sinned" (Rom. 5:12) is very helpful:

> The last clause in verse 12 tells us that we were involved in some way in Adam's sin; it was in some sense also our sin. But what is meant by this? On the one hand it may be understood in terms of federal headship—Adam acted on behalf of all persons. There was a sort of contract between Adam and God as our representative so that what Adam did binds us. Our involvement in Adam's sin might better be understood in terms of natural headship, however . . . the entirety of our human nature, both physical and spiritual, material and immaterial, has been received from our parents and more distant ancestors by way of descent from the first pair of humans. On this basis *we* were actually present within Adam so that we all sinned in his act. There is no unjustice then to our condemnation and death as a result of original sin.[2]

The issue is not that each man commits deeds of sin in the course of his lifetime. That is true, but that is not what is being taught in Romans 5:12. What is being taught is that every member of the human family who has ever been born or will ever be born was related in some way to Adam. When he sinned, the race sinned in him. When Adam sinned, we sinned. He not only represented us, but we sinned in him. The potential of the entire human family was in him, so that what he did, all did in him and through him. Therefore all are guilty and receive the same penalty—death. In another connection Paul said essentially the same thing: "for as in Adam all die" (1 Cor. 15:22). He added, "even so in Christ all shall be made alive."

INHERITED SIN

King David said, "in sin my mother conceived me" (Ps. 51:5). That sinful heart, that corrupt nature which Adam and Eve received when they sinned, they passed on to their children, and they to theirs, and the process continues today. All who are born of woman, with the exception of Christ, are born with the bent toward sin. They are born with the sin nature. Jeremiah, the prophet, stated the human condition like this: "the heart is deceitful above all things, and desperately wicked; who can know it?" (Jer. 17:9).

Paul the apostle was as clear on the matter when he said we "were by nature children of wrath" (Eph. 2:3). Or again, "there is none righteous, no, not one" (Rom. 3:10). All humans are born in a state of separation from God. They are spiritually dead, insensitive to the things of God. All are without God and without hope apart from the redemption provided at Calvary.

INDIVIDUAL SINS

There is a real sense in which the entire human race participated in the sin of Adam. Adam represented all mankind in his actions. More than that, he possessed in himself the potential of all who would ever be born in the human family. As a result, all have sin charged to their account, imputed to them.

35

As a result of imputed sin, all inherit a sin nature from their parents. All are inwardly committed to sin from the very start. No one needs to be educated to sin. It comes quite naturally.

Because we possess a sin nature from conception, all soon become guilty of committing individual sins. These sins, too, serve to condemn us. Outside of Christ we stand condemned before God and in need of His salvation because we commit deeds of sin, and because we have a sin nature inherited from our parents, imputed to us by virtue of our relation to Adam, who represented us and in whom we sinned.

As a result, man stands as a condemned sinner, guilty before God. He is totally depraved, theologians say.[3] This means every facet of man's nature has been polluted or defiled by sin. Man is utterly destitute of all righteousness. Every member of Adam's race is equally depraved. Thankfully, not all manifest their depravity to the same degree or in the same way or even to the fullest extent possible. As a result of this total depravity, this inborn corruption, none is able to do anything to merit favor in the sight of God. None is able to contribute anything, either at the time of salvation or by way of promise for the future. The sinner is spiritually bankrupt and can therefore do absolutely nothing to merit God's favor, His great salvation. God must make the first move and He must provide all the resources if man is ever to be saved from sin. In eternity past, God planned the reconciliation for the sinner, accomplished in Christ in history.

SOCIAL SINS

Up to this point we have talked primarily about individual sins. Adam and Eve sinned as individuals. Every member of the human family except Christ is born with sin already imputed to them because Adam represented all and all were in some sense in him when he sinned. Also, each one is born with a sin nature inherited from his parents. Because all possess imputed sin and inherited sin, all also commit their own acts of sin.

The Bible also refers to collective or group sin, sins of the human race without any particular individuals in view. Powers or influences do not commit sin. People do. Yet Scripture does refer to what might be called social sins. Isaiah, for example, wrote about group sin when he admonished the people as a whole to "wash yourselves, make yourselves clean; put away the evil of your doings from before my eyes. Cease to do evil, learn to do good; seek justice, reprove the oppressor; defend the fatherless, plead for the widow" (1:16–17). "Clearly God is speaking of oppressive conditions for which He holds society responsible. No one individual is responsible for these situations. No single person can alter them. Failures in these areas are sins of society."[4]

A similar emphasis appears in Isaiah 6. The prophet wrote of "a people of unclean lips" (v. 5). He had no particular individual or individuals in mind, but the people of Israel as a whole. This was true of the people even though there were individual exceptions. God told Isaiah to go and warn the people of their sin and God's sure judgment apart from their repentance.

Social Responsibility

We tend to ignore social sins and place responsibility for them upon others. It all seems so distant from us.

Thus, some persons who would never think of killing another human being, taking another's property, or cheating in a business deal may be part of a corporation, nation, or social class which in effect does these very things. Such persons contribute to these evils through financial involvement (by paying

37

taxes or dues), direct approval (by voting), or a tacit consent (by not disapproving or registering opposition).[5]

What can be done about social sins or group sins? Erickson sets forth three different strategies for overcoming social sin: regeneration, reform, and revolution.[6]

Some view group sins as the composite of the sins of individuals. Social problems in this view will never be solved by dealing with society as a unit. Any change in society can only come about as the individuals in it are changed. From the Christian standpoint, only as individuals are regenerated will society be altered. Environmental changes are not what the world needs most but individual, constitutional changes, which in turn will affect the society.

Others insist that since society's problems are larger than individual human wills, the solution must include reforming or changing the structures of society. Those who hold this view usually work for change through the political structure.

Still another strategy for dealing with social sins is revolution. This is the most radical of the three approaches. Destruction and replacement of existing structures is necessary. Terrorism often is acceptable in this approach.

The first of these strategies combined with elements of the second find support in Scripture. Christians need an awakened concern for the social dimension of sin. They need to be actually involved in doing all they can to remove themselves from participation in society's sins. Christians also can become involved in opposing social sins by electing Christians in places of responsible leadership in local, state, and federal governments.

The Decree of Sin

Paul summed up social sin in his declaration that all are "under sin" (Rom. 3:9; Gal. 3:22). This implies that the entire human race is under a decree of sin. There is a judicial

judgment of God upon the human race because of its relation to Adam and because of the sins of each member. There
can be no mistaking, God's verdict upon every member of
the human race. The human family is *guilty*. God's condemnation justly rests upon all of Adam's descendants, even before any particular sins are committed.

WHY EVIL?

Why would God, who is all powerful and good, allow the
entrance and continuance of sin with all its resulting consequences? The question applies equally to what may be called
natural evils, billed as acts of God and eliminated from most
insurance policies, and *moral evils*. Illustrations of the former
include earthquakes, tornadoes, hurricanes, and such dis-
eases as cancer (and AIDS in cases where the victims did not
acquire it because of high risk behavior, e.g., sin).

Moral evils are those brought about by personal choices.
Moral evils can reasonably be argued to come from the consequences of free moral agents to sin. Natural evils, on the
other hand, seem to be contained within God's good creation, completely out of man's control. Why does a great and
good God allow our sins to produce evil in the natural
world?

Romans 8:26 reminds us that the creation is closely associated with the destiny of man. Adam was responsible for the
garden before his fall, and consequently the creation suffered at his fall. No wonder, then, that the creation is now
marred by sin, but also is eagerly anticipating our resurrection. This world touched by calamity is not the world of eternity. God will make a new earth free from natural disaster
for all time. One can explain natural calamity without resort-
ing to manipulating Scripture, as do some forms of extreme
Calvinism,[7] or denying evil, as in Christian Science.[8]

God allowed sin's entrance into His universe, but He also

took sin upon Himself, paying the utmost price for man's redemption from sin, and the world's ultimate deliverance from it. Between now and the time we see our Lord face to face, we must be content to say our God chose the best possible plan, even though that plan included allowing for the entrance and continuance of sin until He ultimately banishes it.

CHAPTER 4 DISCUSSION QUESTIONS

1. How does Romans 5:1–5 explain that we can be assured of God's love for us?

2. Think of the worst sinner you know about (contemporary or historical). If you were God, how would you deal with that person?

3. Think of your own sins. If you were God, how would you deal with someone whose sins are like yours?

4. How do your own ideas of how God should deal with sin differ from God's as revealed in Scripture?

5. What do you consider the worst social sin today?

5

GOD AND THE SINFUL HUMAN RACE

Between God and man there is a great chasm caused by sin. But man often continues to believe that he has righteousness of his own, or that he can contribute to his own salvation. He refuses to accept God's revelation concerning his sin and God's remedy for sin. Man is often willing to accept that he is not perfect, but he will not believe that he is utterly depraved, as the Bible affirms.

MAN'S ESTIMATE OF HIMSELF

The words of the Pharisee as he prayed summarize how most people think of themselves: "God, I thank You that I am not like other men—extortionists, unjust, adulterers, or even as this tax collector" (Luke 18:11). Every human effort toward reconciliation with God is unacceptable to Him and constitutes a rejection of the biblical teaching concerning man's total inability to assist in his own salvation.

Adam and Eve were the first people tempted to do something on their own to find favor with God. The fig leaves they covered themselves with represented an attempt to make themselves acceptable to God. We know from the biblical record the fig leaves were unacceptable to God, not because they did not cover Adam and Eve's nakedness sufficiently, but because they were sinners' attempts to placate God on their own. God rejected their act. They were already dead spiritually. They had lost their relationship with God. Only He could restore it.

From that day to this man has sought to make himself acceptable to God in a thousand different ways, but it still cannot be done. The ladder of human works, including promises, is well-worn but too short. No man has or ever will reach God's presence by climbing its rungs. Every such attempt, however small it may be, is evidence that the condemned sinner does not really believe he stands condemned.

GOD'S ESTIMATE OF MAN

What is God's verdict against humanity? Scripture's answer to this question shows the necessity of Christ's death and of the necessity for the sinner to trust Christ alone for his complete salvation.

God has the only remedy for sinful man: "for the Son of Man has come to seek and to save that which was lost" (Luke 19:10). All people will "perish" apart from salvation (John 3:16). They are already judged by God and in their sinful condition they love darkness rather than light. They commit deeds against God and they hate the light (John 3:17–20). God's wrath abides on all (John 3:36). They are dead in trespasses and sins (Eph. 2:1), and are in the "power of darkness" (Col. 1:13), perishing (2 Cor. 4:3). Satan, the evil one, holds all people who are without Christ in his power (1 John 5:19).

God declares that, from His perspective, people without Christ are:

> . . . filled with all unrighteousness, sexual immorality, covetousness, maliciousness, full of envy, murder, strife, deceit,

evil-mindedness; they are whisperers, backbiters, haters of God, violent, proud, boasters, inventors of evil things, disobedient to parents, undiscerning, untrustworthy, unloving, unforgiving, unmerciful (Rom. 1:29–31).

There are none who are righteous, none who seek for God, none who do good, none who are in awe of God's holiness (Rom. 3:10–18). For example, David confessed he was "brought forth in iniquity and in sin my mother conceived me" (Ps. 51:5). The prophet Jeremiah said, "The heart is deceitful above all things and desperately wicked; who can know it?" (Jer. 17:9).

The Sins of Humanity

God is not saying that each and every sinner is guilty of each and all of the sins named. Rather, such sins characterize the whole human race. Each sinner is, of course, guilty of more than enough personal sin to condemn him. Before anyone can be redeemed, he must accept God's estimate of his sinfulness. God's viewpoint of man as sinner must be received or there will be no salvation. No adjustment of one's behavior can alter this hopeless plight. No self-originating promise to enthrone Christ as Lord will do it either. Only the regenerating work of the Spirit of God can make saints out of sinners. This work of the Spirit is based upon the substitutionary death of Christ alone and is apart from all human effort or commitment. Not every sinner is as wicked as he might be. Not all commit the most wicked deeds possible. But, all do sin and all fail God's standard, demonstrating the destitution of any life or merit before God. It is God's perspective, not man's, which matters and with which the sinner must be concerned.

The Offense of the Gospel

The Gospel is offensive because it strips people of all room for pride in human accomplishment. There is a reproach associated with the message of the Cross because it removes every possibility of self-deliverance. No one can give God anything in exchange for salvation. Nothing the sinner can give is acceptable as a substitute for sin.

THE TRUTH ABOUT SIN

Evangelical Christians are in common agreement on man's exceedingly sinful condition. However, most people who reject the Bible's authority reject this most unpleasant reality about man's sin and alienation from God.

New Age[1] enthusiasts, for example, believe man is himself divine, ultimately perfect, and, in fact, infinite. Man is good. Sin is an illusion. "Mankind and all life is basically good."[2] They reinterpret Christ's glory as the divine power innate in all people: "There is nothing else but God: That we are all part of a great being."[3] One New Age "Christ," Lord Maitreya, claimed, "My purpose is to show man that he need fear no more. That all of light and truth rests within his heart. That when this simple factor is known man will become God."[4]

No matter what sophisticated jargon is used, or how much a New Ager or other unbeliever redefines biblical vocabulary, Truth stands. The Truth is that we are all sinners before the holy God who created us. And only that God can rescue us from the futility of life without Christ. Our Savior is the Lord Himself!

CHAPTER 5 DISCUSSION QUESTIONS

1. What are some ways to help unsaved people see that they are guilty before God?
2. Why do you think God allows evil?
3. Why is the Gospel so offensive to those who need it?

4. Think about one of your non-Christian friends. What do you think his opinion is concerning sin?

5. What do most people in your community think about sin?

SECTION II

The Savior

PART ONE
THE PERSON OF THE SAVIOR

6

LIFE BEFORE BIRTH

With the biblical portrait of man as sinner behind us we are prepared to meet the Lord Jesus Christ, the Savior of sinners. Christ, the God-man, bridged the gap between the holy God and sinful man. Apart from Him there would be no salvation.

This section presents those aspects of Christ's person and work relating to His great work of salvation. This is not a comprehensive treatment of Christology. The areas covered include His eternal status in the Godhead before He came to earth; and the incarnation itself. The Savior came to seek and to save that which was lost. His own life on this sin-cursed planet was sinless. The holy life He lived relates to His substitutionary death. We will also study the Savior's resurrection from the grave and His present intercession on our behalf before the Father.

When we know our Savior, then we can focus on our salvation.

THE PREEXISTENCE OF CHRIST

Jesus Christ is the only person who ever lived before He was conceived. This is true because He is the God-man. In Him absolute deity (eternal) and perfect humanity (incarnational) were united in one divine person forever. Indeed, He is the most unique person who ever lived or ever shall live. Personhood begins for all other humans at conception. But the second person of the Godhead existed eternally. Mary's conception of the Son of God has nothing whatsoever to do with His origin. He always existed. There was never a "time" in eternity past when He was not. The Savior's personal existence was not marked by a beginning. He is equally as eternal as God the Father.

The Savior was conscious of His existence before His birth. On the eve of His death, in His high priestly prayer, Jesus referred to the glory He had shared with the Father before the world was (John 17:5). He was conscious of being loved by God the Father "before the foundation of the world" (John 17:24).

The fact that the second person of the Godhead was involved in the Creation argues for His existence before the work described in Genesis 1 and 2. There are direct statements in Scripture which involve Christ in creation (John 1:3; 1 Cor. 8:4-6; Col. 1:16-17; Heb. 1:2; Rev. 3:14).[1]

THE ETERNAL EXISTENCE OF CHRIST

These Scripture passages demonstrate that the Savior existed not only before His birth in Bethlehem but also before Creation. They assume that He existed eternally. Here we will marshal support for Christ's *eternal* existence, beginning with selected direct scriptural evidence and moving to indirect theological support.

Scripture Evidence

Isaiah, the prophet, described the Savior hundreds of years before He was born as the "eternal Father" or the "Father of eternity" (9:6).[2] The very locality of Christ's incarnation was predicted in the same prophecy as His unoriginated eternal existence: "But you, Bethlehem Ephrathah, though you are little among the thousands of Judah, yet out of you shall come forth to Me the One to be ruler in Israel, whose goings forth have been from of old, from everlasting" (Mic. 5:2). The person involved is none other than Jesus of Nazareth. Chief priests and scribes at the time of His birth even quoted Micah's prophecy in their answer to Herod's question concerning the identity of the Messiah (Matt. 2:4–6).

In the introduction to the Gospel of John the apostle affirms the eternal existence of Christ (John 1:1–2). That the "Word" refers to Him is clear from verse 14, where the incarnation is highlighted. The "beginning" points to a time in eternity past beyond which one cannot go. Under the Spirit's direction John emphasized that the "Word" had no beginning. In the "beginning" He was already existent and therefore unoriginated. He is eternal!

Jesus Himself taught His eternal existence. In conjunction with His claims of deity Jesus said to the Pharisees, "Your father Abraham rejoiced to see My day" (John 8:56). They quickly retorted, "You are not yet fifty years old, and have You seen Abraham?" (v. 57). The Savior answered them, "Before Abraham was, I AM" (v. 58). In this startling statement, Christ was not only claiming to have existed before Abraham lived, but was asserting that He existed eternally. He claimed Jehovah's title, the I AM of Exodus 3:14 (see also Deut. 32:39; Isa. 41:4; 46:4). He used the same Greek term (a predicate absolute) as did the Greek translation of the Old Testament verses. The Jews were familiar with this translation and understood exactly what Jesus was declaring. That was why they picked up stones and tried to kill Him (v. 59).

Indirect Evidence

There are also indirect theological evidences for the eternal existence of Christ. First, every claim for His deity is also a claim of His eternal existence. Some of these claims will be presented later in our discussion of His deity. Second, one cannot affirm the doctrine of the Trinity unless Christ has existed eternally as a divine person. Theological liberals who attempt to straddle the theological fence by affirming a trinity but teaching that Jesus was eternally in God's thoughts are contradictory.

> If Christ is God and as such is distinguished from the Father and the Spirit, preliminary evidence is provided to support the doctrine of the Trinity as normally stated in orthodoxy. It is safe to say that no attack on the doctrine of the Trinity can be made without attacking the person of Christ. It is also true that no attack on the person of Christ can be made without attacking the doctrine of the Trinity, as they stand and fall together. It is for this reason that current liberalism is usually Unitarian, that is, denies the three Persons of the Godhead, or is modalistic, that is, affirming simply that the persons are modes of existence of the one Person and not actual entities.[3]

Third, Christ's heavenly origin necessitates His eternal existence. This is true because of the eternal, personal relationship which existed between the Father and the Son: "I came forth from God," (John 16:27) Christ said. The Father sent Him from His presence into the world. The Savior prayed for the restoration of the glory He had with the Father before He came to earth (John 17:5).

THE ETERNAL SONSHIP OF CHRIST

It has often been assumed that to argue for the preexistence of Christ was to argue for His eternal Sonship. If He existed eternally, He did so as Son. However, among some of the Plymouth Brethren Christians, F. E. Raven categorically denied that Christ was eternally the Son of God. He believed that "Son of God" was only His incarnate title.[4]

52

Arguments Against

Recently this question has surfaced again among evangelicals. Those who deny He was always the Son of God do not deny that He existed eternally as God. What they reject is that He was *eternally* in the position of the Son of God. The title "Son of God" is seen as His incarnate title. According to the argument, His *sonship* had a beginning in time even though *He* always existed as a distinct person in the Trinity.

John MacArthur (popular author, pastor, and conference speaker) is one evangelical who does not believe in the eternal Sonship of Christ. He wrote:

> He was always God but He became Son. He had not always had the title of Son. That is His incarnation title. Eternally He is God, but only from His incarnation has He been Son . . . Christ was *not* Son until His incarnation. Before that He was eternal God . . . His Sonship began in point of time, not in eternity. His life as Son began in this world . . . He was not a Son until He was born into this world through the virgin birth . . . The Sonship of Christ is inextricably connected with His incarnation . . . only after Christ's incarnation did God say, "This is My Son."[5]

MacArthur explained further how he understands the term "son" when applied to Christ:

> *Son* does not refer to Jesus' divine essence . . . in eternity past, though there were always three persons in the Trinity, there were not yet the roles of Father and Son. Those designations apparently came into being only at the incarnation . . . *Son* was a new name never before applied to the second person of the Godhead except prophetically, as in Psalm 2:7 which is interpreted in Hebrews 1:5–6 as referring to the event of the incarnation . . . only when "the Word became flesh and dwelt among us" as "the only begotten God" (John 1:14–18) did He take on the role and function of *Son*.[6]

53

How does this view compare to Scripture? Does it matter a great deal whether we believe Christ was eternally the Son of God or only became such when He became man? Are any other doctrines affected by either of these views of Christ's Sonship?

Arguments For

While there is no verse of Scripture which states in so many words that Christ was always the Son of God, biblical evidence that He was is overwhelming. John 20:28–31, 10:30–48, and 5:18, for example, encompass much more in the term "Son" than MacArthur would like. Before presenting this evidence for the eternal Sonship of Christ we need to understand the meaning of son as applied to Christ.

The title "Son of God" is used of men, angels, and Christ in Scripture. When used of Christ it has nothing to do with His birth, with Mary being His mother. It has everything to do with His eternal relation to the Father. Christ is nowhere in Scripture called a child *(teknos)* of God. The Greek word *teknos* means a child born to parents. Instead the word *huios,* son, is always used of Him. This second term describes an heir destined to receive an inheritance. The following biblical facts must be taken into account to determine whether Christ was always the Son of God or became the Son when He was born of Mary:

(1) The Son of God existed at the time of creation. He had a part in it (Col. 1:13–17; Heb. 1:2).

(2) The Son of God is described as being in the Father's bosom (John 1:18; 1 John 1:1–2).

(3) The Son of God was sent by the Father (Isa. 9:6; John 3:16; 20:21; Rom. 8:32; Gal. 4:4; 1 John 4:10, 14).

54

(4) The Son of God returned to the Father (John 16:28; 17:5, 24).

The term "Son of God" describes the Savior's relationship to God the Father. His relationship to God is eternal and was not affected by the incarnation. "Son of God" is not less, but far more than a name or title. It is another way of setting Christ forth as the only begotten. The second member of the Godhead did become the Son of man, the son of David, and the son of Mary when He became incarnate but He was the Son of God from all eternity. His eternal Sonship became apparent to us in the incarnation (Rom. 1:3, 4; 9:5; Phil. 2:5–11).

John F. Walvoord's summary of the issues of Christ's Sonship is reflective of the biblical teaching:

> The scriptural view of the Sonship of Christ as recognized in many of the great creeds of the church is that Christ was always the Son of God by eternal generation and that He took upon Himself humanity through generation of the Holy Spirit; the human birth was not in order to become a Son of God but because He was the Son of God.[7]

FIRSTBORN AND ONLY BEGOTTEN

Two other titles of Christ relate to an understanding of His Sonship.

Firstborn

Christ is called the "firstborn" (Greek *prototokos*) seven times in the New Testament. Taken together these references present three distinct meanings of this title as used of Christ.[8]

First, Paul described the Savior as "the firstborn among many brethren" (Rom. 8:29) and as "the firstborn of all creation" (Col. 1:15). In the first instance He is being presented as the pre-eminent One, the Head of a new race. He is the one to be acknowledged and glorified as the Son of God. In the Colossians 1:15 passage there is no hint that He became the Son when born of Mary. Rather His priority, pre-eminence, dignity, rank, and position as the Son of God are highlighted. Alford stated it well in these words:

> "Firstborn of every creature" will then imply that Christ was not only firstborn of His mother in the world but first begotten of His Father before the worlds—and that He holds the rank, as compared with every created thing, of firstborn in dignity.[9]

Second, Matthew (1:25) and Luke (2:7) use the title "firstborn" to describe Christ as Mary's firstborn son. In these instances it is used of His incarnate humanity. Christ was indeed Mary's firstborn—first in time and certainly in rank and position within the family. Neither of these passages, however, teach that the Savior became *God's* Son at the time of His birth. Instead, they speak of His relationship within Mary's family.

Third, Christ was the first to be raised from the dead in resurrection, never to die again. He is indeed the "firstborn from the dead" (Col. 1:18; cf. Rev. 1:5). Others had been raised before Him but none of them had received a resurrection body, immortal, never to experience death again. He is the only one with authority or pre-eminence over death (1 Cor. 15:54–57).

Only Begotten

In addition to "firstborn," the title "only begotten" is also used of Christ and is related to His Sonship. It is used of Him five times (John 1:14, 18; 3:16, 18; 1 John 4:9). The Greek word *monogenes*, "begotten," is derived from the roots *genos*, which means kind or class, and *mono*, which means only or unique. There is no concept of generate here. Christ is the only, unique, one-of-a kind Son of God. The uniqueness of Christ's position as Son is what John stresses in each of the references.

> The thought is clearly that Christ is the Begotten of God in the sense that no other is. This is illustrated in the use of the word in regard to Isaac (Heb. 11:17) who was not literally the only begotten of Abraham but was the only begotten of Abraham in the sense that he was the promised seed.[10]

Both of these titles, "firstborn" and "only begotten," describe Christ's eternal relation with the Father. The only exception to this is when He is described as Mary's firstborn. To argue that His divine Sonship began with His birth is to ignore the clear biblical usage of both firstborn and only begotten.

From our brief study we have seen that our Savior is uniquely qualified to act on the Father's behalf for our salvation. He is the eternal Son of God. Since we have already demonstrated that man can do nothing to initiate his own reconciliation to God, it is reasonable and biblical to affirm the Savior's divine, eternal, personal relationship within the Godhead.

CHAPTER 6 DISCUSSION QUESTIONS

1. Why is it important to believe that Jesus Christ is eternal?

2. What are some reasons you have heard for people rejecting the deity of Christ?

3. How would you explain that Jesus Christ is eternal to someone who believes the Bible teaches He is created?

4. What are the two different ways "firstborn" is used to describe Jesus Christ?

5. List a few of the questions you have about Jesus existing eternally, and then list some resources you can use to find answers (this book, friend, pastor, etc.).

7

THE MAN CHRIST JESUS

How do the Savior's virgin birth, His genuine humanity, and His sinlessness relate to sinners and the salvation He provided for them? In the history of the church, liberals have clung to Christ's human side and denied His deity, while evangelicals have concentrated so on proving His deity that they have neglected His true humanity. The Bible, however, presents the Savior as both God and man.

THE VIRGIN BIRTH

The virgin birth,[1] that Mary conceived miraculously by the power of the Holy Spirit without sexual contact with a man, has been a vital and central truth of the historic Christian faith. The virgin birth is a fundamental of orthodoxy. In fact, to deny this truth places one outside orthodoxy.

This doctrine is important because it is a core teaching of Scripture. To deny it, as some professing Christians do, is to reject the inspiration and authority of the Bible which teaches this truth. The virgin birth settles the question of whether we have a natural or supernatural Christ. By means of the virgin birth God the Father united the divine nature with the human nature in one perfect, sinless, divine Person. Because of this Christ qualified to be the sinbearer.

The Old Testament (Isa. 9:6, Mic. 5:2, Dan. 9:24–25) predicts that Christ would be both God and man. The New Testament pronounces that He is both. The only explanation for this union is the virgin birth. It is the inerrant explanation of how God brought His Son into the world.

The Holy Spirit was the efficient cause of Mary's conception. She became pregnant with the Christ child without sexual intercourse. Through the virgin conception the Holy Spirit preserved the perfection of Christ's divine Person, keeping His humanity free from sin. All attempts to explain the virgin birth as a carryover from pagan culture have failed.[2] There simply is no exact parallel in the pages of history.

All the great confessions of the Christian church assert belief in the virgin birth of Christ. This doctrine was a part of orthodoxy from the beginning of the church. Those who have denied this cardinal truth and yet claimed to be Christian have often done so because of their denial of the supernatural. Those who deny the virgin birth on this basis usually also deny the deity, bodily resurrection, and substitutionary death of the Savior.

The Scriptural Basis

What is the scriptural basis for belief in the virgin birth of Christ? We begin with Genesis 3:15. Here we glimpse the unique *importance* of the coming Messiah, the seed of the woman destined to bruise the head of the serpent. (Paul points this out from the basis of the later promise to Abraham [Gen. 12:3] in Galatians 3:16.)

After pointing out the uniqueness of the Messiah's coming birth, the Old Testament affirms that this birth would be *virgin* (Isa. 7:14, especially the Greek version).[3]

In the New Testament, Matthew makes three references to the virgin birth. First, Matthew ends his recitation of Jesus' genealogy by declaring that *Mary* (not *Joseph*) is the one "of whom" was born Jesus. The fact that the feminine singular relative pronoun is used relates the birth of "Jesus who is

60

called Christ" to Mary alone. This is unique within this genealogy as well as unheard of in the patriarchal Jewish society. The relation of Christ to His mother and not to Joseph stands in striking contrast to all the others listed in the genealogy.

Second, Matthew adds that "before they [Joseph and Mary] came together, she was found with child of the Holy Spirit" (Matt. 1:18). Third, Matthew quotes from Isaiah 7:14 and translates "young maiden" as "virgin" (vv. 22–23). He further tells us that Joseph kept Mary a virgin until Christ was born (v. 25).

Luke, the physician in the New Testament, records Mary's concern when the angel told her she would give birth to Israel's Messiah (Luke 1:26–38). Mary insisted that she was a virgin (v. 34), so how could what the angel said be true? She had not known a man in the sense of sexual relations. The angel assured Mary that the One she would give birth to would be the result of the sovereign work of God alone (v. 35) apart from any sexual activity.

What alternatives to the virgin birth of Christ are there for those who claim to believe the Bible? J. Oswald Sanders cites five alternatives if this doctrine is fiction and not fact. He concludes with a challenging summary statement:

1. The New Testament narratives are proved false and the Book is robbed of its authority on other matters also.

2. Mary, instead of being blessed among women, is branded as not chaste, for Joseph asserted that Jesus was not his son.

3. Jesus becomes the natural child of sinful parents, which at once rules out His preexistence with the result there was no real incarnation.

4. We are deprived of any adequate explanation of His unique character and sinless life.

5. If He was begotten of a human father—and that is the only alternative to virgin birth—He was not the second Person of the Trinity as He claimed, and therefore had no power to forgive sin.

6. If this miracle is denied, where do you stop? Logically we should deny all miracles. The question really is are we willing to accept the supernatural claims of Scripture or not?[4]

THE IMPORTANCE OF CHRIST'S HUMANITY

God became man in Christ. The Son of God became the Son of Man in order that the sons of men might become adopted sons of God (Rom. 8:15). The pre-incarnate second Person of the Godhead became the incarnate Christ, Israel's Messiah, and the world's Savior. Nothing is more central to biblical Christianity than the incarnation of the Lord Jesus Christ. It has been correctly observed that upon it "the whole superstructure of Christian theology depends."[5]

The Savior had to be man in order to be the sacrifice for sin (Heb. 9:12–15). "For the validity of the work accomplished in Christ's death, or at least its applicability to us as human beings, depends upon the reality of His humanity, just as the efficacy of it depends upon the genuineness of His deity."[6]

It follows just as certainly that the Savior's full humanity is indispensable to the present ministry He maintains in intercession (1 Tim. 2:5). The humanity with which Christ was clothed in incarnation did not cease to be His when He ascended back to the Father. He now possesses glorified, resurrected humanity, but it is real nonetheless. He is still, and will forever be, the God-man.

A Defense of Christ's Humanity

The Savior was born

The virgin birth encompasses both a virgin conception and Jesus' natural and normal delivery, like any other baby, but from his still virgin mother. The "Word" became "flesh" (John 1:14). Christ was "revealed in the flesh" (1 Tim. 3:16), mystery of mysteries. "Jesus Christ has come in the flesh" (1 John 4:2).

Human names were given to God's Son

He referred to Himself often as "the Son of Man" and identified Himself as "a man" (John 8:40). To Him belonged the human elements of "body" (John 2:21), "soul" (John 12:27), and "spirit" (Luke 23:46). As the incarnate Son of God the Savior experienced human limitations common to man.[7] Like others around Him, He became weary (John 4:6), hungry (Matt. 4:2), thirsty (John 19:28), "sorrowful" (Mark 14:34), and of course, He died (John 19:30).

The Savior also experienced human emotions

He loved (John 13:1), had compassion (Matt. 9:36), felt anger (John 2:13–16), and cried (John 11:35). Human development marked Christ's life on earth. He was knowledgeable (John 7:15) and read from the Old Testament Scriptures (Luke 4:16). His questions baffled the minds of His contemporaries (Luke 2:41–47). Luke summed up the Savior's humanity by saying He "increased in wisdom and stature, and in favor with God and man" (Luke 2:52).

The Nature of Christ's Humanity

He was a real, genuine, though sinless, human (Phil. 2:7–8). It is difficult for us to even think of a sinless person. All the sons of Adam have been tainted with sin. Even the saintliest of people have been marred by sin. The only person without sin ever born of woman is Christ. Evangelical Christians uniformly accept the biblical teaching of the sinlessness of Christ. All concur that He never committed a sin in thought, word, or deed. All agree that the Savior was born without a sin nature.

What evangelicals do not agree on is whether or not Christ *could* have sinned. Those who believe the Savior could not and did not sin affirm what is called the *impeccability* of Christ (from the Latin *peccatum*, sin). Those who hold He did not sin but *could* have affirm the peccability of Christ, or his ability to sin.[8] The issue must be decided on theological

63

grounds since there is no explicit scriptural statement to support either side.

Could Jesus have sinned?

Those who believe the Savior was peccable, that He *could* have sinned, though He *didn't*, believe so for two basic reasons.

First, they do not see how an impeccable person could be genuinely tempted. In other words, if Christ could not have sinned, then He was not really tempted.

In response to this objection it may be said that since Christ did not have a sin nature (all evangelicals agree to this), His temptation was different from that which humans generally experience. His temptation was from without and not from within. Ours is both from within and without.

Second, it is argued that if Christ were truly human, it must have been possible for Him to yield to temptation and thus to sin. If men are able to sin, and if He were true man, why couldn't He have sinned?

An answer is that He was indeed man, but He was more than man. He was also God. His person is one and divine though His natures are two, human and divine.

Jesus could not have sinned

In attempting to arrive at what the Bible teaches in this regard it must be remembered that the Person of Christ is unique. He was and is both God and man. His person cannot be divided. Since the incarnation He must always be viewed as the God-man.

It is argued that the first Adam sinned, and he did not have a sin nature. Why couldn't Christ have done the same? Because He was a divine Person with both a human nature and a divine nature. His absolute, undiminished deity was joined by His divine Person to His perfect humanity. The last Adam was the God-man; the first Adam was only a man.

If Christ could not sin how can He genuinely sympathize with the believer when he is tempted? He can and does, not because our temptation was exactly duplicated in Him, but because He, like us, was genuinely tempted. The genuineness of the temptation is not determined by the susceptibility to yield. One may be tempted to do the impossible. Whether or not it can be done does not determine the reality of the temptation.

The impeccability of Christ can be defended by appealing both to theology and Scripture. First, the Savior was immutable. This means that in His divine nature He could never change. Since His divine nature cannot be divorced from His human nature He could not have sinned. Furthermore, if He could have sinned when He was here on earth, why could He not sin now? In His glorification His natures were not changed. His body was, but not His divine or human natures.

Second, two passages of Scripture, Hebrews 4:15 and 1 John 3:5 lend support to the impeccability of the Savior. In the Hebrew passage the writer seems to be saying that Christ, the believer's High Priest, can and does sympathize with His people even though He did not and could not sin.

A. T. Robertson says of this text:

> *Without sin (choris hamartias)*. This is the outstanding difference that must never be overlooked in considering the actual humanity of Jesus. He did not yield to sin but more than this is true. There was no latent sin in Jesus to be stirred by temptation and no habits of sin to be overcome.[9]

The whole problem of the relation of sin to the Savior raises the question, why was He tempted? From God's perspective He was tempted to prove to us that He could not sin. Satan's purpose in tempting Christ was to get Christ to bypass Calvary. The Savior was tempted as proof of His sinlessness. The reality of His temptation at the hands of Satan is the basis upon which He can sympathize with His people. But none of us will ever be tempted in exactly the same manner that He was.

THE MAN CHRIST JESUS

The man Christ Jesus is unique. He was fully God and yet fully man. The one divine Person encompassed two natures, perfectly bridging the infinite moral gap of sin between sinful man and the holy God.

We can trust this God-man for our salvation because He is perfect and sinless in both His deity and His humanity.

He can reconcile us to God as no mere, sinful descendant of Adam could ever do. He can identify with our human condition as the perfect man. In the Savior all of God's plan of salvation is ordained.

CHAPTER 7 DISCUSSION QUESTIONS

1. Do you believe in the Virgin Birth? Why or why not?

2. How would you explain the Virgin Birth to someone who laughs at the idea?

3. Why is it important to understand and accept the Virgin Birth?

4. In what ways is Jesus' humanity like ours?

5. In what ways is Jesus' humanity different from ours?

8

VERY GOD OF VERY GOD

We live in a time when there is a lot of God-talk. Terms and phrases like divinity, deity, Son of God, Savior and even God are applied to Christ with different meanings than they ever had before. There was a time when these terms described the unique, absolute, and undiminished deity of the Savior. This is no longer true.[1]

In this chapter *deity of Christ* means He is truly and fully God, not merely Godlike. It does not mean that He is nearer to God than anyone else ever was. He is absolute God, just as much God as the Father is God. Also, He is just as much God since His incarnation as He was before it.

THE IMPORTANCE

An attack upon the deity of the Savior of sinners is an attack upon Christianity itself. There is no room for difference or debate here. To deny that Jesus of Nazareth was fully God is to remove oneself from the historic, orthodox Christian faith. (The same is true, as we have seen already, with regard to the humanity of Christ.)

Denial of the deity of Christ does not merely weaken and water down Christianity. It is an anti-Christian point of view.[2] The question of Jesus' identity is the most basic and far-reaching that could ever be asked. Is He God? Or is He not?

> If Jesus is not God then there is no Christianity, and we who worship Him are nothing more than idolators. Conversely if He is God, those who say He was merely a good man, or even the best of men, are blasphemers. More serious still, if He is not God then *He* is a blasphemer in the fullest sense of the word. If He is not God He is not even good.
>
> It has already been maintained that there is no stopping between Unitarism and rationalism after Christ. The deity of Christ is the key doctrine of Scripture. Reject it, and the Bible becomes a confused jumble of words void of any unifying theme. Accept it, and the Bible becomes an intelligible and ordered revelation of God, in the person of Jesus Christ. Christ is the centre of Christianity and the conception we form of Christianity is therefore the conception we have of Him.[3]

THEORIES OPPOSED TO CHRIST'S DEITY

The Early Church

First it must be said that the post-apostolic fathers of the second century such as Clement of Alexandria, Ignatius of Antioch, and Polycarp of Smyrna all believed Christ was as fully God as He was man. In the same general time period, however, others deviated from this New Testament concept of the eternally existing person of God the Son. The Ebionites, heretical Jews, also denied the deity of Christ. The Gnostics viewed Christ as the highest of created intelligences, but not as God.

Later

Later in the history of the church men such as Clement of Rome, Origen, and Tertullian rejected any view which denied the full humanity of Christ and they also held tenaciously to the absolute deity of Christ.

Airus, an heretical Presbyter in Alexandria, insisted contrarily that Christ was not eternal and by no means equal with God the Father. Christ was of a different substance from the Father, he argued. The Council of Nicaea was called by the civil power to resolve the issue (A.D. 326). The Nicaean Creed, accepted throughout the Church, developed from this council and affirms the deity of Christ.[4] But this did not mean all parties at the time agreed. The controversy continued, until the orthodox view triumphed, and the Church then maintained belief that Christ was fully human and fully divine, joined in one Person.

The Reformation

While there was little development of the doctrine of Christ in the Middle Ages (A.D. 600–1500) the Reformers continued to hold to the true deity and humanity of Christ. During the eighteenth century a noticeable change in the value and role of the New Testament in affirming a doctrine of Christ developed. With the rise of secular agnositicism and its denial of the supernatural and of the Bible as God's Word, liberal church theologians also attacked the deity of Christ while still claiming to be Christian.

Today

A confusing picture of the person of Christ emerges as we turn to the contemporary scene. Docetism and Ebionitism are both very much present but the latter is dominant. Pannenberg, in jettisoning the doctrine of the two natures, maintains that Jesus was a real man who lived completely in and for the future, that is, in and for God. He begins not with the incarnation of our Lord but with His resurrection and avers that this event gives us the clue to the status as the one who anticipates and embodies the future of world history. J. A. T. Robinson affirms the full humanity of Jesus but not His deity except in a functional sense. Jesus represents God to man. He is but the parable or sign by which it is possible to recognize Christ in others. Allen Flessman, a Dutch theologian, in his book *Believing Today*, has a similar view: "The Son Jesus Christ is not God,

but a man who was so one with God that in Him I meet God."
Thomas O'Meara regards Jesus as "the climax of man." The
culminating point in human evolution, He is "not the creator
of salvation but its prophet." For Ernst Fuchs Jesus should be
considered "a man who dares to act in God's stead." In
Schoonenberg's *Christology* Jesus is basically a human person
who embodies and reveals the presence of God rather than a
divine person who assumes human nature. Hans Kung de-
picts Jesus as "God's advocate and deputy." The man who by
His words and deeds attests God's love for us. The impact of
positivistic historicism is clearly evident in his attempt to show
what can be believed and what can be discarded in the life of
Jesus. John Cobb rejects the traditional idea of Jesus Christ as a
supernatural being in human form and contends instead that
He was an extraordinary prophetic figure who fully realized
the divine creative urge to fulfillment within Him.[5]

SCRIPTURAL DEFENSE OF
THE DEITY OF CHRIST

Louis Berkhof has given an excellent summary of the biblical evidence for the deity of Christ:

> We find that Scripture (1) *explicitly asserts the deity of the Son*
> in such passages as John 1:1; 20:28; Romans 9:5; Philippians
> 2:6; Titus 2:13; 1 John 5:20; (2) *applies divine names to Him,*
> Isaiah 9:6; 40:3; Jeremiah 23:5–6; Joel 2:32 (cf. Acts 2:21);
> 1 Timothy 3:16; (3) *ascribes to Him divine attributes* such as eter-
> nal existence, Isaiah 9:6; John 1:1, 2; Revelation 1:8; 22:13, om-
> nipresence, Matthew 18:20; 28:20; John 3:13, omniscience,
> John 2:24, 25; 21:17; Revelation 2:23, omnipotence, Isaiah 9:6;
> Philippians 3:21; Revelation 1:8, immutability, Hebrews 1:10–
> 12; 13:8, and in general every attribute belonging to the Father,
> Colossians 2:9; (4) *speaks of Him as doing divine works* as cre-
> ation, John 1:3, 10; Colossians 1:16; Hebrews 1:2, 10, provi-
> dence, Luke 10:22; John 3:35; 17:2; Ephesians 1:22; Colossians
> 1:17; Hebrews 1:3, forgiveness of sins, Matthew 9:2–7; Mark
> 2:7–10; Colossians 3:13; resurrection and judgment, Matthew
> 25:31, 32; John 5:19–29; Acts 10:42; 17:31; Philippians 3:31;

2 Timothy 4:1, the final disillusion and renewal of all things, Hebrews 1:10–12; Philippians 3:21; Revelation 21:5, and (5) *accords Him divine honor*, John 5:22, 23; 14:1; 1 Corinthians 5:15–19; 2 Corinthians 13:13; Hebrews 1:6; Matthew 28:19.[6]

Three additional passages not a part of the above summary should be included. The writer of Hebrews exalts Christ qualitatively above angels. In contrast to the way angels are related to God, the Son is called God by the Father: "But to the Son He says, 'Your throne, O God, is forever and ever'" (1:8). This is the Father's view of His Son. To His critics Jesus said, "If you do not believe that I am He, you will die in your sins" (John 8:24). And again, "Before Abraham was, I AM" (v. 58). In both cases the Savior was claiming to be equal with the Jehovah God of the Old Testament (Ex. 3:14; Isa. 44:8, etc.).

VERY GOD

Abundant scriptural evidence supports the deity of Christ. The arguments against His deity have been answered repeatedly through the centuries. No one who claims to follow Christ and His word can deny His absolute deity. To confess that He is "very God of very God" affirms one's allegiance to the Lord of lords and King of kings (1 Tim. 6:15; cf. Deut. 10:17), God Almighty.

CHAPTER 8 DISCUSSION QUESTIONS

1. Why do you think many people who deny the deity of Christ still call themselves Christians?

2. Can you think of any cults or sects today that say they believe the Bible, but reject the deity of Christ?

3. Why do you believe in the deity of Christ?

4. Do you think someone can become a Christian who does not believe Christ is fully God?

5. How does your belief in the deity of Christ affect your confidence in your salvation?

9

THE GOD-MAN

In chapters 7 and 8, we concluded that the Savior came to save sinners. God's Son was truly and fully human and truly and fully divine. Before that in Section I, we saw that God and man were separated because of man's sin. Man is alienated from God because of his involvement by representation in Adam's specific sin, his own inherited *sin nature*, and his own specific sins.

Bridging the gap between God and man depends upon the union of humanity and deity in Christ. The redemption the Savior provided at Calvary could not avail if He were not truly and fully human, able to be fully representative of humanity. On the other hand, His work on the cross could not atone for sin either if He were not truly and fully God, able to represent the One against whom we sin. His sacrifice could not be lacking in either deity or humanity. In this chapter we explore the crucial though difficult subject of the union of the divine and human in our Savior.

NATURE AND PERSON

In order to understand the union of deity and humanity in one person in Christ we need to understand what is meant by *nature* and *person*. John Walvoord's comments are helpful:

The English word 'nature' is derived from the Latin *natura* and is the equivalent of the Greek *physis* (cf. Rom. 2:14; Gal. 2:15; 4:8; Eph. 2:3; 2 Peter 1:4). . . . As this refers to the Person of Christ, nature is seen to be the sum of all the attributes and their relationship to each other.[1]

J. Oliver Buswell defines "nature" as "a complex of attributes."[2] Everything belonging to Christ's humanity describes His human nature. By the same token, everything belonging to His deity describes His divine nature.

Nature is the real essence, the inward properties, the essential qualities of being. *Person* describes nature, or as in the case of Christ, natures, *and* independent subsistence or reality. "The single person of the incarnate Christ retained the total complex of divine attributes and possessed all the complex of human attributes essential to a perfect human being."[3]

When God the Son became incarnate, perfect humanity and absolute, undiminished deity were united in one person forever. There was not a loss of the separate identity of each or a confusing of the attributes of each. The attributes of both the divine and human natures belong to the one person. The unique union of humanity and deity formed at the incarnation continues now and will continue always.

The union of the divine and human in Christ is abundantly supported by Scripture, even though it is a complex concept. Paul described the incarnation of God's Son as a mystery (1 Tim. 3:16). He also said Christ Himself is "the mystery of God" (Col. 2:2).

When the Son of God became man, deity did not permeate humanity, nor did humanity simply become absorbed in deity. Confusing man with God is pantheism, characteristic of the New Age Movement rather than Christianity. The Son of God was not changed into a human being. He did not even unite Himself with a human person, but with a human nature. The Savior always acted as a single person because that is what He was. He was not acting sometimes as man and at other times as God, although at various times His words or actions highlighted either His humanity or His deity.

GOD AND MAN

The Son of God was *theanthropic* in His person. The word is from two Greek words for God and man. Not only is Christ God through all eternity, the humanity the Savior embraced continues forever. His humanity is in perpetuity, theologians say. The incarnation began at a point in time, but Christ is still incarnate. The only change which occurred is that humanity was glorified with His resurrection and is no longer subject to and restricted by time and space.

The Lord Jesus Christ, the Savior of sinners, was the most unique person who ever lived or will ever live. Being the God-man, He was hungry and yet fed multitudes. The same One who was so human He slept was so divine the waves of the sea obeyed Him. He was thirsty Himself and yet turned water into wine. This One who wept at the death of His friend Lazarus also raised the dead. He Himself died and came forth from the grave three days later. Such actions seem contradictory, but are not, stemming from His two natures. There was a communion, but not a mixture, of the attributes in the person of Christ.

FALSE THEORIES

From the early centuries of the church, and throughout the history of the church to the present, false theories regarding the relation of the human and divine in Christ have prevailed.

The apostle John refers to a heresy similar to incipient Gnosticism when he emphasizes Christ's genuine humanity

(1 John 4:1–3). Some heretics said Christ only appeared to be human. This view led to a form of Gnosticism called Doceticism (from the Greek *dokeo*, to seem).

The deity of Christ was denied by heretics called Ebionites already in the second century. They said Christ was a man chosen to be God's Son, who became such at His baptism by John.

Jesus was called "begotten," and the heretic Arius misinterpreted that term to mean He was a created "being." Christ's "divine" nature was not the same as God's.

In the fifth century of the church the Nestorians divided Christ into two persons. Many other heresies concerning Christ's divinity and humanity cropped up through the centuries. Today liberal theology, for example, embraces the human Jesus while rejecting His necessary deity. John A. T. Robinson's view of how he understands Christ as a man of God is representative of a contemporary nonevangelical point of view.

> In other words the formula that we presuppose is not of one superhuman person with two natures, divine and human, but of one human person of whom we must use two languages, man language and God language. Jesus is wholly and completely a man, but a man who 'speaks true' not simply of humanity but of God. He is not a man plus a man fitted as it were with a second engine—which would mean that he was *not* a man in any genuine sense. He is a man who in all that He says and does as man is the personal representative of God: He stands in God's place. He *is* God to us and for us.[4]

In contrast, the orthodox believers have always maintained His absolute deity and His genuine humanity in one person.

SCRIPTURAL SUPPORT FOR THE UNION

There is no indication in Scripture that the Lord Jesus Christ is anything other than one person. He is always spoken of in the singular. There are many Scriptures defending His deity and His humanity, but none stating or implying that He is two persons. Every description of His being and all His actions, including His death and resurrection, present Him as one person. It is true that at times a human title is used of Him in a passage concerning His deity (John 3:13; 6:62) and yet at other times the divine title is used in a passage concerning His humanity (1 Cor. 2:8; Col. 1:13–14). This in no way conflicts with the singularity of His person, which includes deity and humanity.

On the positive side there are three central texts representing both natures united in one person:

> Paul, a servant of Jesus Christ, called to be an apostle, separated to the gospel of God which He promised before through His prophets in the Holy Scriptures, concerning His Son Jesus Christ our Lord, who was born of the seed of David according to the flesh, and declared to be the Son of God with power, according to the Spirit of holiness by the resurrection from the dead, through whom we have received grace and apostleship for obedience to the faith among all nations for His name . . . (Rom. 1:1–5).

"Christ Jesus" in verse 1 is God's Son (v. 2) but also a "descendant of David" (v. 3). He is just as much the one as the other, just as much God as man.

> But when the fulness of the time had come, God sent forth His Son, born of a woman, born under the law, to redeem those who were under the law, that we might receive the adoption as sons (Gal. 4:4–5).

Here God's Son was born of woman. How much clearer could the singularity of His person yet the duality of His natures be set forth?

> Let this mind be in you which was also in Christ Jesus, who, being in the form of God, did not consider it robbery to be equal with God, but made Himself of no reputation, taking the

form of a servant, and coming in the likeness of men. And being found in appearance as a man, He humbled Himself and became obedient to the point of death, even the death of the cross (Phil. 2:5–8).

The Savior, before His incarnation, existed in the "form of God" and was equal with God. Yet He was made "in the likeness of men." His work described in these verses is not attributed to either His deity or His humanity, but to Him as a divine human person.

The passage is often said to describe the self-emptying of Christ. It is called the *kenosis* passage. *Kenosis* is the Greek word in Philippians 2:7 which means self-emptying. Christ emptied Himself of something, laid aside something when He became man. The question is, of what did He empty Himself? What did He lay aside?

GOD WAS IN CHRIST

In view of the clear teaching of Scripture affirming the Savior's deity, evangelicals rightly insist He did not surrender or lay aside His deity. To surrender any of His divine authority would have been to surrender His deity. Of what then did He empty Himself when He became man?

John Calvin said Christ laid aside His preincarnate glory: "He laid aside His glory in the view of men, not by lessening it, but by concealing it. The abasement of the flesh was, notwithstanding, like a veil, by which his divine majesty was concealed."[5] What this means, at least in part, is that while He was here on earth Christ did not look like God. He laid aside His godly appearance and took on the form or appearance of man, but without sin.

Baptist theologian Augustus Hopkins Strong believed Christ surrendered "the independent exercise of the divine attributers."[6] Many evangelicals followed Strong's lead. Some have objected, thinking it implies a time when Christ

78

acted independently of the other members of the Godhead.

It seems to me there is validity and truth in both of the above declarations. Charles Ryrie's view seems to include these, but adds another necessary dimension: ". . . the emptying concerned becoming a man to be able to die. Thus the *kenosis* means leaving His preincarnate position and taking a servant-humanity."[7]

Christ is personal. We can trust Him as a divine Person who is able to fulfill whatever He promises. He is God, representing divine holiness in judgment against sin. And He is man, reconciling us to the Father through His sacrifice. In Jesus Christ the God-man, "God was in Christ, reconciling the world to Himself" (2 Cor. 5:19).

CHAPTER 9 DISCUSSION QUESTIONS

1. Why was it necessary for Christ to be both God and man?

2. How long will Christ's humanity continue?

3. If someone asked you to explain how Christ could be both God and man, what would you answer?

4. A particular sect uses the picture of a tea bag being permeated by hot water and producing hot tea as an example of Christ being God and man. Do you think this is good example? Why or why not?

5. Was Christ two persons since He had two natures?

10

PROPHET, PRIEST, KING

The Savior of sinners is also Prophet, Priest, and King. He occupies these three offices simultaneously and in a way infinitely superior to any others who have ever held them or who will ever hold them. All three relate to both the incarnation and the ministry, death, and resurrection of the Son of God.

> Taken together, the three offices of Christ as Prophet, Priest, and King are the key to the incarnation. His prophetic office was concerned with the revelation of the truth of God; His priestly office was related to His work as Savior and Mediator; His kingly office had in view His right to reign over Israel and over the entire earth. In Christ the supreme dignity of these offices is reached.[1]

THE SAVIOR AS PROPHET

Deuteronomy 18:15 predicted that God would raise up a prophet like Himself. This prophecy was fulfilled in the Lord Jesus Christ (Acts 3:22–26). He not only gave forth God's revelation, He was God's revelation. Those who saw Him and heard Him preach called Him a prophet (Matt. 21:11). His fiercest critics, the Pharisees, wanted to arrest Him but they were afraid to do so because they knew the multitudes viewed Him with the high regard of a prophet (Matt. 21:46).

Prophets in biblical times were those who foretold—predicted future events, and those who forth-told—declared God's message or taught His truth. The Savior was a prophet in both senses. He foretold His own death and resurrection (John 2:19–22) and the destruction of Jerusalem (Matt. 24:2), for example.

Three extended messages of Jesus illustrate His role as prophet in the forth-telling sense. These are the Sermon on the Mount (Matt. 5–7), the Upper Room Discourse (John 13–17); and the Olivet Discourse (Matt. 24–25). The teachings of Christ are not as easy to understand as they first appear to be. The primary reason for this is because He lived and taught during such a unique period of time, the bridge between the kingdom and the church. The Law of Moses was still operative and He, of course, kept it perfectly and brought it to conclusion as a rule of life with His death. John the Baptist announced the imminency of the Davidic kingdom with his message, "Repent for the kingdom of heaven is at hand" (Matt. 3:2). During His teaching ministry the Savior also promised to build His church, against which the gates of hell would not prevail (Matt. 16:18). As prophet the Savior gave forth God's revelation while at the same time He was God's revelation (John 1:4–18).

Christ was the Prophet of God throughout His life and even in His dying moments on the cross. Since God's revelation to man has been completed, Christ is not now functioning as a prophet. Neither does there seem to be any need for Him to function as prophet in the future.

THE SAVIOR AS PRIEST

Prophets represented God to the people. Priests represented the people to God. Christ was a priest, not after the order of Aaron, since Jesus was from the tribe of Judah instead of Levi, but after the order of Melchizedek (Heb. 7:1–3). The Savior met the qualifications of the Old Testa-

81

ment priesthood. As Hodge points out, He was "a man duly appointed to act for men in things which pertained to God. . . . A priest is appointed to offer gifts and sacrifices . . . he makes intercession for the people."[2] In the Book of Hebrews Christ is presented as the believer's great High Priest. He was fully qualified for the office (3:1–6), He was appointed by God (5:1–10) and was of the right order (5:6, 10). Christ was able to offer sacrifice and make intercession (7:23–28). Further, His priesthood was eternal, in contrast to the work of the priests of the Aaronic order (7:24).

When did Christ become a priest of God? Lewis Sperry Chafer has Christ anointed and consecrated as priest at His baptism by John.[3] Two facts seem to conflict with such a view. One, Christ was not of the Aaronic order of priests and, therefore, would not harmonize with John's role. Two, unless one says Christ's life is part of His sacrifice for sin, which Chafer does not agree with, His priestly ministry could not begin when John baptized Him.

It seems better to acknowledge that the Savior was God's Priest when He became incarnate. He did not function as a priest with respect to sacrifice for sin, however, until His death. At the present time He functions as priest. He ever lives to make intercession for His own. He is the one and only mediator between God and man. The Savior's present priestly ministry is based upon His past sacrifice for sin at Calvary and does not involve continuous sacrifice.

THE SAVIOR AS KING

As we have noted earlier, one of the primary purposes for Christ's coming was to offer Himself as Israel's king and to bring to fulfillment the Davidic Covenant. The Twelve and the Seventy all proclaimed the same message John the Baptist did—"Repent for the kingdom of heaven is at hand."

The Old Testament Scriptures promise a king to rule on the throne of David (2 Sam. 7:16; Ps. 2; 45; 72; 110). Isaiah's prophecy, the Christmas story familiar to us from Handel's "Hallelujah Chorus," has it that the Messiah would institute and rule on the throne of David (Isa. 9:7). Mary was told by Gabriel that God "will give [Jesus] the throne of His father David. And He will reign over the house of Jacob for ever" (Luke 1:32–33). But these promises of reigning were not fulfilled literally when Christ was born or during His life on earth. This is why premillennialists believe they will be fulfilled in the future, just as God promised. As the Savior ministered on earth, His Davidic kingship was announced and offered to Israel but was rejected by them (Matt. 2:2; 27:11; John 12:13).

Jesus was born King of the Jews. He did not function as king because He was rejected by His own people. The Savior is not now reigning on David's throne as King. He will in the future when He returns to earth and puts down all opposing rule.

> Because the King was rejected the Messianic, Davidic kingdom was (from a human viewpoint) postponed. Though He never ceases to be king and, of course, is king today as always, Christ is never designated as king of the church (Acts 17:7 and 1 Tim. 1:17 are no exceptions and Rev. 15:3, "king of saints" *KJV*, is "King of nations" in the critical majority texts). Though Christ is a king today He does not rule as king. This awaits His second coming. Then the Davidic kingdom will be realized (Matt. 25:31; Rev. 19:15; 20). Then the priest will sit on His throne, bringing to this earth the long-awaited golden age (Ps. 110).[4]

The rejection of Christ brought His prophetic ministry to completion. His priestly ministry began to function at His death with respect to sacrifice for sin. His kingly ministry in the future has its foundation in His death also. The Messiah was predicted the One who would rule and also the One who would atone for the sins of the people.

The fulfillment of God's ministry of reconciliation and communion with man is embodied in Jesus Christ. As our

The Offices Of Christ

Prophet
Matt. 24-2

Priest
Hebrews

King
John 18:37; Rev. 20:1-6

prophet He secures our knowledge of God and the future. As our priest He accomplishes atonement for our sin and reconciliation to God. As our King we look forward to the time when the world will submit to Him, when "at the name of Jesus every knee should bow, of those in heaven, and of those on earth, and of those under the earth" (Phil. 2:10).

CHAPTER 10 DISCUSSION QUESTIONS

1. How is Christ your prophet?

2. How is Christ your priest?

3. How is Christ your king?

4. Think about the Old Testament priests. How do they picture Christ's priestly activities?

5. Look at Deuteronomy 13:1–3 and 18:18–21. What are two tests of a true prophet? Did Christ fulfill both?

PART TWO
THE WORK OF THE SAVIOR

11
OBEDIENCE AND SUFFERING IN LIFE

The Savior's obedience to the Law of God and His sufferings in life before He went to the cross are often neglected, and sometimes their significance is distorted.[1] The truthfulness of the scriptural accounts is not the issue with those who embrace the authority of the Bible. The question, rather, is one of the theological import of Christ's life of obedience and suffering.

Evangelicals are united in their agreement that Christ obeyed the Law of God perfectly and suffered at the hands of sinners in His life on earth. There is some disagreement, though, as to the purpose and the effects of these things. Did Christ's obedience and suffering in life, sometimes called His active obedience, provide substitution for sin *as well as* His passive obedience, His suffering, and His death on the cross? How does Christ's obedience and suffering in life relate to His obedience and suffering in death? First we will establish the reality of His life of obedience and suffering.

THE REALITY OF CHRIST'S OBEDIENCE AND SUFFERING

Obedience to the Law of God

The Savior obeyed every precept of the Law of God. This can be demonstrated first by acknowledging that He was born under the Law's rule. He was "born under the Law" (Gal. 4:4). Not once did He ever violate any of God's Law. He was "without sin" (Heb. 4:15) and was in fact "the end of the law" (Rom. 10:4). The Savior came not to abolish the Law, but to fulfill it (Matt. 5:17). The writer to the Hebrews said Christ, the Savior, "learned obedience by the things which He suffered" (Heb. 5:8). In no way does this imply there were times when He did not obey God's Law. Rather, it means that during His life of humiliation on earth He came to know what obedience costs. When the Son of God became man, He voluntarily subjected Himself to a new and unique role in relation to the Father. The new relationship involved submission.

Suffering Because of His Humanity

The union of God with man necessarily involved the suffering associated with humanity. The physical properties common to man were His also. He experienced pain; grew hungry, thirsty, and tired as a man. As a vital part of His humiliation, when He clothed Himself with humanity He voluntarily subjected Himself to the limitations of humanity (Phil. 2:7–8). He was the sinless One among sinners, the obedient One among the disobedient. In short, the Savior suffered in life because He was genuinely human.

Suffering Caused by Satan

Scripture records that Jesus was "led up by the Spirit into the wilderness to be tempted by the devil" (Matt. 4:1). Though the Holy Spirit providentially arranged for

His temptation in the wilderness, the devil was the instrument used to do the testing. Also, Matthew reveals that the devil left Him as he found Him, the sinless, spotless Savior (cf. Matt. 4:11).

The Bible clearly states that Christ did not sin when tested by Satan in that unique and peculiar experience, nor on any other occasion. There is a difference of opinion, though, as to whether or not Christ could have sinned, as we have learned in chapter 7. Even though the Savior did not sin, could He have sinned? The answer to that question must be an emphatic *no*. He could not sin because He was one divine Person with two natures: human (but without sin) and divine.

Suffering at the Hands of His Foes

The very ones who would be expected to have received Christ are the ones who rejected and opposed Him the most. The Sadducees and the Herodians, the influential Jews, opposed Him by rejecting His identity as the Messiah and dismissing His ministry until His popularity with the people threatened their power and alarmed their Roman overlords.

The reaction of the Scribes and Pharisees, the spiritual leaders, to Christ's claims was very different. They did not ignore Him. Instead they persecuted Him and mocked His teachings relentlessly. These religious leaders were respected by the people as the orthodox religious spokesmen of the day, and yet they were the very ones who rejected, repudiated, and eventually crucified the Lord of glory. Their sin had so blinded their spiritual eyes (2 Cor. 3:14–16) that they could not see Him as their Messiah even though they were students of the Old Testament Scriptures, which clearly spoke of Him. This brought suffering and sadness to the Savior. These who should have been His friends were His fiercest foes.

Suffering at the Hands of His Friends

Neglect and rejection of Christ could be expected from His foes. Those who refused to accept Him as Israel's Messiah would naturally spurn Him and bring heart-rending suffering to Him. But the Savior also suffered at the hands of His friends—the Twelve whom He had chosen for unique ministry. In His parting words to His own, Christ told them, "You are My friends if you do whatever I command you" (John 15:14). But they brought suffering to Him through withdrawal, denial, and betrayal.

The withdrawal of His own climaxed when they all "forsook Him and fled" (Matt. 26:56), although it started long before that awful moment became a reality. Even though they had forsaken all to follow Him, they often failed to exercise faith in Him. On one such occasion Jesus said the reason for their powerlessness in serving Him was because of their unbelief (Matt. 17:20).

Unconcern

The disciples were also sometimes unconcerned. At a most crucial moment in the Garden of Gethsemane, when they should have been praying, they were asleep (Matt. 26:40). Pride crept into their lives, too, on occasion. Anticipating as they did the establishment of the Messianic rule on earth, and having heard the Savior say that He would be killed and then raised from the dead, they evidently assumed He would then institute the kingdom promised to the fathers. They disputed among themselves, "who would be the greatest" (Mark 9:34). Two of the disciples in particular gave vent to their unholy ambition. James and John, through their mother, asked to be especially favored by the Lord. They wanted one to sit on His right hand and the other on His left hand (Mark 10:37). This must have grieved the heart of the Son of God. Surely their unconcern and unholy ambition brought suffering to Him.

Abandonment

No doubt the most severe suffering came when, after they all, along with Peter (Mark 14:31), said they would not deny the Lord, and then soon afterward "they all forsook Him and fled" (Mark 14:50). Here was the climax. His own had withdrawn from Him. Peter's denial of his Lord brought extreme suffering to the Savior. The Lord knew it would come to pass, for He had predicted it (Matt. 26:34). Peter probably thought it impossible. How could he, the spokesman for the Twelve, ever do such a thing? And yet that is exactly what he did before individuals and the crowds gathered to accuse the Savior (Matt. 26:69–75).

Betrayal

The startling and difficult words of Christ to His own, "Did I not choose you, the twelve, and one of you is a devil?" (John 6:70), must have puzzled the Twelve often. Who could it be? Speaking for the entire group Peter had just said, "Lord, to whom shall we go? You have the words of eternal life" (John 6:68). It seemed impossible that one of the Twelve would ever act as an adversary of the Savior. As history unfolded, however, that is precisely what took place; Judas did betray the Savior. Through treachery and deceit Christ was betrayed by one of His own followers, one whom He had chosen and loved. Just as His own nation, which He had come to exalt, and over which He was to reign as King, and for whom He was to bring everlasting peace and righteousness, had officially rejected Him, so now one of that small, select company betrayed Him into the hands of His executioners (Matt. 26:47–56).

The suffering and agony in life which accompanied Christ's perfect humanity cannot be denied. The questions remain: Why did He suffer in life? Of what value were His life sufferings? Were these the ways in which Christ made atonement for sin?

THE REASONS FOR HIS LIFE SUFFERINGS

The query propounded by the psalmist and the prophet, "Why do the righteous suffer?" is no more demanding of an answer than when asked concerning the Lord Jesus Christ. That He suffered in life is as certain and undeniable as that He suffered in death. Truly He was "a Man of sorrows and acquainted with grief" (Isa. 53:3) and "He was wounded for our transgressions" (Isa. 53:5).

Students of theology are usually divided into two classes in answer to the question, "What was the purpose of Christ's suffering in life?" Dispensationalists usually hold to one view and nondispensationalists to another. In fact, one's view of the value of Christ's life sufferings and obedience to the Law is directly related to acceptance or rejection of Covenant theology. If it can be conceded, as Covenant theology contends, that God made a covenant with Adam promising him eternal life for his obedience, and if this covenant is the basis for all God's redemptive dealing with man for all ages, then belief in the substitutionary nature of Christ's sufferings in life is a natural corollary. This is so because just as the first Adam represented his posterity, so Christ, the last Adam, represented the same group. Because the first Adam sinned he plunged the entire human race into sin. Christ as the last Adam, in addition to coming to die for our sins, came to do for the race what the first Adam failed to do—obey God and thus fulfill His part of the covenant.

The Vicarious Atoning View

Those who hold to Reformed or Covenant theology subscribe to this position. They classify Christ's obedience into active obedience and passive obedience. While some distinction is made between these two by making the active refer to Christ's obedience in life and the passive to His obedience in death, it is conceded that the two cannot be separated. "The two accompany each other at every point in the Savior's life."[2]

Definition

Berkhof explains his view of the vicarious nature of Christ's life sufferings by showing the relation of the first Adam to Christ, the last Adam.

> The first Adam was by nature under the Law of God and the keeping of it as such gave him no claim to a reward. It was only when God graciously entered into a covenant with him and promised him life in the way of obedience that the keeping of the Law was made the condition of obtaining eternal life for himself and his descendants. And when Christ voluntarily entered into the federal relationship of the last Adam, the keeping of the Law naturally required the same significance for Him and for those whom the Father had given Him.[3]

Charles Hodge states the view very clearly as he explains the meaning of Christ being made under the Law, saying, "This subjection to the Law was not only voluntary but vicarious."[4]

Murray, a more contemporary adherent to the view, also presents the idea that what Christ suffered in life was as vicarious and substitutionary as what He endured on the cross.

> Christ's obedience was vicarious in the bearing of the full judgment of God upon sin and it was vicarious in the full discharge of the demands of righteousness. His obedience becomes the ground of the remission of sin and of actual justification.[5]

A classic orthodox writer on the atonement gives clear expression to this concept.

> Most readers who merely read the narrative of Christ's life as they do a common history see nothing more in these suffer-

93

ings than the opposition of ungodly men to the cause of God or limit the endurance of the curse on the part of Jesus to the hours when He hung on the cross. But the curse-bearing career of Christ was by no means of that nature nor limited to that time.[6]

Those who hold to this view make Christ's life sufferings as substitutionary as His death sufferings, though they insist that the one would not be complete without the other. Too, the view is normally tied in with belief in a covenant of works which God is said to have made with Adam, promising him eternal life for obedience and death for disobedience. Since Adam failed God in the covenant relationship, Christ, the last Adam, came to obey God's Law for man, thus gaining for him eternal life by His acts of obedience in life as well as by His death on the cross.

Criticism

This view of the life sufferings of Christ bristles with biblical and theological problems. The orthodoxy and sincerity of those who subscribe to it is genuine and need not be questioned. But the view contains serious weaknesses which make it unacceptable to me.

First, the view fails to take into account that before the fall, Adam did not have a sin nature. Instead it assumes that to be rightly related to God, Adam and his posterity were required to render perfect obedience to the commands of God. Boettner stated this view well when she said: "We believe that the requirement for salvation now, as originally, is prefect obedience."[7]

The whole concept of the vicarious nature of Christ's active obedience rests primarily on the idea of the covenant of works. The covenant promised eternal life for obedience and, since Adam disobeyed and all his posterity in him, Christ, the last Adam, came to accomplish what the first Adam failed to do.

The fact that Adam came from the hands of the Creator sinlessly perfect must not be overlooked. The command of God to obey Him was not designed to produce eternal life in him or to relate him rightly to God. He already enjoyed a state of sinlessness and the proper relation to his Creator. Human effort is never presented as a condition of salvation in Scripture. Rather the command of God to Adam was designed to *demonstrate* his obedience to the authority of God.

Second, the view amounts to a minimizing of the work of Christ on the cross:

> A moment's reflection should convince us that the suffering and death of Christ, although fully effective in paying the debt which His people owed to divine justice, was in a sense only a negative service. Being of the nature of a penalty it could relieve His people from the liability under which they labored but it could not provide them a positive reward. Its effect was to bring them back up to the zero point, back to the position in which Adam stood before the Fall. It provided for their rescue from sin and its consequences but it did not provide for their establishment in heaven. By His passive obedience they have been rescued from hell and by His active obedience they are given entrance into heaven.[8]

This distraction from the death of Christ is also seen in the words of Berkhof:

> And finally if Christ had suffered only the penalty imposed on man, those who shared in the fruits of His work would have been left exactly where Adam was before the Fall. . . . By His active obedience, however, He carried His people beyond that point and gave them a claim to everlasting life.[9]

According to this view the death of Christ was not the sole basis upon which God provided redemption and everlasting life for man. If the life sufferings are viewed as substitutionary and vicarious, then the Savior's passive obedience in the shedding of His blood on the cross must be viewed as less

95

than the total or complete means by which God through His Son atoned for sin. The blood shed at Calvary would then constitute only part of the payment for sin.

The third and most serious weakness of all is the stark fact that no Scripture assigns substitution to the life sufferings of Christ. On the contrary, Scripture abounds with evidence that, through His substitutionary death on the cross, and that alone, He took the sinner's place and died in the sinner's stead (Isa. 53:6-7; Rom. 3:18, 24-25; 5:19; 2 Cor. 5:14-21; 1 Peter 2:24).

Evaluation

Scriptural proof of the vicarious nature of Christ's active obedience or His suffering in life is conspicuous by its absence. A few passages are usually cited, however (e.g., Matt. 3:15; 5:17-18; John 15:10; Gal. 4:4-5; Heb. 10:7-9). Not one of these passages, or any other passage for that matter, teaches or even implies that Christ's life sufferings were vicarious.

Christ submitted Himself to John in baptism to fulfill all righteousness (Matt. 3:15) and He came to fulfill the Law (Matt. 5:17-18), but that He by these acts was being a substitute for sin is foreign to Scripture. He kept the Father's commandments (John 15:10, but the text does not indicate that He did this as an act of substitution in place of the sinner. It is simply assumed that, as the God-Man, He could do nothing but obey. Galatians 4:4-5 does not say that Christ's obedience to the Law was vicarious. Rather, it teaches that He was born under the Law in order to redeem those under the Law. Likewise, Hebrews 10:7-9 says nothing about Christ's life being substitutionary. In fact the verses which follow make it crystal clear that it was the *one* offering of His body (on the cross) which constituted the *one* sacrifice for sin (Heb. 10:10-12).

The Nonatoning View

Without detracting from the reality or intensity of Christ's suffering in life or from the sinlessness of His person and His absolute obedience to the Law of God, the nonatoning view denies that the active obedience of the Savior was in any way vicarious or atoning. Those who subscribe to this view reserve the substitionary work of Christ to His death on the cross and to that alone. It was not the blood shed when He was circumcised, or even when He prayed in Gethsemane, which made atonement for sin. Only as He became a curse, as He hung on the accursed tree and cried "It is finished," did He become the full and final sacrifice for sin as He took the sinner's place. All the contradictions of sinners which the Savior endured in life were real and cannot be viewed lightly. Though genuine and without comparison, they were not vicarious.

Two basic things were accomplished by the Savior's suffering in life:

The proof of His sinless character

To prove that the Paschal lamb was without blemish it was confined from the tenth day of the month until the fourteenth (Ex. 12:3, 6). During this time the lamb was not a sacrifice for sin, but this time was needed to demonstrate its qualifications as a sacrifice to be offered. The Paschal lamb was a type of Christ. His life of suffering with all that it involved served to prove His eligibility as an offerer and as the offering for sin. His sufferings in life did not provide a sacrifice, or even make Him eligible to offer one, but they did demonstrate His right to be the sacrifice. They proved He was eligible to offer the one eternal sacrifice for sin. Though tested often, and on all points, He remains the sinless, spotless Savior. Thus His sinless life of suffering was a natural and necessary prelude to His cross work.

97

The apostle Peter showed the relation of the life sufferings and death sufferings of Christ. In a context dealing with the believer's responsibility to submit to human government rather than to misuse individual liberty (1 Peter 2:11–20), he uses the example of Christ (1 Peter 2:21–25). In His life, "Christ also suffered for us, leaving us an example, that you should follow His steps: Who committed no sin, nor was guile found in His mouth" (1 Peter 2:21–22). On the cross, "when He was reviled, did not revile in return; when He suffered, He did not threaten, but committed Himself to Him who judges righteously" (1 Peter 2:23). It was there alone that He "bore our sins in His own body on the tree, that we, having died to sin, might live for righteousness—by whose stripes you were healed" (1 Peter 2:24).

The suffering of Christ in life proved and demonstrated His impeccability. Through them all He "committed no sin, and no deceit was found in His mouth." In the midst of all the sin and corruption around Him, His sinless person was preserved, though often offended.

The preparation for His sacrificial death

One minute infraction of the Law by Christ would have disqualified Him as the sin bearer. Like the priest under the Levitical system, He would have had to provide a sacrifice for Himself before He could have offered one for sinners. Furthermore, He would have had to repeat the sacrifice continually as those priests did. In fact, His sacrifice would have been no different than theirs. The contrast to the repeated sacrifices of the old economy and in contradiction of the view that His life sufferings were vicarious, Peter declares: "Christ also suffered once for sins, the just for the unjust, that He might bring us to God, being put to death in the flesh but made alive by the Spirit" (1 Peter 3:18).

Again, the Scripture provides the relation between the Savior's sinless life and His sacrificial death. Paul put it this way: "He made Him who knew no sin to be sin for us, that we might become the righteousness of God in Him" (2 Cor. 5:21). True, He knew no sin—He obeyed the Law perfectly—but it was not His sinless life which the Father accepted as the sacrifice for sin. The context of this passage bears abundant testimony to the fact that through death alone (vv. 14–15) He bore the penalty of our sin. In death He was so closely identified with the sinner and the guilt of His sin that the Father viewed His death as the sin offering.

CHRIST'S OBEDIENCE

True to the prophecy of Isaiah, the Savior "is despised and rejected by men, a Man of sorrows and acquainted with grief; and we hid, as it were, our faces from Him; He was despised, and we did not esteem Him. Surely He has borne our griefs and carried our sorrows" (Isa. 53:3–4a; cf. Matt. 8:17). However, it was only when He was "stricken, smitten by God, and afflicted" that He was "wounded for our transgressions" and was "bruised for our iniquities." It was only in death that the Lord "laid on Him the iniquity of us all" (Isa. 53:4b–6).

CHAPTER 11 DISCUSSION QUESTIONS

1. What are some lessons about obedience you can learn from the Savior's obedience to the Father?

2. What kinds of emotions do you think Christ felt when His disciples fell asleep instead of praying for Him in the Garden?

3. Think about a time when a close friend let you down. How did you feel? How was the situation resolved?

4. What are some principles you can learn from the way

99

Christ responded when He was betrayed by Judas? How should we react to betrayal?

5. Why did the Savior suffer during His lifetime?

12

OBEDIENCE AND SUFFERING IN DEATH

Christ was "obedient to the point of death, even the death of the cross" (Phil. 2:8). The major conflict between the Savior and the Pharisees was over His origin. He told them plainly, ". . . you do not know where I come from and where I am going" (John 8:14). They refused to believe He was eternally with the Father and sent to earth by Him on a divine mission. Because they didn't know the Son of God, they didn't know the Father either. In view of their unbelief the Savior said to His critics plainly, "you . . . will die in your sins" (v. 24).

In His coming to earth the Savior was obedient to the Father's will. That is not to say He came reluctantly or against His own will. It does mean that what He came to do was a part of the divine plan, and He carried it out willingly and gladly. The Savior also told the Pharisees He spoke only those things He heard from the Father (John 8:26), and He did only those things which were pleasing to Him (v. 29). Hundreds of years before the Savior came, the prophet wrote that "it pleased the LORD to bruise Him" (Isa. 53:10) in death.

GLOOM AND GLORY

The Cross of Christ demonstrates two extremes. It declares the immensity of God's love in giving His Son and the enor-

OF MT. TABOR

mity of man's guilt in crucifying the Lord of glory. Calvary has two sides—the side of gloom and the side of glory. There is man's side and there is God's side.

The side of gloom is unveiled when we learn that the sinless Christ died at the hands of sinful men. No greater crime has ever been committed or recorded in all the annals of history—sacred or secular. Not only are crime and gloom seen in that wicked and sinful men put the sinless and perfect Lamb of God to death, they are also revealed by the reaction of heaven and earth to the brutal business done at Calvary. The heavens displayed shame by becoming dark for three hours. The earth quaked and trembled in anger. It seemed as though the earth was threatening to swallow the creatures who had put the Creator to death (Matt. 27:45–51). The crucifixion was a crime of stupendous proportion and from the perspective of the unregenerate that is all it was—a human tragedy.

But the cross was not an accident which defeated the purpose of God or caught Him off guard. It is true that Christ was crucified by wicked hands, but it is also true that He was "delivered by the determined counsel and foreknowledge of God" (Acts 2:23). The glory is seen in the divine accomplishments and exaltation of the Savior. The Father took Christ, the rejected One, and brought triumph to Himself through the very event men view as a tragedy. He took the gloom and sorrow and turned it into glory and grace and salvation. The very One whom sinful men spit upon and debased, that One the Sovereign God raised from the dead, exalted to His own right hand, and gave a name above every other name (Phil. 2:9–11).

Not only is mankind responsible for the death of Christ, but according to Scripture, the very necessity of the atonement arises from man's sin. Why did the Father smite His Son, the very one He loved and in whom He was well pleased? The answer to this baffling question was given by the apostle Paul. Speaking of Christ he said:

. . . whom God set forth to be a propitiation by His blood, through faith, to demonstrate His righteousness, because in His forbearance God had passed over the sins that were previously committed, to demonstrate at the present time His righteousness, that He might be just and justifier of the one who has faith in Jesus (Rom. 3:25–26).

Here Paul not only declared the nature of the atonement—Christ, "whom God set forth to be a propitiation by His blood"—but also the necessity of the atonement "to demonstrate His righteousness . . . that He might be just and justifier of the one who has faith in Jesus." That is, the Father would not have been just nor could He have been the justifier apart from Christ's death in the place of sinners. Therefore it was man's sin, sin for which man alone is responsible, that made necessary the death of Christ.

Four topics are addressed in this chapter to explain the Savior's obedience in suffering and death: theories as to why He died, the purpose for His death, the accomplishment of His death, and the extent of His work on the cross.

THEORIES OF THE SAVIOR'S DEATH

Men have devised many heretical, unbiblical theories as to why Christ died. Diagram 1 compares some of these theories. All deny the substitutionary sacrifice declared in Scripture.

Ransom and Recapitulation

The early church was plagued with the false notion that Christ's death was a ransom paid to Satan so that Satan's hold on man could be released. Others in the early church (such as Irenaeus) believed Christ recapitulated in Himself or went through all the stages of human life, including those which involved sin.

Satisfaction

In the eleventh century the satisfaction or commercial theory was advanced by Anselm. He believed the honor of God was robbed by the sin of man, and thus Christ died to vindicate God's honor. In this view, God could have done this either by punishment or satisfaction, and He chose the latter through the gift of His Son. This theory's greatest weakness is it grounds the necessity of the atonement in God's honor rather than in His justice.

Moral Influence

The theory of Abelard rose in opposition to Anselm's theory. Abelard's moral influence theory finds many advocates today.

> The fundamental idea is that there is no principle of the divine nature which necessarily calls for satisfaction on the part of the sinner and that the death of Christ should not be regarded as an expiation for sin. It was merely a manifestation of the love of God suffering in and with His sinful creatures and taking upon Himself their woes and griefs.[1]

Example

About the sixteenth century the Socinians postulated the idea that Christ died as an example. This they did in opposition to the view of the Reformers that Christ atoned vicariously for sinners. In this example theory, Christ did not atone for sin in any sense. Salvation comes to man by Christ's example of faith and obedience.

Governmental

As a compromise view between that of the Reformers and the Socinians, a view called the governmental theory was adopted. An adherent of this view advocated that God altered His demands, and although sinners deserved death

MAJOR THEORIES OF THE ATONEMENT

THEORIES	ORIGINAL EXPONENTS	MAJOR TEACHING
Recapitulation	Irenaeus (130-202 A.D.)	Christ recapitulated in Himself all the stages of human life that related to sin. In this way He reversed the course on which Adam, by his sin, started humanity.
Ransom to Satan	Origen (185-254 A.D.)	Christ's death was a ransom paid to Satan for claims he had on man.
Satisfaction	Anselm (1033-1109 A.D.)	Christ's death rendered satisfaction to God's honor.
Moral Influence	Abelard (1079-1142 A.D.)	Christ's death was a manifestation of God's love. The suffering love of Christ awakens a responsive love in sinners.
Example	Socinus (1539-1604 A.D.)	Christ's death did not atone for sin. By His teaching in life and example in death, Christ brought salvation to man.
Governmental	Grotius (1583-1645 A.D.)	Sin disrupted God's government. By His death Christ demonstrated the high estimate God placed on His law and government.
Mystical	Schleirmacher (1768-1834 A.D.)	Christ's death exercises some influence to change man. Christ's unbroken unity with God enabled Him to bring a potential mystical influence for good to man through His death.
Vicarious Repentance	McLeod Campbell (1800-1872 A.D.)	By His death Christ offered to God a perfect and vicarious repentance which man could not do but from which he benefits.

because of sin, He allowed Christ to render a kind of satis-faction. He accepted it to show His displeasure with sin, but it was not the only kind of satisfaction He could have de-manded.

Mystical

There is a great deal of similarity between the moral influ-ence theory and the mystical theory. In fact, some view the mystical idea as a modern variation of the moral influence idea. The purpose of the Incarnation was to lift man to the plane of the divine. While Christ possessed a human nature that was corrupt, the Holy Spirit kept Him from manifesting the corruption and thus purified human nature so that, in His death, He could remove original depravity.

Vicarious Repentance

Perhaps the most subtle theory in the history of the church was proposed by McLeod Campbell. His view of vi-carious repentance, as the title indicates, includes the idea of substitution. However, the substitutionary element relates to Christ's death as a confession or repentance for man's guilt, not to Christ's death as the actual payment for sin. Thus, only the repentance is substitutionary, not the death itself.

Response

Most of these views emphasize only one aspect of truth and either neglect or deny other truths, resulting in heresy. They all fail to ascribe to Christ's death what He and the writers of the New Testament ascribe to it—substitution. While it is true that Christ was a perfect example and that He satisfied God's honor in government, the purpose of His death goes far beyond these, according to Scripture, where we are told that He died *in the stead of* and *in the place of* sin-ners.

This stems from weak views of sin and man's total inability. If man is not seen as a rebel against God and sin is not seen as an infinitely heinous crime against God, the necessity of the vicarious atonement of Christ will, of course, be nullified. And man today (like the men who introduced these theories of the atonement into the church) rejects the biblical concept of man as destitute of righteousness. He then rejects the need for a substitutionary atonement.

One such nonevangelical spokesman for contemporary theology said, "That man sins no one will deny. . . . But that a curse is upon man because of the sin of the first man is to me an immoral absurdity."[2] With such a rejection of man's absolute sinfulness, this same writer could say of Christ's atonement, "I have never been able to carry the idea of justice to the place where someone else can vicariously pay for what I have done in order to clean the slate. . . . It simply does not make sense to me. It is rather an offense. It offends my moral sense."[3]

Another with equal fervor and dogmatism rejects the idea of substitution by Christ by saying, "Certainly we ought to repudiate the notion that God is unwilling to forgive any sin until blood has been spilled as propitiation."[4] Today there is widespread rejection of what the Bible actually has to say on the matters in question.

PURPOSE OF THE SAVIOR'S DEATH

The question before us now relates to the nature of the atonement. Why did God the Son die on the accursed tree?

There are three basic answers.

The Arminian Answer

James Arminius (1560–1609) was a noted professor of theology at the University of Leyden in Leyden, Holland. Soon after his appointment to answer the attacks being made upon supralap sarianism, or hyper-Calvinism, he accepted a less severe form of Calvinism. He became the central figure in the theological controversy of his day in the Dutch Reformed Church.[5] As is usually the case, the followers of Arminius have distorted his views. What passes today as Arminianism would hardly be identifiable with what Arminius set forth in his Declaration of Sentiments delivered in October 1608.

One year after his death, his followers drew up five articles of faith in the form of a protest. They are commonly called the *Remonstrance* or the *Five Arminian Articles*. These articles were in opposition to what came to be known as the five points of Calvinism as they were later set forth at the Synod of Dort (1618–1619).

Remonstrance

The divine design or purpose of the atonement according to the Remonstrance reads as follows:

> That . . . Jesus Christ the Savior of the world died for all men and for every man so that He has *obtained for them all by His death on the cross redemption and the forgiveness of sins* [italics mine]; yet that no one actually enjoys this forgiveness of sins except the believer, according to the word of the Gospel of John 3:16, "God so loved the world that He gave His only begotten Son that whosoever believeth in Him should not perish but have ever lasting life" and in the 1 Epistle of John 2:2, "And He is the propitiation for our sins and not for ours only but also for the sins of the whole world."[6]

The crucial point of this statement regarding the purpose and extent of the atonement centers in the word "obtained." This is precisely the Arminian view, not only that Christ's death *provided* for all but that His death *obtained* it for all. This explains why Arminianism believes each member of Adam's race possesses sufficient grace to be saved. God has endowed every man with the grace or favor which enables him to repent and believe, if he will.[7]

From the confession of the Arminian Remonstrance comes this statement which clarifies the above observation. Although there is the greatest diversity in the degrees in which grace is bestowed in accordance with the divine plan, yet the holy Spirit confers, or at least is ready to confer, upon all and each to whom the Word is ordinarily preached as much grace as is sufficient for generating faith and carrying forward their conversion in its successive stages. Sufficient faith for grace and conviction is allotted not only to those who actually believe and are converted but *also to those who do not actually believe* and are not in fact converted.[8]

This means that on the basis of Christ's death, and because He *obtained* forgiveness of sins for all, everyone now has a degree of grace sufficient to generate faith and repentance. But this view removes God too much from the great work of salvation. Instead of salvation being a work of God, it becomes a work of God *and* man. It places God on the periphery as a bystander, having given all men a measure of grace which may or may not become effectual, depending solely upon how they respond to it.

Total depravity

The above also strikes at the very heart of the great biblical doctrine of total depravity. Total depravity means that man possesses nothing, nor can he do anything, to merit favor before God. He is totally unacceptable to God, is a sinner by nature and by choice. Scripture is abundantly clear on this point, as we have seen earlier.

Strange as it may seem, Arminians nevertheless speak frequently of man's lost condition. Watson, an outstanding Arminian theologian, cites abundant testimony from history and then from Scripture for the corrupt and degenerate condition of all men.[9]

While the Arminian acknowledges the scriptural teaching of man's lost condition, he softens that teaching by his doctrine of sufficient grace. This is what Watson explains:

It is allowed and all scriptural advocates of the universal redemption of mankind will join with the Calvinists in maintain-
ing the doctrine, that every disposition and inclination to good
which originally existed in the nature of man is lost by the Fall;
that all men, in their simply *natural* state, are "dead in trespasses and sins" and have neither the will nor the power to
turn to God; that no one is sufficient of himself to think or do
anything of the saving tendency. But, as all men are required to
do those things which have a saving tendency we contend that
the grace to do them has been bestowed upon all.[10]

The Strict Calvinistic Answer

The views of the Remonstrance were rejected as heretical
at a National Synod in Dort 1618–1619. The Synod also set
out to present the true Calvinistic teaching in regard to the
five matters called into question. They stated what we know
today as the five points of Calvinism. The term *Calvinism*
was derived from the great reformer John Calvin (1509 to
1564), who along with many others, expounded these
views.

The five points

The "five points of Calvinism" presented at the Synod are
as follows: (1) total depravity, (2) unconditional election,
(3) limited atonement or particular redemption, (4) irresistible grace or the efficacious call of the Spirit, and (5) perseverance of the saints or eternal security.

Concerning the third point, that of limited atonement, the
Synod of Dort declared:

> For this was with the Sovereign counsel and most gracious
> will and purpose of God the Father, that the quickening and
> saving efficacy of the most precious death of His Son should
> extend to all the elect for bestowing upon them alone the gift of
> justifying faith, thereby to bring them infallibly to salvation.[11]

Many Calvinists understand this to teach limited or particular atonement. The design of the atonement, according

to Calvinists, was to secure the salvation of the elect. Calvinists confine the atonement to the elect and view all men in their natural state as totally depraved, lacking in the ability to cooperate with God in anything. The design of the atonement was to save those for whom Christ died. John Owen, the Calvinist of Calvinists, put it this way:

> . . . Jesus Christ according to the counsel and will of His Father, did offer Himself upon the cross, to the procurement of those things before recounted and maketh continual intercession, with this intent and purpose: *that all the good things so procured by His death might be actually and infallibly bestowed on, and applied to, all and everyone for whom He died* [italics mine], according to the will and purpose of God.[12]

R. B. Kuiper said, "Calvinism on the contrary insists that the atonement saves all it was intended to save."[13]

Calvinists see the divine design and intent of the atonement as not merely to provide salvation, but actually to secure it for the elect with no provision whatsoever for the nonelect. They view the work of Christ on the cross as efficacious in itself. The atoning work of Christ on the cross saves.

Summarizing the Arminian and Calvinistic views of the divine purpose of Christ's death: the divine purpose in the Arminian view was to obtain redemption and the forgiveness of sins for all men by supplying sufficient grace to all to believe if they will. The Calvinistic answer to the question "Why did Christ die?" is that the Savior died for the elect only, and that by His death He not only provided salvation for that limited number, but also infallibly secured their salvation—saved them.

The Moderate Calvinistic Answer

The Godhead will affect all that was designed in the atonement. The question is, "What is the divine design?" While the Arminians and Calvinists view the design of the atonement similarly, they view its extent very differently.

111

The moderate Calvinist view (which I accept) lies between these two. Christ died to secure the salvation of those who believe—the elect—and it is our conviction that the Bible teaches that Christ died to provide a basis of salvation for all men. To those who are elect and who therefore believe in Christ, this provision secures for them their eternal salvation when they believe. For those who do not believe and thus evidence the fact that they are the nonelect, the provisions exist as a basis of condemnation. The eternal destiny of men, according to the Bible, is not determined by the extent of the atonement or by man's relationship to Adam and his sin, but by man's relationship to Jesus Christ who died for sin and sins—the root and the fruit (Rom. 6:10; 1 Cor. 15:3).

We reject the idea that Christ died to secure the salvation of all or that He provided every man with sufficient grace to cooperate with God. If this were true, God would be defeated, because all will not be saved. We also reject the idea that Christ died to secure the salvation of the elect only. If that were true, the Cross could no longer be the basis of condemnation for those who do not believe (John 3:18). We believe that the twofold testimony of the Scripture can be harmonized by understanding that Christ died to make possible the certain salvation of those who believe.

Mediating position

Strict Calvinists have not allowed for this mediating, and we believe biblical, position. (It is a mediating position not because it is partly biblical and partly nonbiblical, but because it is between the strict Calvinist and the strict Arminian views.)

A. A. Hodge, a strict Calvinist, speaks as though there were only two choices:

> Did Christ die with the design and effect of making the salvation of all men indifferently possible and the salvation of none certain, or did He die in pursuance of an eternal covenant

112

between the Father and Himself for the purpose as well with the result of effecting the salvation of His own people?"[14]

We must reject both of these views because neither one of them is altogether biblical. Christ did die for all men (John 3:16; 2 Cor. 5:19; 2 Peter 2:1; 1 John 2:2). And He also died to secure and make certain the salvation of His own (John 10:15; Eph. 5:25). There are difficulties in harmonizing the Scripture with either the Arminian or Calvinistic concepts. Scripture teaches the total inability of man to move toward God. The Arminian rejection of this concept is unscriptural and totally unacceptable. On the other hand, the strict Calvinist position which insists that Christ's death of itself saved the elect makes faith, the sole biblical condition of salvation, virtually unnecessary. Another difficulty facing both of these views relates to the matter of imputation. Arminianism, because of its incorporation of the governmental theory of the atonement, objects to the imputation of the sins of the race to Christ. Calvinism objects to this same imputation for putting over to Christ's account the totality of the sin of the race.

Imputation

The Bible teaches very clearly that Adam's sin was imputed to the race (Rom. 5:12–20). The sin of the race was imputed or reckoned over to Christ (Isa. 53:5, 6, 11; 1 Peter 3:18; 1 Peter 2:24, 25; 2 Peter 5:21) and the righteousness of Christ is imputed to the believing sinner (Rom. 3:21, 22; 2 Cor. 5:21; Heb. 10:14).

The Arminian solution to the problem ascribes to all men sufficient grace enabling them to believe. The strict Calvinistic solution restricts the extent of the atonement to the elect and makes Christ's death the only saving instrumentality. Neither of these solutions is biblical. Would it not be better to face Scripture objectively, accepting not only its clear teaching of man's native sinfulness and total inability to please

God, but also its equally clear emphasis upon the unlimited provisionary nature of the atonement and the necessary condition of faith for salvation?

Arminianism and Calvinism Compared

"Why did Christ die?"

Moderate Calvinists acknowledge and accept fully the vicarious nature of the atonement, but they insist that the Bible makes that full and complete sacrifice provisionary. They do not believe the Cross applies its own benefits, but that God has conditioned His full and free salvation upon personal faith in order to appropriate its accomplishments to the individual. This faith which men must exercise is not a work whereby man contributes his part to his salvation. Nor does faith, in the moderate view, improve in any way the final and complete sacrifice of Calvary. It is simply the method of applying Calvary's benefits which the sovereign God has designed to use in His all-wise plan of salvation.

For the moderate Calvinist the basis upon which sinners will be eternally lost is not only their sin in Adam, but also because of their rejection of the provision of salvation for them in Christ. To the believer the Cross becomes his means of salvation when he believes. And to the unbeliever it remains a basis of condemnation.

ACCOMPLISHMENTS OF THE SAVIOR'S DEATH

The accomplishments of God the Son on Calvary are many. Christ and His cross are central to Christianity.

"It is finished" was Christ's cry from the cross. That proclamation from the lips of the dying Savior is fraught with meaning. Surely the Lord was doing more than announcing the termination of His physical. Somehow, in spite of the sin of the brutal business at Calvary, God through Christ had completed the final sacrifice for sin.

We might translate the words "It is finished" as "It stands finished." That is, the work was finished then and will remain finished in the future. The same Greek tense is used with this word as was used when Christ replied to Satan, "It is written" or "It stands written." On the cross the Son was announcing that the eternal plan of God for the salvation of sinners had now been enacted in time, and that the fruits of it would extend into the future for all eternity.

Substitution for Sin

Every provision for living the spiritual life has its source in the work of Christ on the cross. However, without doubt the most important accomplishment of Christ's death, and the one on which all the others depend, was His substitution for sin and sinners. He did not die merely to demonstrate bravery in the hour of death. He did not die simply for the benefit of mankind. Nor did He die as a victim of His persecutors. Rather, He died in the place of sinners. His death was vicarious in that He was the sinless vicar intervening for humans. The Savior took the sinner's place and thus acted as the sinner's substitute. The certainty and finality of this substitution is true whether anyone ever appropriates it by faith or not. In other words, its reality and value do not depend upon its application to the individual.

The Scriptures use two Greek words which denote substitution—*anti* and *huper*. The Savior used the stronger of these two words—*anti*—as He spoke to the disciples concerning His purpose in giving His life. When tempted to exalt themselves, they were to remember that the one desiring to be greatest among them was to be their servant: "just as the Son of Man did not come to be served, but to serve, and to give His life a ransom for many" (Matt. 20:28; Mark 10:45). Here the Greek preposition *anti* is translated "for." This word clearly denotes substitution, "in the place of," or "instead of" another. It was so used in the Septuagint or

Greek translation of the Old Testament. For example, ". . . God has appointed another seed for me *instead of* Abel, whom Cain killed" (Gen. 4:25). Or, ". . . Joseph gave them bread *in exchange for* the horses, the flocks, the cattle" (Gen. 47:17) [italics mine]. There are numerous other passages where the idea of substitution is the only possible meaning of *anti*.

In the New Testament this preposition is employed in the same sense. ". . . Archelaus was reigning over Judea instead of his father Herod . . ." (Matt. 2:22). "You have heard that it was said 'An eye for an eye and a tooth for a tooth'" (Matt. 5:38). "Repay no one evil for evil" (Rom. 12:17). It should be noted that in the instances cited above, as well as many others, *anti* is used in passages totally unrelated to redemption and has the same meaning of substitution.

> Nor is it less so assuredly in our Lord's statement, "the Son of man is come to give His life a ransom for many . . ." Indeed were there any room for doubt as to the proper import of the preposition in the present instance the doubt would be at once removed by its connection with the word *lutron* which indicates that the life of the Son of man was the ransom given for many, or the price paid to redeem their forfeited lives."[15]

The basic meaning of *huper* is "for the benefit of" or "on behalf of." But it also means in some contexts what *anti* means—substitution, in the place of or in stead of. In John 13:37 when Peter said to the Lord, "I will lay down my life for Your sake," he used *huper* and obviously meant in behalf of or for the benefit of. When the Savior said, "pray for those who spitefully use you and persecute you" (Matt. 5:44), He meant pray on behalf of them or for their benefit.

Huper also denotes the idea of substitution, as proved not only from its use in the Greek classics but also from the New Testament itself. Paul used the word in his epistle to Philemon regarding Onesimus: ". . . whom I wished to keep with me, that on your behalf [*huper*] he might minister to me" (Philem. 13). While *anti* only connotes substitution, *huper* connotes both the idea of benefit ("on behalf of" another) and also the idea of substitution. This latter meaning is clear in such statements as "[Christ] gave Himself as a ransom for all" (1 Tim. 2:6); Christ tasted "death for everyone" (Heb. 2:9); Christ "suffered once for sins, the just for the unjust" (1 Peter 3:18); and "He made Him who knew no sin to be sin for us, that we might become the righteousness of God in Him" (2 Cor. 5:21).

Redemption—Price Paid

Christ's death atoned for sin. The means of redemption from sin in Scripture is always through the shed blood of Christ, related to His death (Gal. 3:13; Eph. 1:7; Col. 1:14; Heb. 9:12, 15; 1 Peter 1:18, 19; Rev. 5:9).

Old Testament and New Testament words for redemption all have essentially the same idea—freedom by the payment of a price. Three related and progressive ideas are in the New Testament words translated redeem, redemption, bought, etc.

Purchase

First is the concept of purchase. This is found in 2 Peter 2:1: "But there were also false prophets among the people, even as there will be false teachers among you, who will secretly bring in destructive heresies, even denying the Lord who bought them, and bring on themselves swift destruction." The Lord bought, redeemed, or purchased even those who deny Him. The purchase price of His blood is paid even for the false prophets and teachers who deny the only possible thing that can save them. Therefore, they are never saved. This word was used of the purchase of slaves in the slave market as the purchase money was paid.

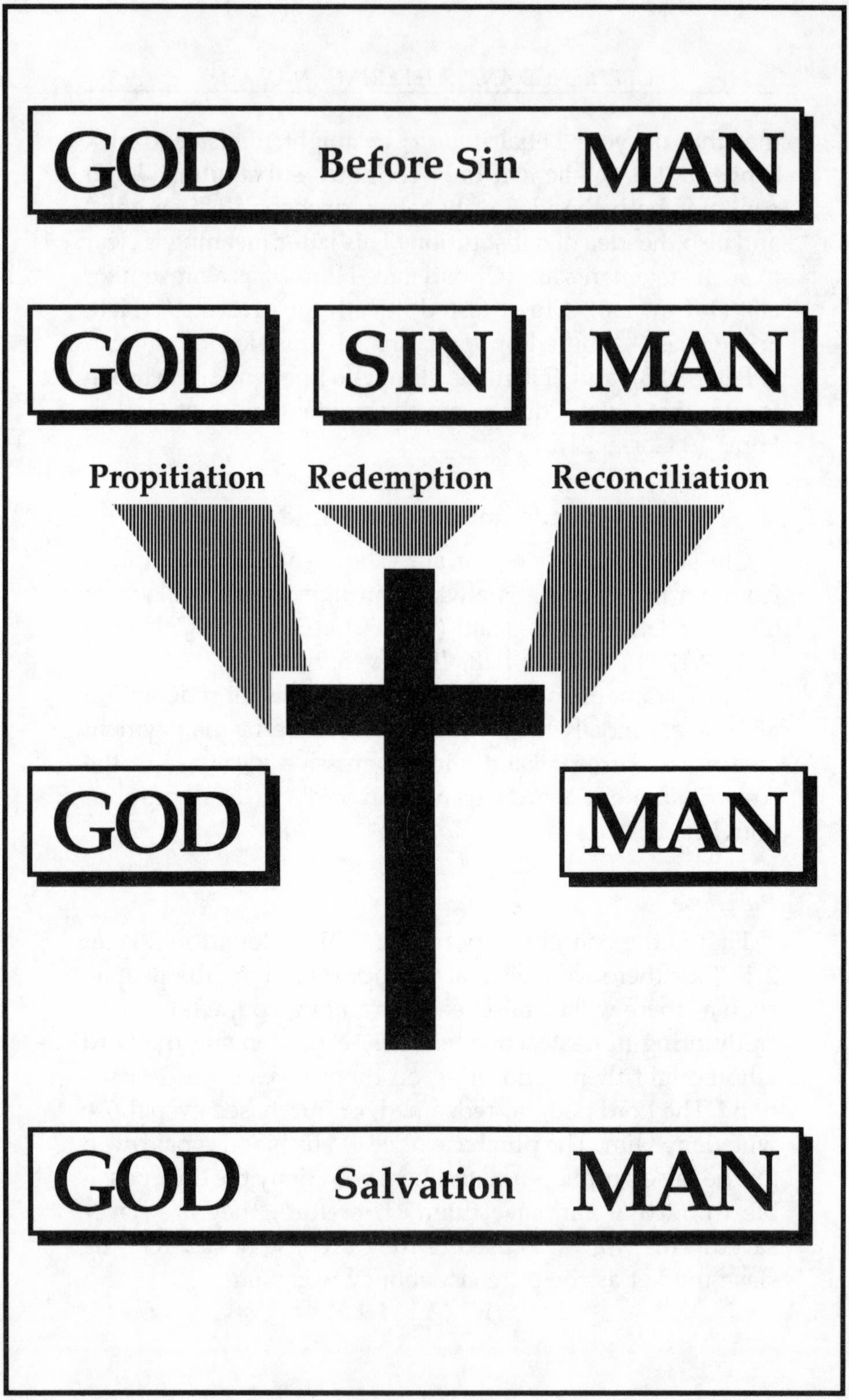
GOD
Before Sin
MAN
GOD
SIN
MAN
Propitiation
Redemption
Reconciliation
GOD
MAN
GOD
Salvation
MAN

Security

Second, there is the idea of security. This occurs in a passage like Galatians 3:13: "Christ has redeemed us from the curse of the law, having become a curse for us—(for it is written), 'cursed is everyone who hangs on a tree.'" This word is even more intensive than the word used in 2 Peter 2:1 and means that the purchased one is removed from the market never to be put on sale again. Paying the price is one thing that was done by Christ for the whole world. Removing the redeemed from the slave market of sin is another that was also done by the Savior but only for those who believe.

Freedom

Third, freedom is taught from another word. The word is used in 1 Peter 1:18: "knowing that you were not redeemed with corruptible things, like silver or gold, from your aimless conduct received by tradition from your fathers." As used by the Greeks, the word implied that the purchased one who is taken from the slave market is ransomed or released and set free. The believer need no longer be a slave, in bondage to sin and Satan. Because of the acceptance of the purchased redemption, he is now delivered from sin's fetters and has a new Master, Christ.

Redemption is concerned with that which Christ accomplished in regard to sin. The message or results of it, therefore, include many positive things regarding the position of the believer before God.

According to Galatians 3:13, all the guilt and penalty revealed by the Law has been met by Christ's death. We have been redeemed from the law. Forgiveness of sin for the unsaved one comes as he trusts Christ. Our redemption is through His blood (Eph. 1:7; Col. 1:14). Also through the redemptive work of Christ the believer is declared righteous—justified (Rom. 3:24–25). To Titus Paul stated clearly the purpose of redemption: It is so that God might

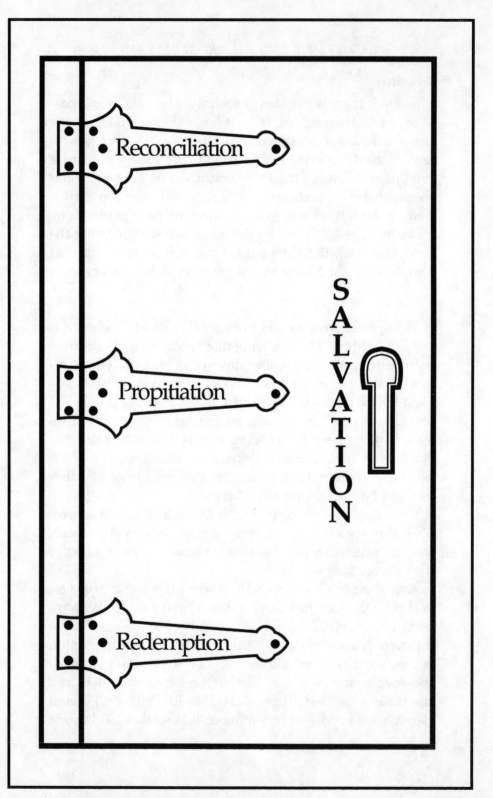

"purify for Himself His own special people, zealous for good works" (Titus 2:14).

Propitiation—the Father Satisfied

The death of Christ satisfied the righteous demands of God the Father. Because of sin His holiness had been offended and only a sinless sacrifice could meet His righteous demands. Jesus Christ the righteous One provided in Himself just that sacrifice. Proof of the Father's acceptance of the Son's sacrifice is found in Christ's resurrection from the dead.

The word *propitiation* occurs four times in the New Testament: (1) Romans 3:25. Here Christ is said to be set forth as the propitiation for the remission of sins. (2) In Hebrews 9:5, the same word is translated "mercy seat" and refers to that appointed place where a holy God could meet sinful man. Because of the blood which was shed, Paul tells us Christ is now our place of meeting—the mercy seat. (3) 1 John 2:2 and (4) 1 John 4:10. In these references John calls Christ a propitiation for sin. As in the case of redemption (i.e., 2 Peter 2:1), so in the matter of propitiation—the work reaches to the entire world (i.e., 1 John 2:1–2). John also associated this particular work of Christ with the Father's love (i.e., 1 John 4:10).

The need for propitiation stems from the sin of man and the holiness of God. It is man who needs to be reinstated or reconciled with God. God's holiness and righteous demands remain unchanged. However, they must be the basis on which God receives sinners. Satisfaction must be made for sin and propitiation provided such a basis through the death of Christ.

Reconciliation—the World Changed

At the end of each month, banks usually issue statements to all those who have checking accounts. The purpose of these is to be sure that our record of deposits, checks, and charges agree with that of the bank. Occasionally a person finds that his figures do not agree with the bank's. He or someone else has made a mistake. Reconciliation takes place when his figures and the bank's match.

Because of sin in Adam the entire human race is out of balance, and God's work of reconciliation through the death of Christ extends to the entire world (2 Cor. 5:19)—in a provisional way and in an experiential and personal way to those who believe (2 Cor. 5:18).

When both the Old and New Testament words translated by "reconcile" or "reconciliation" are taken into account, it is clear that reconciliation is God's work through the death of Christ by which the sinner is brought back to spiritual fellowship and harmony with God.

According to Greek lexicographer Thayer, the New Testament word translated "reconciled" means "to change" or "exchange." Often reconciliation consisted of an agreement or arrangement in which both parties contributed in the renewal of relationships (cf. 1 Cor. 7:11). It is important to note, however, that whenever this doctrine of reconciliation is referred to in connection with salvation, every reference speaks of man as the one reconciled. God is never said to be reconciled in Scripture. His standards and demands of holiness and righteousness remain the same. Reconciliation is manward. Through Christ's work of redemption the price for sin was paid. God the Father accepted this sacrifice. His demands were satisfied. This is propitiation.

As in the case of redemption and propitiation, reconciliation is twofold. There is provisional reconciliation for every member of Adam's race. Before this great work can benefit the individual, however, it must be appropriated by faith. At this time and not before, the individual who does nothing but trust Christ as Savior is reconciled to God and no longer under condemnation.

There are two principal passages which deal extensively with reconciliation: 2 Corinthians 5:14–21 and Romans 5:6–11. The message of reconciliation is stated clearly in verse 19 of 2 Corinthians 5. The desired result of God's work of reconciliation is that those who accept it be ambassadors (v. 20). Of great importance to the ambassador is the worldwide extent of the reconciliation (2 Cor. 5:14–15, 19).

A fourfold need of reconciliation may be seen from the passage in Romans 5: (1) Man's total inability (without strength) (v. 6); (2) man's lack of merit (ungodly) (v. 6); (3) man's guilt toward God (sinners) (v. 8); (d) man at complete enmity toward God and separated from Him (enemies) (v. 10).[16]

EXTENT OF THE SAVIOR'S CROSS WORK

Evangelicals are divided in their answers to the question, "For whom did Christ die?"[17] Some believe the Savior died as a substitute for every member of the human family. Their view is often described as the unlimited atonement or general redemption view. Others say Christ died only for those who believe in Him, the elect. Their view is the limited view of the atonement or particular redemption view.

Those who believe in limited atonement insist that if one believes in the other four essential points of Calvinism—total depravity, unconditional election, irresistible grace, and the perseverance of the saints—he should also believe in limited atonement. It is true that many who reject limited atonement also reject the other four points. However, there are many who find scriptural support for the four points named above but believe support is lacking for the doctrine of limited atonement. These might be called four-point Calvinists or moderate Calvinists.

Our earlier discussion of the divine purpose for the Savior's death relates directly to the question of the extent of the atonement. The divine purpose in the death of Christ is the real issue. One who believes in limited atonement put it succinctly when he said, "The nature of the atonement settles its extent."[18]

If one believes the Savior died as a substitute for the elect only and to secure their salvation, it follows that He died only for this group. On the other hand, if Christ died as a substitute for and to make provision for all, elect and non-elect, then it must be said His death extended to all.

Those who believe in limited atonement appeal to a few specific texts of Scripture. Those who believe in unlimited atonement believe Scripture abounds with evidence for the universality of Christ's death. Let's look at some passages on both sides of this issue first and then try to draw some theological conclusions:

Christ died for specific individuals
(italics added)

Isaiah 53:5: He was wounded *for our transgressions*.
Matthew 1:21: He who will save *His people*.
John 10:15: I lay down My life *for the sheep*.
Ephesians 5:25: Christ also loved the church and *gave Himself for it*.
Acts 20:28: *the church of God* which He purchased with His own blood.

Christ died for all
(italics added)

John 1:29: Behold! The Lamb of God who *takes away the sin of the world!*
2 Corinthians 5:19: God was in Christ *reconciling the world to Himself*.
1 John 4:14: the Father has sent the Son as *Savior of the world*.
Luke 19:10: The Son of man has come to *seek and to save that which was lost*.
Romans 5:6: Christ died for *the ungodly*.
1 Timothy 2:6: [Christ] gave Himself a *ransom for all*.

Hebrews 2:9: [Christ tasted] *death for everyone*.

1 John 2:2: [Christ . . . is the propitiation for] the sins of *the whole world*.

2 Peter 2:1: Denying the Lord who *bought them*.

The Whole Truth

Taking all the Scripture bearing on the subject into consideration, the divine purpose in the atonement was to provide redemption, reconciliation, and propitiation for all. The Cross is not the only saving instrument in the Father's plan of redemption, for apart from faith it saves no one. Salvation is impossible without the Cross and so is it impossible without faith.

Believing that Christ died for all produces no difficulty with the Scriptures that specify His death for the elect. The biblical extent of the atonement is settled by answering the question of the Father's purpose in the death of His Son. If His purpose was to justify all those for whom Christ died apart from any other consideration, then, of course, He died only for some because all will not be saved. However, if the Father's purpose was to *provide* a redemption for all which was dependent upon faith for its personal implication, then His death must be extended to all. The Bible surely speaks of the completed work and absolute salvation secured by Christ. But it speaks with equal emphasis of the absolute necessity of faith before any of the benefits of that finished work are personalized.

We have tried to face the problems on both sides of the question. The solutions presented may not satisfy everyone, but if what has been said stimulates more Bible study on the subject it will have been well worth the effort. I find deep and perplexing difficulties with the limited view of the atonement. Limited atonement is quite consistent with the other points of Calvinism, but it is irreconcilable with the whole of Scripture.

What confidence for the soul winner to know that the Sav-

125

ior has not only commissioned His servants to take the Gospel, but has also taught that His purpose in coming into the world is to call "sinners, to repentance" (Luke 5:32) and "to seek and to save that which was lost" (Luke 19:10). Unless only the elect are "sinners" and unless they are the only ones who constitute the "lost," it must be admitted that according to Christ's own testimony His death reached out beyond the elect. Paul, the greatest missionary apart from Christ, and who gave us more information on the sovereignty of God and election than any other New Testament writer, also extended the benefits of Calvary beyond the elect to include the whole world (2 Cor. 5:17–19).

The question of the extent of the Savior's work on the cross directly relates to the gospel message we are to share with the non-Christian. They must believe the Savior died for them, in their place, as their substitute. But if in fact the Savior did not die for all, it would be dishonest to tell all indiscriminately that Christ died for them when in fact He only died for some.

If we believe in limited atonement we cannot personalize the Gospel. Each and every member of the human family has sinned in Adam and is a guilty sinner, but if limited atonement is true, Christ did not die for each and every sinner. What brings salvation to sinners is not their belief that Christ died for sinners in general, but that He died for them in particular and paid the debt they owed.

CHRIST DIED FOR US

The death Christ died was a death in the place of all—a death which accomplished a work that completely satisfied God the Father. It was a death which provided life for every member of Adam's lost race who has ever lived or ever shall live—a death that made it possible for the Father to be just and at the same time the justifier of any sinner who does nothing more than receive Christ as personal Savior.

CHAPTER 12 DISCUSSION QUESTIONS

1. What do you think is the most important accomplishment of Christ's death? Why?

2. Explain *redemption* in your own words.

3. Explain *propitiation* in your own words.

4. Explain *reconciliation* in your own words.

5. If a non-Christian friend asked you why Jesus had to die for our sins, how would you explain it to him?

13

LIFE AFTER DEATH

Three great ministries of the Savior of sinners are studied in this chapter. Each of them relates directly to the salvation the Son of God gives to sinners who trust Him alone as their sin bearer.

THE SAVIOR'S RESURRECTION

We began this second section of our study on the Savior by thinking about His life before His birth—His eternal existence as the Son of God. Now as we conclude the section, it is appropriate that we study His life after His death.

The physical, bodily resurrection of the Savior is a most crucial doctrine of the historic Christian faith. Without His physical and bodily resurrection, which He Himself predicted, His birth and work on the cross would have no special meaning. The only way His birth and death can be understood is through His resurrection.

> Of all the great religions Christianity alone bases its claim to acceptance on the resurrection of its Founder. If it is not a fact our preaching is emptied of content. Instead of it being a dynamic message, it merely enshrines a fragrant memory. Our faith is without a factual basis and is therefore empty. The Scripture writers become purveyors of intentional lies and

128

the Scriptures themselves are unreliable. Deliverance from the penalty and power of sin is no more than a mirage, and the future life still shrouded in midnight darkness. Thus Paul makes Christianity answer with its life for the truth of the resurrection.[1]

Resurrection Related to Life

The resurrection of Christ is indispensable to the meaning and significance of life for man. Without it man has absolutely no hope of finding his way back to God. Man is now indeed what Loren Eiseley called the Cosmic Orphan.[2]

In the process of evaluating Eiseley's philosophy of life in contrast to the biblical view, William Craig made this pointed observation:

> Now the question is, Which if any of these views of life and death is correct? If we could wait until history's end, then we could see if the biblical view of resurrection is indeed true. But by then it would be too late. Fortunately in this case, however, we have a very peculiar circumstance that allows us to determine now the truth of the biblical doctrine of resurrection; namely, the biblical conviction that man has been raised from the dead by God *in advance* as the basis and pattern for our future resurrection. That man was, of course, Jesus of Nazareth. If historical evidence is sufficient to indicate that He did in fact rise from the dead then we have sufficient grounds for affirming the truth of the biblical view.
>
> Thus, the historicity of the resurrection of Jesus becomes of paramount importance to modern man. If it is true, then the Cosmic Orphan has found his home; for the resurrection of Jesus gives him both God and immortality at once.[3]

The bodily resurrection of Christ is absolutely indispensable to the Gospel (1 Cor. 15:1–5) and to the whole Christian faith (1 Cor. 15:1–19). There simply is no salvation apart from it (Rom. 4:25; 10:9). Satan was not defeated and man is without hope if the Savior did not rise from the dead as He said He would. The Savior's physical and bodily resurrec-

129

tion three days after He was crucified was the fulfillment of His own predictions that He would die and rise from the dead (John 2:19; Matt. 12:40; 17:9).

Resurrection and the Gospel

The message of the resurrected Christ was both the center and the circumference of the message the earliest Christians preached. They had seen the empty tomb and the resurrected Christ, touched Him, walked with Him and talked with Him, and even ate food with Him. All this made an indelible impression upon those who before His resurrection were timid and fearful and even unbelieving.

Nature of the Resurrection

Until recently those who were evangelical in their faith held as a cardinal doctrine that Christ rose from the grave in the same physical body in which He was crucified. They acknowledged that His resurrected body was immortal, but physical nonetheless. All the historical and evangelical creeds and confessions reflect this view when they refer to Christ's bodily resurrection.

Today, some in the evangelical community who still use the term bodily resurrection mean something quite different than what has been historically understood by that phrase. Norman Geisler, contemporary apologist for the historic Christian faith, described this new view this way:

> Some are now contending that the resurrected body was only "spiritual" or immaterial. They deny that the resurrection was empirically observable or historically verifiable. This platonic "Gnostic" tendency to "spiritualize" or allegorize the literal truth of Scripture is not new. What is new is that those who claim to be evangelicals apply it to fundamental doctrines of the Christian faith such as the inspiration of the Bible and the resurrection of Christ.[4]

Eight features identifying the resurrected body of Christ as the same body laid in the tomb have been set forth by John F. Walvoord.[5] The nail prints were still in the resurrected body (John 20:25–29). The wound in Christ's side was still there (John 20:27). His disciples recognized their Lord as the same one who had died and had been buried. In the upper room the Savior ate food with His disciples to show that He was not just a spirit (Luke 24:39–43). The resurrected body of Christ was clearly visible to the natural eye. The resurrected body of Christ had the ability to breathe (John 20:22). The Savior said His resurrected body had flesh and bones (Luke 24:39–40).

There were several new qualities of Christ's resurrected body, however: It was not subject to the normal limitations of our bodies. Christ could pass through closed doors (John 20:19). He could appear suddenly and disappear just as suddenly. Distance was no restriction to Him. His resurrected body was not sustained by blood and did not require rest. The most distinctive feature of Christ's resurrected body is that it will never again be subjected to death (Rom. 6:9).

Agents of the Resurrection

Each member of the Godhead was involved in raising Christ from the dead. Clearly the Father's part is seen in such passages as Psalm 16, Acts 2:24, and Ephesians 1:19–20. The Son's promise that He would raise Himself from the dead is also clear (John 2:19; 10:17–18). The role of the Holy Spirit is less clear in Scripture. Passages usually cited in support of the Spirit's part in raising Christ from the dead are Romans 1:4; 8:11; and 1 Peter 3:18. (There are questions, however, about the correct interpretation of each of these.[6])

Evidences of the Resurrection

Those who accept the Bible's historical reliability find in it conclusive evidence to support the historic orthodox Christian belief in the bodily resurrection of Christ from the dead. After all, people witnessed Christ's resurrection and sinners came to believe it before the New Testament was written. The Resurrection as historic fact is buttressed by the following lines of support:

(1) The tomb in which Jesus Christ was placed was empty on the third day.

(2) Jesus Christ appeared to a large number of people after His death, most of whom had access to the empty tomb: Mary Magdalene, John 20:14–17; other women, Matt. 28:9–10; Peter, Luke 24:34; two on the road to Emmaus, Luke 24:13–35; ten disciples, John 20:19–23; Luke 24:36–43; eleven disciples, John 20:26–29; seven disciples by the sea, John 21:1–3; more than five hundred brethren, 1 Cor. 15:6; James the Lord's half brother, 1 Cor. 15:7; eleven on the mountain in Galilee, Matt. 28:16–20; disciples at the time of the ascension, Acts 1:3–9; and Paul, Acts 9:3–6, 26–30; 20:24; 23:11.

(3) There was a definite change in the disciples after the Resurrection, especially noticeable in Peter.

(4) After the resurrection of Christ the first day of the week rather than the seventh day became a special day of worship.

(5) On the day of Pentecost, fifty days after the Passover, Peter preached to thousands who had access to the tomb owned by Joseph of Arimathea. If his message about the resurrection of Christ was false, why did not someone disprove him?

THE SAVIOR'S ASCENSION

The Savior's work in heaven began with His ascension. When He was "carried up into heaven" (Luke 24:51), the period of His humiliation came to an end. He finished the work He had come to earth to do and began the state of His exaltation.

On two different occasions the psalmist wrote of the Savior's ascension. What David said about ascension in Psalm 68:18 the apostle Paul applied to Christ's ascension (Eph. 4:8). Peter asserted that what David wrote in Psalm 110:1 was not about his own ascension but the Lord's (Acts 2:34). Christ Himself did not hide from His own that He would not only die and be raised, but that He would also go back to the Father (John 14:12, 28; 16:5). He made a specific reference to His ascension twice (John 6:62; 20:17).

The historic event of the ascension of Christ is recorded three times in Scripture: Mark 16:19–20;[7] Luke 24:50–53; Acts 1:6–11. As a climax of His life and resurrection from the dead, Christ returned to His Father.[8]

THE SAVIOR'S PRESENT MINISTRY

The division of the post-ascension ministries of Christ into past, present, and future is warranted.[9]

On the eve of His death Christ promised His own that He would send them the Holy Spirit, who would minister to them in unique ways. He called the Spirit the believers' Helper, who would be another of the same kind as He. This One would bring to remembrance what the Savior had taught His disciples and cause them also to understand it. Furthermore, He would also baptize them and take up residence in them and remain with them permanently (Acts 1:5; John 14:16–18; 15:26; 16:7). Not until the Savior had ascended and returned to the Father would all this take place.

Christ did return to the Father. The Holy Spirit did come as promised. He came on the day of Pentecost (Acts 2) in fulfillment of Christ's promise. Peter wasted no time telling the people gathered on the day of Pentecost that the Spirit's ministries they were witnessing were the result of Christ's post-ascension work (Acts 2:32–34).

Presently, Christ is seated at the right hand of the Father (Rom. 8:34; Eph. 1:20; Col. 3:1; Heb. 1:3–13).

> This position is obviously one of highest possible honor and involves possession of the throne without dispossession of the Father. The implication is that all glory, authority, and power is shared by the Father with the Son. The throne is definitely a heavenly throne, not the Davidic throne and not an earthly throne. He is over all the universe and its creatures.
>
> One of the constant assumptions of the postmillennial and amillennial interpreters is that the throne which Christ is now occupying is the throne of David. An examination of the New Testament discloses that not a single instance can be found where the present position of Christ is identified with David's throne. In view of the many references to the fact that Christ is now seated at the right hand of the Father it is inconceivable that these two positions are identical as none of the passages cited above use the expression "throne of David" as a proper representation of the present position of Christ. If Christ is now on the throne of David it is without any scriptural support whatever.[10]

The other appearances of the resurrected Savior demonstrate beyond doubt that He had indeed conquered death, and tell that His appearance and departure at the time of the ascension were different. The transition period was past. A new era was to begin. That little band of believers gathered at Bethany knew they were not to expect the Son of God to appear again until He came to gather them to be with Him forever. Until that time, theirs was the responsibility of being witnesses to Him in the power of the Holy Spirit (Acts 1:8, 11).

Just as surely as Christ came to earth the first time, so He will come again. The Savior taught this to His own before He went to the cross (Matt. 24:30; John 14:28). The angels who appeared at the time of His ascension proclaimed the same. They said to those gathered, "This same Jesus, who was taken up from you into heaven, will so come in like manner as you saw Him go into heaven" (Acts 1:11).

The Savior will perform three great ministries in the future. First, at His voice all will rise from the dead (John 5:28–29). Those rightly related to God will be raised to eternal life. Those who are not will be raised to eternal death.

> Though we know from other Scriptures that both groups will not be raised at the same time, His voice calling them will be the cause of the resurrection of all. Believers of the church age will be raised at the Rapture of the church (1 Thess. 4:14–18). Old Testament saints will apparently be raised at the Second Coming (Dan. 12:2). The unbelieving dead of all time will not be raised until after the millennium (Rev. 20:5).[11]

Second, Christ will also judge all (John 5:22, 27).

> Believers will be judged by Him at the judgment seat of Christ (1 Cor. 3:1–15; 2 Cor. 5:10) after the Rapture of the church. The outcome of this judgment for all will be heaven, though with a varying number of rewards . . . unbelievers will be judged at the Great White Throne at the conclusion of the millennial kingdom (Rev. 20:11–15). All will be rewarded for their deeds by being cast into the lake of fire.[12]

Third, when Christ comes to establish His kingdom on earth He will "strike the nations. And He Himself will rule them with a rod of iron. He Himself treads the winepress of the fierceness and wrath of Almighty God" (Rev. 19:15). During the Savior's rule from the throne of David there will be perfect peace on earth at last. The Savior is not only the substitute for man's sin, He is also the King of kings and the Lord of lords.

135

CHAPTER 13 DISCUSSION QUESTIONS

1. How is Christianity different from all other world religions?

2. Why is it important to believe in the *bodily* resurrection of Christ?

3. What promise do believers have because of Christ's resurrection?

4. How do you think Christ's resurrection differs from myths and legends of other cultures?

5. Why do you think Paul said we would be foolish if Christ is not raised (1 Cor. 15)?

SECTION III

Salvation

14
GOD'S PLAN OF SALVATION

Salvation is from the Lord. It is His work from start to finish. The writer of Hebrews described this marvelous undertaking, which is all from God, as "so great a salvation" (Heb. 2:3). There simply is no greater or more wonderful accomplishment man could ever experience. Salvation from sin is God's work on behalf of humans only. No other creatures experience God's salvation. The Son of God did not die for the angels that sinned. In contrast to humans, God's grace was not extended to those angelic beings who followed Satan in his rebellion.

As we have seen in Section I, the Bible presents an ugly picture of man as sinner. All sinned in Adam. All received a sinful nature or disposition from their parents and all commit deeds of sin very early in life. All are without God and without hope. The unregenerate rebel against the idea of their inability to make some contribution to their eternal welfare. Even the regenerate often chaff at the thought of presenting to sinners the Gospel of God's grace plus absolutely nothing. "Results" seem to come much easier and faster, and today are said to be more genuine, if we allow the sinner even an infinitesimally small part in his salvation. But Scripture will not support such a view. It views all humans in the same way—without any merit before a holy God and, therefore, unable to make any contribution toward their salvation.

This last section sets forth a biblical soteriology in harmony with the biblical doctrines of sin and the Savior already studied. In the process of doing this we will address some of the contemporary issues related to soteriology—lordship salvation, universalism, and annihilationism.

Three major themes occupy our attention in this chapter—the demand for the plan, the designer of the plan, and the development of the plan.

THE DEMAND FOR THE PLAN

Guilty sinners dead in trespasses and sin and without any merit before God will not and cannot initiate contact with God. God must make the first move if ever He and wayward sinners are to be reunited. He has initiated a plan to bring sinners back to Himself. Both Scripture and reason argue for the divine plan of salvation. To disbelieve this is to dishonor the all-wise God.

God is a God of design and order. He is also a God of justice. He created man in His image and to enjoy His fellowship. But man sinned. If ever the sinner is to be restored to a right relationship with God, God must devise a plan of salvation, and He has done so. If we may say it reverently, God had a problem and He solved it.

The Divine Problem

Man's sin not only affected him; it affected God too. All sin affects God. We observed earlier how sin made its mark upon Adam and Eve and through them upon the whole human race. Very severe penalties were inflicted upon the sinners in the garden, upon the serpent, and even upon the ground because of man's sin. The question remains, what relationship, if any, did Adam's sin and our sin in him have upon God?

Sin is an offense against God. He is the norm, the standard, the criterion of judging right from wrong. Therefore sin is an offense against His holy character. Sin did not surprise God or intrude into His universe unnoticed.

God's ineffable purity cannot tolerate sin. He is of purer eyes than to behold evil. How then can man ever come before Him? How can God "be just and the justifier of the one who has faith in Jesus" (Rom. 3:26)? God is righteous and always deals righteously with the sinner. The solution is in Christ's cross. Here it was that God's love was poured out and at the same time all His just demands were met.

The Divine Solution

God solved the problem man's sin presented to Him. He is the only One who could. After man's fall God the Father began in time the plan of salvation He ordained in eternity past. This divine plan centered in His divine Son: "He gave His only begotten Son" because He "so loved the world" (John 3:16). "He laid down His life for us" (1 John 3:16).

From the time God clothed Adam and Eve with the skins of the slain animals, the great program of redemption through blood was begun in time. Genesis 3:15 in particular anticipates the coming of the Seed of the woman who was to inflict a fatal wound upon Satan: "he shall bruise your head." This Seed was none other than Jesus Christ the Messiah. The sacrifices of the Old Testament were types of Him who was to come—God clothed in human flesh—to become the substitute for every member of Adam's lost race.

Christ alone

In the divine solution, Christ was the righteous one who alone could satisfy every demand of the offended righteousness of God. The cross of Christ is presented in holy Scripture as the declaration of the very righteousness of God (Rom. 3:25). Through that cross, God was in Christ reconcil-

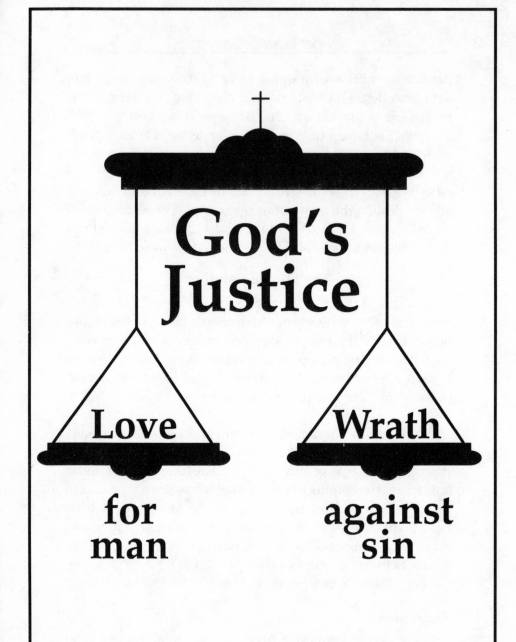

ing the world unto Himself (2 Cor. 5:19). Since Calvary, the question before lost humans is not one concerned primarily with their original sin. It is now a question of what they will do with Christ the Son, who died for them. There is only one condition they must meet to be made right with God.

God's plan

The divine plan of salvation, formulated in eternity past, allowed for the entrance and continuance of sin until the day appointed by God when sin and the author of it shall be banished forever. In his sermon on the day of Pentecost, Peter, speaking of Christ said that this man "delivered by the determined counsel and foreknowledge of God, you have taken by lawless hands, have crucified, and put to death" (Acts 2:23). On another occasion as Peter and John preached, it was said that those who had gathered to crucify Christ were doing "whatever Your hand and Your purpose determined before to be done" (Acts 4:28). The same apostle also said Christ "was foreordained before the foundation of the world, but was manifest in these last times for you" (1 Peter 1:20).

If the historic death of Christ was a part of the divine plan as the solution to the sin question, the entrance of sin which made that death necessary was also known and permitted.

THE DESIGNER OF THE PLAN

Each of the three members of the holy Trinity—Father, Son, and Holy Spirit—has a vital part in man's salvation. The three are referred to in relation to man's salvation in the first chapter of Ephesians. The Father and the Son are highlighted in the first twelve verses, and the Spirit in verses 13–14.

The Father "chose us" (Eph. 1:4) in Christ and "predestined us" (v. 5). All of this is to the "good pleasure of His will" (v. 5) and to the "glory of His grace" (v. 6). He is the one who has made us accepted "in the Beloved" (v. 6). The Son is the beloved One in whom "we have redemption" and "forgiveness of sins" (v. 7). The Spirit seals the believer (v. 13) and is the "guarantee of our inheritance" (v. 14). Throughout Scripture various roles related to man's salvation are ascribed to the different persons of the Godhead.

There is a danger of compartmentalizing the redemptive work of the members of the Godhead. This usually shows up when the Father's love of sinners is stressed. The implication often left in doing this is that the Son came because it was His Father's will, and not because He too loves sinners. There is complete harmony among the members of the Trinity. While each one has specific functions (i.e., the Son died, not the Father), there is always concurrence and mutual involvement in what is done. There is a subordination of office but not a subordination of essence.

Birth

The complex miracle of physical birth requires a divine plan and planner. This is even more true of the miracle of spiritual birth into the family of God. The Author of the plan of redemption is none other than God Himself. The Creator of the universe and of man who spoke and brought all things into existence deigned to devise a plan of salvation for His disobedient and fallen creatures. God the Father's love and grace is displayed beautifully and abundantly in His plan of salvation.

John declared that those who received Christ as Savior are the recipients of the very power of God and in fact they are born of God (John 1:12–13). We are told by Paul that Christ, the Savior, is the wisdom of God (1 Cor. 1:30). He reminds us that it was God the Father who displayed His Son publicly as a propitiation or satisfaction for man's sin. It was through the work on the cross by the Savior that the Father could remain just and at the same time the one who could justify all who believe in Christ as Savior (Rom. 3:25–26).

Eternal Plan

Salvation must never be viewed as an afterthought, as the only possible way out of a hopeless dilemma which God faced. The great plan of salvation is as eternal as God is and as ordered as He is too. God was certainly not shocked when Adam and Eve sinned and plunged the whole human race in sin, guilt, and degradation.

Every possible human instrument in the plan of salvation is eliminated. John the apostle said it was not of blood (not of human lineage), not of the will of the flesh, nor even of the will or desire of man (John 1:13). No, it is all of God. It is His plan from start to finish. Salvation is indeed of the Lord.

THE DEVELOPMENT OF THE PLAN

The plan of redemption the Father designed in eternity past before He even created man has been realized in time. In His infinite wisdom God solved the problem man's sin caused. His solution involved the choice of sinful humans on whom He would bestow His grace and salvation.

The Basis of the Plan

The foundation of God's plan of salvation is His justice, holiness, mercy, and grace.

God's holiness means He possesses absolute perfection in every detail and is completely separate from evil, both in His person and in His relationships with sinners.

To say God is righteous and just is to speak of His holiness as He relates to His creatures—humans. God's own nature is His standard to which He demands conformity.

God never violates His holiness and neither does He allow His creatures to violate it without full payment and satisfaction. That is what Scripture means when it ascribes justice to God.

The grace of God has to do with the undeserved favor He displays toward sinners.

145

His mercy is His withholding of merited judgment. The Author of the plan of salvation is the God of love, holiness, justice, mercy, and grace.

We often feel that everything about our salvation began when we made our decision to trust Christ as Savior. The fact is, God was at work on our behalf long before that moment of decision. We did not, we could not, initiate the salvation we enjoy in Christ. Scripture declares that we were chosen in Christ "before the foundation of the world" (Eph. 1:4). Peter told the scattered Christians they were chosen "according to the foreknowledge of God the Father (1 Peter 1:2). Paul, the apostle to the Gentiles, put it this way: "For whom He foreknew, He also predestined to be conformed to the image of His Son" (Rom. 8:29). And again, "God from the beginning chose you for salvation through sanctification by the Spirit and faith in the truth" (2 Thess. 2:13). The Savior Himself spoke of the sovereign electing work of God the Father to the multitudes who came to Him to hear Him: "All that the Father gives Me will come to Me, and the one who comes to Me I will by no means cast out, . . . No one can come to Me unless the Father who sent Me draws Him; and I will raise him up at the last day" (John 6:37, 44).

The Purpose of the Plan

We do not understand why God has been pleased to do the things He has. Why were we chosen and brought to faith in Christ and many others were not? Why were many called but only a few chosen (Matt. 22:14)? We will never know the answers to many of our queries until we see the Savior face to face. One thing we do know, however. We know that God's plan is the best possible plan to bring the most possible glory now and eternally to His name. It is our knowledge of Him from His Word that tells us. He is "too good to be unkind and too wise to make mistakes."

Evangelical Christians who take seriously the scriptural

teaching on election are divided over how it should be understood. There are basically three viewpoints on this important doctrine.

Some believe God has elected sinners to be saved on the basis of the faith He knew they would have. God "chose those who He foreknew would accept Christ."[1] This is a popular explanation among those Christians who think at all about election. The major weakness in the view is that it seems to view God's foreknowledge merely as foresight.

What might be called corporate or group election is another view becoming quite popular. The idea here is of God's election of the church in Christ rather than individuals being elected before the foundation of the world. Those who believe in Christ become a part of the elect group and can therefore be called elect ones. A contemporary spokesman for this view stated it this way:

> Christ is the chosen One in and through whom in corporate solidarity with Him the church is selected to be God's own. No one is ever chosen *on his own*, that is, outside of Christ, or apart from incorporation into the church.[2]

The major weakness with this view is its failure to deal adequately with those Scriptures which relate election to individuals.

Among Calvinists (four-point and five-point Calvinists) election is seen as "that eternal act of God whereby He, in His sovereign good pleasure, and on account of no foreseen merit in them" chooses a certain number of men to be the recipients of special grace and of eternal salvation.[3]

Those who hold this view often fail to take into account the fact that Scripture does sometimes speak of what might be called group election—the church—in addition to individual election. Also Scripture does involve God's foreknowledge in His election (cf. 1 Peter 1:1-2).

It seems most in harmony with the totality of Scripture to

148

believe in personal, pre-temporal election as well as a corporate election of the church. God's foreknowledge of human faith in His election both of individuals and the church must be included. He did predestine those He foreknew (Rom. 8:29). And He did choose according to His foreknowledge (1 Peter 1:1-2). We are not told what it was in God's foreknowledge which moved Him to choose. It is going beyond what Scripture says to say it was His knowledge of the sinner's faith which caused Him to make the choice.

The precious truths of election and salvation will not make one self-absorbed, and unconcerned for the lost, if rightly understood and balanced with God's commands involving human responsibilities. His plan is the result of His infinite wisdom and love and is in keeping with His absolute holiness, justice, mercy, and grace.

The Human Agents in the Plan

The eternal plan of salvation includes not only the end—a redeemed company in glory—but the means to the end as well. It includes a holy, loving, and intelligent Being behind it. These things set this plan in contrast to fatalism, which does not include the means, nor does it have an intelligent being behind it.

Scripture does not present God's plan as incompatible with man's will. The sovereign plan includes the actions and responsibilities of man. It is all part of His plan.

Paul associated the matter of his call to salvation with his responsibility to serve Christ (Gal. 1:15-16). God's choice of us becomes the motivating force for our service to Him. These truths concerning our salvation ought to humble us.

A proper understanding of these glorious truths will bring us where Paul was brought after his long discourse on the subject. His hymn of praise should be made our own:

> Oh, the depth of the riches both of the wisdom and knowledge of God! How unsearchable are His judgments and His

ways past finding out! "For who has known the mind of the Lord? Or who has become His counselor? Or who has first given to Him and it shall be repaid to Him?" For of Him and through Him and to Him are all things, to whom be glory forever. Amen (Rom. 11:33–36).

CHAPTER 14 DISCUSSION QUESTIONS

1. Think about when you first became a Christian. How did you hear about the Gospel?

2. How does 1 Corinthians 15:1–4 define the Gospel?

3. Can you think of other "gospels" preached by cults or sects today?

4. Think about your closest friend who is not a Christian. How would you explain the Gospel to him?

5. How has God's "plan" been worked out in your own life?

15

THE HOLY SPIRIT'S ROLE IN SALVATION

Apart from the Father's work there would have been no plan of salvation. We studied this plan in chapter 14. Without the Son's work there would have been no provision of salvation, as we have already seen.

Apart from the Spirit's work there would be no application of this great salvation to man's needs. It is the third member of the Godhead who procures salvation for all who believe. He applies the finished work of Christ to the believing sinner who was chosen by God.

There are two major works of the Holy Spirit in man's salvation which we will study in this chapter—His general work upon the unregenerate and His specific work in salvation.

THE HOLY SPIRIT'S GENERAL WORK

By the Spirit's general work is meant His ministry upon all people everywhere, without distinction of their knowledge, spiritual experience, or relationship to God. Charles Hodge defined this work of the Spirit:

> The Holy Spirit, as the Spirit of truth, of holiness and of life in all its forms is present with every human mind enforcing truth, restraining from evil, exciting to good, and imparting

wisdom or strength when, where, and in what measure seemeth to Him good . . . this is what in theology is called common grace.[1]

Referring to the work of the Spirit as "grace" does not mean that it provides the sinner with abilities or capabilities, thereby enabling him to move toward the Savior. It certainly does not mean that because of this work of the Spirit man can now make some contribution—add his part—to his salvation. The general work of the Spirit upon the unregenerate, or common grace, simply refers to God's undeserved favor displayed toward all.

Necessity

Three things explain the reality and need for this gracious activity of the Spirit. First, God's sovereignty and providence imply such a ministry. Since He is the supreme ruler, sustainer, and preserver of life, it follows naturally that He would exhibit such an attitude toward His creatures.

Second, this work of the Spirit is absolutely essential since man is the sinner he is. On his own the natural or unregenerate person cannot receive spiritual truth (1 Cor. 2:14). To him the Gospel is foolishness (1 Cor. 1:18). In other words, apart from the work of the Spirit the unregenerate have no hope whatsoever.

Third, mankind could not survive the results of his own sinfulness and Satan's power were it not for the restraining work of the Spirit of God. Satan's power and wickedness demand a divine power to counter and supersede it. The Holy Spirit is that power. He holds back the full onslaught of wickedness in this world and will continue to do so until the divinely appointed time.

Description

There are three specific activities of the Holy Spirit which illustrate His general work on the unregenerate.

The most general of these is His providential care over His creatures. The Spirit of God has compassion on all and showers many natural blessings upon them universally. The rain and sunshine, for example, come to the just and to the unjust. The laws of nature (i.e., seed time and harvest) hold true for all. Both Old and New Testaments make this clear (i.e., Ps. 145:9; Matt. 5:45; Luke 6:35; Acts 14:17).

A second illustration of the general work of the Holy Spirit upon the unregenerate involves His restraint of sin. Striving in Genesis 6:3 means the Spirit holds back. He restrains sin in the world. God kept Satan from having total control over Job. He restrained sin. Paul wrote to the Thessalonian believers about one "who now restrains" (2 Thess. 2:7). While interpreters differ over who this one is, it seems certain to be the Holy Spirit since He is the restrainer of sin in the Old Testament. Also, He is in the immediate context and is a member of the Godhead, which would be required to withstand Satan to such a degree.

The Holy Spirit's conviction of sin is the third illustration of His work of common grace. Jesus said the Spirit He would send would "convict the world of sin, and of righteousness, and of judgment" (John 16:8). This means the Holy Spirit would give demonstrable proof of the truth of the gospel message. Humans are in a state of sin (note the singular "sin" in John 16:8) because they do not believe in Christ. The Spirit proves that Christ is righteous because He rose from the dead and returned to the Father. The Spirit proves that judgment is sure to come because it has come in the past through the judgment of Satan at the Cross.

In this way the Holy Spirit enlightens the mind of the unsaved, which is blinded by Satan (2 Cor. 4:4). Not all who are thus enlightened respond in faith, however. This work by itself is not sufficient for salvation, but it does provide the sinner with proof of the truthfulness of the gospel message. If and when that message is received, the Spirit's work of giving life becomes operative.

How, we might ask, does the Spirit do these things where the Gospel has not been taken? We are not told. Perhaps in such cases God the Spirit performs this work through God's revelation of Himself in nature and in man's conscience. Some attempt to solve this problem by restricting the meaning of the "world" in John 16 to the world of the elect. There does not seem to be any reason, however, in the text or context for doing this.

THE HOLY SPIRIT'S SPECIFIC WORK IN SALVATION

All the general ministries of the Spirit with the unregenerate discussed above fall short of actual salvation. God did not intend that they should save. What the general ministries of the Spirit do is show man his need of salvation; they leave him without excuse before God. They are genuine ministries of God but they precede the Spirit's saving work by preparing the way for salvation.

His Work Accomplishing Salvation

Salvation becomes a reality when, at the moment of faith, the Holy Spirit imparts life to the believing sinner. When the Holy Spirit moves in this way upon the individual, His ministry is always 100 percent effective (note in Rom. 8:28–30 that those called are glorified). This work of the Spirit in moving sinners to trust in Christ, the sin bearer, has been called irresistible grace, efficacious grace, or effectual grace. All the other works of the Holy Spirit described above come before this saving work. They involve a process continuing over a period of time. However, that work of the Spirit which results in the individual's acceptance of Christ as Savior is not a process. Rather it is an instantaneous act simultaneous with faith. Scriptural support for this effectual work of the Spirit is found in the following passages: Rom. 1:1; 8:28; 1 Tim. 6:12; 2 Peter 1:3, 10.

The work of the Spirit that accomplishes salvation produces regeneration. Though the word regeneration appears only twice in Scripture (Matt. 19:28; Titus 3:5), the concept of being born again occurs often. Regeneration means just that—to be born again. It has to do with the impartation of life from God to the sinner.

The means by which regeneration is accomplished eliminates all human endeavor. Though personal faith in Christ the Savior is necessary, faith does not produce the new life. Human faith and divine regeneration occur at the same time, but one is man's responsibility as he is enabled by the Holy Spirit and the other is the work of God imparting the divine life.

The work of regeneration is ascribed to each member of the Godhead (e.g., John 5:21; Titus 3:5; James 1:17–18). It is not based on experience, though the life of one who has been regenerated will surely be different. The results of this instantaneous sovereign work of the Spirit include a new nature (2 Cor. 5:17), new righteousness (Rom. 5:19), new life (e.g., John 3:9; 4:7; 5:1), and eternal life (Phil. 1:6).

His Work Accompanying Salvation

There are many riches of God's grace which are a part of salvation. Here we want to consider only those which are the result of the Holy Spirit's work at the time of salvation.

First, the Spirit baptizes or identifies the believing sinner with Christ, the head of the body, and with every other member of that body. There is much confusion abroad today over this work of the Spirit. Confusion usually centers around two errors. One of these is to make Spirit baptism a ministry which comes after salvation. The other error relates to making speaking in tongues a sign of the baptism.[2]

These and many other problems will be eliminated if the following truths are accepted. The baptism of the Spirit is peculiar to the church age. It cannot be found in any other dispensation. Every reference to it in the Gospels and even in Acts 1:5 is future. All believers of this dispensation are baptized by the Holy Spirit:

> For as the body is one and has many members, but all the members of that one body, being many, are one body, so also is Christ. For by one Spirit we were all baptized into one body—whether Jews or Greeks, whether slaves or free—and have all been made to drink into one Spirit (1 Cor. 12:12–13).

No command is ever given to be baptized by the Spirit. This is a divine work which accompanies salvation, whereby the Holy Spirit identifies the believing sinner with Christ and His work (Rom. 6:1–10) and makes him a member of the body of Christ. Because of the tense used in 1 Corinthians 12:13, and since the work of the Spirit effects a union with Christ and His body, it is experienced only once by each believer. It cannot be repeated. This work of the Spirit is based upon human experience or derived from it. This means the individual need not be conscious of it or experience some great emotional stir to be assured of it.

The baptism by the Spirit is not to be confused with the filling of the Spirit. This latter ministry is repeatable and involves human cooperation (Acts 2:4; 4:31; Eph. 5:18; where the present tense is used to indicate continuous action). Neither is it true that all who were baptized with the Spirit spoke with tongues (see 1 Cor. 12:13 and compare with 1 Cor. 12:30).

Second, the Spirit indwells the people of God. He takes up residence in each and every believer (1 Cor. 6:19).

Third, the Spirit seals the sinner who trusts the Savior. At the same time as salvation and the two ministries listed above, the Holy Spirit seals the believing sinner. He is the seal (2 Cor. 1:22; Eph. 1:13; 4:30). This guarantee of eternal security is true of each and every believer. This spiritual ministry is performed at the time of salvation and without any human effort.

A threefold significance describes the intent of this sealing. First is the certainty of possession by God. Second, there is the certainty of the promise of His salvation, for there is no power greater than God who could break the seal, and God Himself has promised never to break it. Third, the seal gives us the certainty of His purpose to keep us until the day of redemption.[3]

Two things need to be emphasized in relation to the Holy Spirit's role in salvation. First, the general work of the Spirit upon the unregenerate should encourage the believer to share his faith with others. The Spirit is at work preparing the way. He is the only one who convicts and draws sinners to the Savior. Second, the Spirit of God is the one who brings life to the sinner and who accomplishes all the other works enabling the child of God to live to the glory of God. These works of the Spirit are totally unrelated to human merit or accomplishment and are eternal in nature. The Holy Spirit's role in salvation empowers us to fruitful evangelism and enables the sinner to come to salvation.

CHAPTER 15 DISCUSSION QUESTIONS

1. Jesus calls the Holy Spirit our "Helper." How is He your Helper?

2   List a few of the ways the Holy Spirit gives general grace to the world.

3. Read Romans 8. What are some of the activities of the Holy Spirit in the believer's life?

4. What does *regeneration* mean?

5. How are you "sealed" by the Holy Spirit?

16

THE HUMAN CONDITION OF SALVATION

"What must I do to be saved?" the jailer at Philippi asked Paul and Silas (Acts 16:30). When you are lost, proper directions are very important. How terrible to give wrong directions to someone transporting a dying person to the hospital! How much more terrible to give sinners the wrong directions to heaven!

Although Scripture repeatedly declares that salvation is by faith alone, plus *nothing,* various conditions have been added to the Gospel from time to time in the history of the church. Some groups, even within evangelicalism, are known for their insistence on certain human actions or attitudes in addition to faith for salvation.

Today the evangelical community is divided over whether Christ must be received as Lord of the sinner's life as well as Savior or Substitute for sin. (This issue will be addressed separately in chapter 18).

There is also a growing sympathy among evangelicals for what is called "biblical universalism" and also a form of annihilationism. We will address these issues in this chapter, after we review the one condition of salvation clearly stated in Scripture.

THE ONE CONDITION OF SALVATION

The condition of salvation must be understood to apply to those who are mentally capable of meeting that condition. The question regarding the salvation of those who die before they reach decision-making status, though not specifically addressed in Scripture, is discussed in this chapter.

How is God's great plan of salvation to benefit the individual sinner? The Father planned it all. The Son of God, the last Adam, gave Himself as a substitute for the descendants of the first Adam. The Spirit uses the Word of God to convict the sinner and draw him to the Savior. But what part does the sinner play in all of this? What must he or she do to be saved? In our answer we will divide time into two periods.

The Condition in the Present Dispensation

The present dispensation[1] (a distinctive epoch of God's testing of man) refers to the time from the birth of the church on the day of Pentecost (Acts 2) until the rapture of the church (1 Thess. 4:13–18). Dispensationalists are frequently wrongly accused of believing in a different way of salvation for each dispensation, but dispensations involve testing, each one showing the necessity of God's one plan of salvation.

Personal faith in the Lord Jesus Christ alone as Savior is the one and only condition for human salvation. Over one hundred times in the New Testament, faith in Christ, for those who are capable of exercising it, is made the one human requirement for receiving eternal life.

There are one hundred and fifteen passages at least wherein the word *believe* is used alone and apart from every other condition as the only way of salvation. In addition to this there are upwards of 35 passages wherein its synonym *faith* is used.[2]

To be sure, there are essentials the sinner must know before he can be saved—he is a guilty sinner (Rom. 3:23), sin's wages is death (Rom. 6:23), Christ died in the sinner's place (Rom. 5:8; 1 Cor. 15:3), the sinner must trust Christ alone as his sin bearer (John 3:16; Acts 16:31). These are the essentials of the Gospel. Yet mere knowledge of them does not bring the new birth. Only at the point of personal reception and acceptance of Christ alone as Savior, by the drawing power of the Holy Spirit, does the guilty sinner pass from death unto life and into the family of God.

Without faith

"Without faith it is impossible to please" God (Heb. 11:6). That is as true when it comes to salvation as it is in every other area and yet it must be emphasized that it is not man's faith which saves him. Man's faith is not the cause of his salvation. It is Jesus Christ, the *object* of our faith, who saves us. Christ and Christ alone saves sinners; faith does not. Salvation, however, is always *through* faith by God's marvelous grace.

The Gospel is sometimes presented as though some special kind or amount of faith is required for salvation. Satan often comes to the newborn child of God and brings doubts as to whether he had enough faith or has believed in the right way. As far as Scripture is concerned, God simply requires all the faith or trust one has and that one's faith be in Jesus Christ. The sinner's reception of God's great gift of salvation adds nothing to the completed work of Christ. Were that true it would be Christ's substitutionary atonement plus faith in Christ which saves. Christ's work alone saves, but unless His Person and work are received by faith, no benefit comes to the individual sinner.

Man's faith must have the proper object before salvation results. God does not simply demand belief in the ultimate triumph of good, or faith in the evangelical church, or even

160

faith in His own existence and power, as that which brings salvation. It is always faith in God's Son as the divine substitute for sin which brings life to the spiritually dead sinner.

The stigma

This involves Christ's death on the cross. According to Scripture there is an offense, a stigma, attached to the cross. God has done everything and man makes no contribution whatsoever to the finished work of Christ or to his own salvation. Paul indicated that the offense of the cross was the absence of human work from God's way of salvation (Gal. 5:11). Man desires to make some contribution, however small, but he cannot—it is finished. Faith in Christ is not a work. "Faith consists not in doing something but in receiving something."[3]

Think about getting a gift or giving a gift. A gift does not cease to be a gift just because the one to whom it is given receives it. Salvation is a gift—God's gift—and it remains a gift even after it is received by faith.

The person who is truly born again will want to serve Christ. Life cannot be hidden very long. Life issues in growth. The growth evidences itself in service. Paul's exhortation to Titus is applicable to all believers. Every child of God must be careful to maintain good works (Titus 3:8). This is not so that one might be saved or remain saved but rather because he *is* saved.

The Condition in Other Dispensations

The Bible knows of only one way of salvation. It makes no difference which period of time one refers to. The salvation of a sinner has always been and will always be by God's grace through faith. The basis upon which God forgives sin has always been the substitutionary death of Christ. People have not always known what we know about the Person and work of Christ simply because all that has been revealed in the New Testament was not made known to the men of God who wrote the Old Testament. Therefore, while God has always required personal faith as a condition of salvation, the complexity of that faith has not always been the same. Those who lived before Calvary knew very little about the finished work of Christ so vividly portrayed in the New Testament. Many of the Old Testament sacrifices and offerings were types of the Savior and of the final and complete work He would do. However, even though the people may not have known all that was involved when they believed God and His promises, He accounted their faith to them for righteousness because He accepted the work of His Son as already finished. The resurrection of Christ is proof of this acceptance.

The only difference between other dispensations and this one, as it relates to salvation, is the complexity of faith, that which was believed by the sinner. Before the full revelation of Scripture was given, faith was placed in the person and promises of God made known up to that time (Rom. 4:3). Since God has made known to man the meaning of the death of His Son, faith is now placed in His person and work. Salvation in any age is a work of God on behalf of the believing sinner, apart from human works of any kind.

HUMAN ADDITIONS TO THE ONE CONDITION

Water Baptism

Many people depend on ritual baptism, received either as infants or as adults, for their salvation. This is an entirely false hope. All the water in the world could not take away even one sin. Nowhere does Scripture make water baptism a condition for salvation. The Bible teaches that an obedient believer will obey the Lord and His Word and be baptized, identifying himself with a Bible-believing church.

Water baptism, however, symbolically but not literally

identifies one with Christ in His death, burial, and resurrection. Water baptism gives public demonstration to the fact that the believer has already been identified with Christ, having trusted Him as personal Savior.

Several passages of Scripture, taken by themselves, seem to include water baptism as a condition of salvation. The following are the major problem passages used by those who believe water baptism is essential for salvation.

A generally acknowledged rule of Bible interpretation is to arrive at a biblical teaching based upon the clear and undisputed texts. Whatever problem texts exist must then be viewed in relation to the clear ones. The difficult passages must not be ignored or twisted, or given an interpretation which will not stand up under rigorous scrutiny. Rather, the interpreter's obligation is to see if the problem passages will yield to an interpretation which is in harmony with the clear passages. If this cannot be done, the existing conflict between the clear texts and the problem ones must be allowed to stand until further light comes. The disputed text must not become dominant over the undisputed one. In other words, we do not build a doctrine on problematic texts and then adjust the clear ones to fit that doctrine. It is really the other way around.

Mark 16:15–16

And He said to them, "Go into all the world and preach the gospel to every creature. He who believes and is baptized will be saved, but he who does not believe will be condemned.

The above passage is included in a longer passage—Mark 16:9–20—which appears in the *Textus Receptus* version of the Greek New Testament. This text is the basis of the King James Version of the Scriptures. Many New Testament scholars, however, do not believe these verses were a part of Mark's Gospel originally, but were added later and therefore were not part of the inspired canon of Scripture. If that is the case, the passage is not problematic with respect to the issue at hand.

It is beyond our purpose here to debate the issue of the *Textus Receptus* text versus the older texts, upon which many modern translations are based. Even if we grant the validity of the passage in question, it can be easily harmonized with those which do not include baptism as a condition for salvation. This is done by taking seriously the concluding summary statement in verse 16. Here, lack of baptism is not included as a basis for condemnation, but only disbelief: "He who does not believe will be condemned" (Mark 16:16).

John 3:3–5

Jesus answered and said to him, "Most assuredly, I say to you, unless one is born again, he cannot see the kingdom of God." Nicodemus said to Him, "How can a man be born when he is old? Can he enter a second time into his mother's womb and be born?" Jesus answered, "Most assuredly, I say to you, unless one is born of water and the Spirit, he cannot enter the kingdom of God."

Those who believe in baptismal regeneration frequently come to this passage for support.

Given the probability that "water" in John 3:5 refers to Christian baptism and given the fact that "born again" and "kingdom of God" refer to salvation, we cannot avoid the conclusion that baptism is inseparable from the new birth and thus is a condition for salvation. This is in full agreement with the teaching of Mark 16:16.[4]

Contextually, it is much better to take the "water" in the passage to refer to the water or amniotic fluid which surrounds the fetus in the womb. After all, Nicodemus did make it plain by his question that he was thinking about physical birth (v. 4). The response Jesus gave him shows that is precisely how Jesus understood him (v. 6). "Water" also sometimes refers symbolically to the Holy Spirit (cf. John 7:37–39), another valid interpretation not referring to water baptism.

One objection to this belief is often that in the amniotic fluid explanation Jesus is saying the obvious—of course one has to be born the first time before he can be born the second time from above. At first this sounds like a valid objection. But don't we have something similar in John 11:16? There Jesus said to Martha, "Everyone who lives and believes in me shall never die." Didn't the Savior know no one could believe in Him who did not first live?

Acts 2:38–39

> Then Peter said to them, "Repent, and let every one of you be baptized in the name of Jesus Christ for the remission of sins; and you shall receive the gift of the Holy Spirit. For the promise is to you and to your children, and to all who are afar off, as many as the Lord our God will call."

It has been said that this verse states clearly that baptism is the focal point of God's promises of forgiveness and the gift of the Holy Spirit. "The conditions for receiving 'double cure' according to Acts 2:38 are repentance and baptism, plus an implied faith . . . part of what a sinner must do to bring about forgiveness of his sins is to be baptized."[5]

There are alternative ways of understanding this verse which harmonize it with the rest of Scripture. It has been suggested that the word "believing" should be supplied, in keeping with the context. This would make the verse read "repent and be baptized every one of you [believing] in the name of Jesus Christ for the remission of sins."

An even better solution is found in the text itself. The phrase translated "for the remission of sins" can mean "because of" or "for the purpose of" the remission of sins (cf. Matt. 12:41 where the same construction appears). Gram-

165

matically it could be either. Since the consistent testimony of Scripture makes faith the only condition for salvation, and since there are biblical examples where baptism was not performed for salvation (i.e., the thief on the cross), it seems best to translate the phrase "because of the remission" here. In this way the interpreter is true to the text and is in harmony with the rest of Scripture.

Acts 22:16

And now why are you waiting? Arise and be baptized, and wash away your sins, calling on the name of the Lord.

Cottrell speaks for those who believe in baptismal regeneration when he makes this comment:

Thus Ananias's instruction does no less than confirm the anonymous biblical testimony to the saving significance of baptism. God has promised to save us—to give us forgiveness of sins and the gift of the Holy Spirit—in Christian baptism.[6]

Charles Ryrie has summarized the opposing view. His interpretation is exegetically sound and harmonizes this passage with those which make faith the sole condition for salvation.

The verse contains four segments: (a) arise (which is a participle, arising), (b) be baptized (an imperative), (c) wash away your sins (another imperative), and (d) calling on the name of the Lord (another participle). To make the verse teach baptism is necessary for salvation necessitates connecting parts two and three—be baptized and wash away. But rather than being connected to each other, each of those commands is actually connected with the participle. Arising is necessary before baptism and calling before sins can be washing away. Thus the verse should be read this way: Arising, be baptized; washing away your sins, calling on the Lord. The verse correctly understood does not teach baptismal regeneration.[7]

Repentance

Usually those who see water baptism as a condition for salvation in addition to faith see repentance in the same way. Some feel including repentance in addition to faith in the Gospel serves to reduce the number of "easy believism" converts. "Easy believism" refers to those who "accept Christ" but whose lives reveal no commitment, fruit, or obedience to Christ.

Many have read into the meaning of the word *repentance* the idea of sorrow, and have thereby implied that sorrow for sin is the same as repentance for sin. There is no doubt but that genuine repentance will be accompanied by sorrow, but it is also true that one can be sorrowful without repenting.

The word *repentance* means a change of mind. Because of the confusion described above many make repentance a *separate and additional* condition of salvation. This is not true in the Word. There is no question about it: repentance is necessary for salvation. However, Scripture views repentance as included in believing and not as an additional and separate condition to faith. All who have trusted Christ as Savior have changed their minds regarding Him and their sin. (Of course, it would be impossible to change one's mind without trusting the Savior.[8])

According to scriptural usage repentance is almost a synonym for faith.[9] Paul said he declared to both the Jews and the Greeks "repentance toward God and faith toward our Lord Jesus Christ" (Acts 20:21; cf. 11:21). God the Holy Spirit uses the facts of Scripture and causes the sinner to change his mind about himself, his sin, and the Savior. At the same time the Holy Spirit shows him his need of trusting Christ for salvation. In repentance the sinner turns from himself and his sin. In faith the sinner turns to the Savior for salvation.

Public Confession

Some people say that a public confession of Christ is necessary for salvation. Romans 10:9–10 is used to support this view.

> . . . that if you confess with your mouth the Lord Jesus, and believe in your heart that God has raised Him from the dead, you will be saved. For with the heart one believes to righteousness, and with the mouth confession is made to salvation.

But nothing about public confession is included in the verses. The confession referred to could just as well be a private confession to God. This has to do with one's open acknowledgment of his need and Christ's salvation. To confess Christ to others is the normal Christian experience, the result of new life within. One who has received Christ will usually want to make his faith known to others. But this is not a requirement for salvation. Rather, the sinner makes the confession because he has salvation.

If public confession is in view here as a condition of salvation, what of the many who have been saved under circumstances which made a public testimony impossible (i.e., what of the deaf and dumb or deathbed conversions)? The condition of salvation must be the same for all who can meet it. Note also how verse 10 clarifies the whole matter. It is through faith alone that the sinner is declared righteous. Confession is not *for* salvation but is *because* of it.

Jesus and others in the New Testament constantly invited others to accept Him and the salvation He offered. It seems just as valid to make the invitation in a church service as in private. The confession in either case, however, is not what brings salvation. Christ does, since He alone is the Savior of sinners.

Prayer

Sincere Christians often tell the unsaved to beg God for mercy. Appeal is frequently made to Luke 18:13 and the

Salvation

Faith in Christ

Repentance toward God

Acts 11:21
Acts 20:21

Sinner

prayer of the publican, "God, be merciful to me a sinner." But this prayer was prayed before the accomplishments of Calvary were a reality in time. The publican asked God to provide satisfaction for his sin. God has done just that in the Person of Jesus Christ. In fact, God can be no more merciful than He has been at the cross. The work is finished. All that remains now is for man to believe. How simple. Salvation is free to the sinner. Absolutely free.[10]

Prayer must never be viewed as a condition for salvation. The newborn child of God will no doubt express his faith in prayer. Prayer does not save, however. Multitudes of people "pray" who are not saved. Scripture does not condition salvation upon prayer. Prayer is for the child of God. It is his means of communing with his heavenly Father. The calling in Romans 10:13 need not be understood as an audible prayer. Rather, in context it refers to the call or cry of the heart to God in faith.

Isaiah 55:6 is sometimes used to stress the need of seeking the Lord for salvation. This was said not to the church, but to the nation of Israel and meant that they, as God's chosen people, were to return to Him. The New Testament reveals that Christ came to seek and to save that which was lost (Luke 19:10).

The unsaved are often told to confess their sin to be saved, and John's exhortation in 1 John 1:9 is used for scriptural support. However, this text relates to Christians only. The unsaved are never told to confess their sins to be saved. They are called only to believe on the Lord Jesus Christ, and God says they will be saved (Acts 16:31; John 3:18).

WHAT ABOUT BIBLICAL UNIVERSALISM?

In order to understand "biblical universalism" or "qualified universalism"[11] it must be seen in contrast both to the biblical doctrine of everlasting punishment and to classic or absolute universalism. Absolute universalism or "universalism proper" believes in the eventual actual salvation of all rational beings.

Clark Pinnock and others believe qualified universalism is a middle option with regard to the destiny of those who have never responded to the Gospel:

> However, there is a third possibility. The "fire" of God's judgment consumes the lost. According to this understanding God does not raise the wicked in order to torture them consciously forever but rather to declare His judgment upon the wicked and to condemn them to extinction, which is the second death (Rev. 20:11–15).[12]

Though Pinnock does not call his view "biblical universalism," he does seek to defend the same view from the Bible.

He first appeals to verses in Matthew's gospel. There John the Baptist refers to the wicked as branches and chaff which are eventually *destroyed* in the fire of God's judgment (Matt. 3:10, 12). Even the Lord Himself, Pinnock points out, appealed to *Gehenna* and related it to the fiery pit outside the city where useless things were destroyed by the fire. Jesus likened this to the destiny of the wicked (Matt. 5:22). God is to be feared, Jesus said, because He alone could destroy both the soul and body in hell (Matt. 10:28).

Pinnock raises a good question of his own view when he says, "But what about the eternal punishment of Matthew 25:46?"[13] His answer to his own question is that the punishment referred to there is not everlasting but eternal:

> God sentences the lost to a final, irrevocable, definite death. It is indeed an everlasting punishment. The fire of hell does not torment but rather consumes the wicked. As Paul put it the wages of sin is death (Rom. 6:23).[14]

Such a view is simply a revised form of annihilationism. This is the belief that at death the souls of those who have not trusted Christ cease to exist and therefore do not suffer eternal punishment. Pinnock embraces this view because he believes it is more biblical than everlasting conscious punishment. He also rejects the latter view because he believes it is based upon the ancient Greek view of the immortality of the soul.

A similar view regarding the eternal destiny of the unredeemed is called "conditional immortality." Immortality was offered to Adam and Eve if they would obey God's word to them. Since they sinned, it was never given to them or their posterity, but was made available through Christ. Nicole, who rejects the view, explains it this way: "Those therefore who are not found in Christ inevitably fall into nonexistence either immediately at death or after a limited period of serious punishment after death."[15]

With justification Jon Braun calls annihilationism and conditional immortality "hitchhikers to universalism" or "subschemes universalism has spawned."[16] By universalism here he means the classic absolute universalism referred to above.

> As universalism slowly gained prominence, there were those who wanted to be universalists but just couldn't bring themselves to justify it. Agreeing with universalists in rejecting future punishment for the wicked, they couldn't quite swallow the notion that all men will ultimately be saved. This led to the creation of some variations, conditionalism and annihilationism, as attractive options. These doctrinal "first cousins" to universalism differ in that they allow for an eternal state of bliss and blessing for some but eternal punishment and torment for none.[17]

Neil Punt calls his own view regarding those who will be saved and those who will not "biblical universalism."[18] His premise is that the traditional view (all except Christ are children of wrath and deserving of eternal damnation) led our forefathers to place all outside of Christ except those the

Bible declares will be saved. He insists this is not really the biblical portrait. Rather, he says, the Bible presents the good news that "all persons are elect in Christ except those whom the Scripture expressly declares will be finally lost."[19]

Punt believes his "qualified universalism" or "biblical universalism" provides the answer for the apparent conflict between those texts of Scripture which speak of God's certain judgments upon the lost, and those which seem to imply universalism.

The major difference between Punt's view and that of his denomination (Christian Reformed) is that Punt's view emphasizes that all are elect in Christ except those whom Scripture says are lost. The traditional view places stress upon the lostness and inability of all rather than upon the election of almost all. Punt believes the electing grace of God has intervened on behalf of all except those who "willfully, personally, and finally refuse to have God in their knowledge."[20]

Evangelicals who support "biblical universalism" seem to be increasing. Some are more vocal than others as they differ from the traditional, biblical view.

> It [the New Testament] does not tell that God will damn out of hand those who have never heard. That accords ill with various hints of the New Testament, but supremely with the nature of God who has revealed Himself in Christ, the God who loved men enough to be crucified for them and by them. We may reverently be agnostic about the destiny of the unevangelized: that lies in the hands of God, the God of infinite compassion and strict justice. We can have confidence in Him but we have no right to sidestep the commission whilst we consider the problem . . . I have seen, as no doubt you have, people from Buddhist and Hindu and Muslim faiths coming to respond to Jesus Christ as their Truth and Redeemer. But I have not generally found them wishing to repudiate their past as if it were of no account. They have too strong a conviction that the living and true God was drawing and dealing with them in the days of their pre-Christian wrestlings.[21]

Some evangelicals believe that some of the unevangelized are saved and some are lost, depending on their response to the revelation of God to them in nature and conscience.

> They may be saved simply by responding to the knowledge all men have, however limited it may be . . . because they have all been given a knowledge of God and are being held accountable for what they do with that general revelation, it must follow that man can be saved on the basis of that revelation, depending on his response.[22]

What Does Scripture Say?

Those who believe in some form of "biblical universalism," "conditionalism," or "annihilationism," build their case on two major premises. "They believe they alone do justice to the reality of God's love and Christ's victory on the cross."[23] Appeal also is made to Scripture. Other arguments are also used, such as the universal saving will of God (John 3:16–17), "the restoration of all things" (Acts 3:21), and death as eventually "destroyed" (1 Cor. 15:26).

> Scriptures like these, when considered in isolation, constitute a fairly strong case, especially when combined with a deep yearning in our hearts for an ultimate abolishment of evil. We do not, however, have the luxury of dealing with any Scripture in isolation. Specifically, we must note the expressions used to denote the faith of the impenitent.[24]

Nicole follows the above words with a survey of the biblical terms used to speak of the eternal destiny of the unregenerate—separation from God, destruction and death, fire, darkness, the worms that will not die, trouble, distress, torment, agony, shame and everlasting contempt, everlasting chains and gloomy dungeons, futility, the wrath of God.

The Old Testament speaks of the eternal destiny of the ungodly in no uncertain terms. The key word is *sheol*, a term which appears sixty-four times. Sometimes the word is used for the grave and sometimes for eternal punishment.

> A final forever devouring, silent, purposeless, most distant place from God's heaven, shining with darkness, and gloom, seeking all it may devour—that is the picture of the place of eternal punishment as it was understood by the people of the Old Testament.[25]

The New Testament is even clearer than the Old in its teaching of eternal punishment.[26] While Jesus was by no means the only one to speak about eternal damnation, He did say more about it than anyone else. He spoke of "everlasting fire" (Matt. 25:41) and "everlasting punishment" (Matt. 25:46). Hell, He said, was "the fire that shall never be quenched" (Mark 9:43) and place of "torments" (Luke 16:23), a place of "wailing and gnashing of teeth" (Matt. 13:50).

A normal interpretation of Scripture requires belief in eternal punishment of those capable of responding who are outside of Christ. Any appeal to God's universal love for man and Christ's death for all as a basis for denying eternal punishment is unjustified. Scripture also requires the sinner to respond in faith before he can realize the saving merit of God's love and the Savior's death in his place. God's love and Christ's death save no one apart from the responsible individual's response in faith and trust in the Savior and His substitutionary death. The Cross does not apply its own benefits.

WHAT ABOUT THE UNEVANGELIZED?

Sometimes those who have not heard the Gospel of God's saving grace in Christ are called heathen. It may be better to refer to them as unevangelized.[27] The term "heathen" may imply barbaric people which is not true of all who have not been exposed to the message of salvation. And not all who have in fact heard the true Gospel have a clear understanding of how to prepare for heaven.

> There are more people being born into the world than there are people being born again. In fact the increase in the world's population is about twenty-seven times faster than the increase in the number of Christians. . . . Less than seven percent of the world has accepted the gospel message. About one-half of the world's population still does not know who Jesus Christ is. . . . approximately three-fourths of the world's population do not have a clear understanding of the gospel (clear enough to be able [to] understand the atonement process for their sins).[28]

Needless to say, these realities are sobering. The Bible is silent on the question. The only reasonable answer which can be given must be the result of one's theological view.

We know God is sovereign and that He will always do what is right. He is a loving God and according to Scripture always responds to the open and receptive heart.

We know too that God has revealed Himself in man (Rom. 1:19) and in nature (Ps. 19; Rom. 1:20), and all responsible humans are therefore without excuse. Scripture makes it clear that salvation is only through Christ (Acts 4:12; 1 Tim. 2:5) and that no one can come to God except through Him (John 14:6). Belief or trust in Him is essential to salvation (John 3:16).

What shall we say about the multitudes who die without ever hearing the name of Christ as the Savior of sinners? The compassionate heart wants to say God will make an exception in their case and somehow apply the finished work of Christ to them whether they ever hear the Gospel and respond to it or not. But there simply is no biblical basis for such a conclusion. We must rest in God's sovereign wisdom and goodness and leave the mystery of His will and ways with Him.

It seems in harmony with Scripture and human reason to conclude the following: God grants to those who respond positively to the revelation of God in themselves and in nature the opportunity to hear the Gospel. Sovereignly He sees to it that the message of God's gift of salvation through Christ comes to them so they can believe and become children of God. It is here that God's people have the responsibility to take the message of salvation to the lost. The unevangelized are not always in some far-off distant land. Some of them live in our neighborhoods. Some of them are our friends.

CHAPTER 16 DISCUSSION QUESTIONS

1. How much did you need to do in order to be saved?

2. Talk to someone you know who is not a Christian. Ask what he or she thinks God requires for anyone to be saved. Record the answer below.

3. How were people saved in Old Testament times?

4. How are people saved today?

5. Talk to your non-Christian friend again. Explain what the Bible says about what you must do to be saved. Record his response to your presentation.

17

WHAT ABOUT THOSE WHO CAN'T BELIEVE?

By those who can't believe we mean not only infants and young children, but also all who experience physical death before they are capable of making a decision either for or against the Savior.[1] Those individuals who are mentally incompetent or incapacitated, and have therefore never been able to believe, are also included. Human life begins at conception. Those who can't believe also include babies aborted naturally or by human instigation.

PREVIOUS ANSWERS

In the history of the church a number of views have been set forth in defense of the salvation of those who can't believe. Most of these views are still held today in some form or other.

Some have argued for the sinlessness or moral innocence of these individuals as the basis for their salvation. Such a view is in conflict with Scripture, which teaches the universality of sin.

God is love, others have said, and therefore, purely on the basis of His love He saves all who cannot believe. True, God is love but He is also holy and just. Unless His demands are met no one can enter heaven.

God is the universal Father of all. All are His children. Believing this, some insist those who can't believe are most certainly saved. Scripture, however, simply does not teach that God is the Father of all in a saving, or spiritual, sense. Only as Creator is He Father of all.

Others believe that through baptism those who can't believe are saved. Some who hold this view say those who die without being baptized are damned. The Roman Catholic Church teaches that those infants who die unbaptized enter *limbus infantum*, which is neither heaven nor hell. But the Bible does not teach salvation through water baptism for either those who can or those who can't believe.

Some believe that since Christ died for all, His death removed the guilt from all. Therefore, those who die before they can believe go to heaven. Although Christ died for all, it does not follow that His death removed the guilt from all. Even though the Lord Jesus Christ died for all, all are still guilty before God. Only when Christ's death is appropriated can its benefits be applied to the individual. Only when the finished work of Christ is applied to the person is he declared righteous by God.

Still others base the salvation of all who die before they can believe on God's election. They believe God's election was a redeeming act, as was Christ's death for those elected. Faith in this view is not what results in salvation and eternal life but is "the first conscious act of the quickened soul."[2] The Bible does not teach that God's electing choice is redemptive or that Christ died only for the elect. Neither does it teach that one believes or receives Christ as Savior because He has been regenerated. It is always the other way around in the Bible. Personal faith in Christ as Savior results in salvation. It is not the result of it.

THE PROBLEM

Those who can't believe are born to Christian and non-Christian parents. They are born in America as well as every

179

other part of the world. To whom they are born makes no difference when it comes to the question of their eternal destiny.

Most Christians believe those who cannot meet God's requirement of man for salvation and die in that state are taken to safety and bliss in God's heaven. But few know why they believe as they do. Sooner or later the problem of eternal destiny of those who can't believe touches most believers.

How many ways of salvation are there? Only one. Jesus said, "I am the way and the truth and the life" (John 14:6). Not many ways, or even two ways, but only one way has been opened whereby man, the guilty one, can be accepted by God. That one way is through the Lord Jesus Christ. God's Son. He alone is the Savior. There is no other. The sinner, regardless of age or mental ability, must be related to Jesus the Savior if he is to spend eternity in God's heaven. Unless the benefits of the shed blood of the Redeemer are applied to the guilty one, he will remain forever outside the family of God and therefore outside heaven.

There is but one human condition the sinner must meet in order to enter into salvation in Christ. Personal faith—individual trust—is presented many, many times in Scriptures as the sole condition for salvation. "What must I do to be saved?" the Philippian jailer asked. Through the Spirit Paul and Silas gave the divine answer, "Believe on the Lord Jesus Christ, and you will be saved" (Acts 16:31). Millions the world over have experienced this great salvation. They have acknowledged themselves as sinners and Christ as the only Savior and have accepted Him as their own substitute, as the one who paid the full price for all their sin.

The Bible makes it clear that whosoever will may come and drink of the water of life freely. The door of God's grace and mercy always stands ajar. All the sinner needs to do is receive the Savior as His own. There is room in heaven for as many as will obey the Spirit's call and respond to His work in the heart. No one will ever be turned away who responds in faith to God's salvation.

But what about those who can't believe, those who can't consciously receive salvation? How about all those who either die before they are capable of decision making or who remain unable to respond to God's great and grand invitation to all? Are these all damned to hell because they did not respond in faith to God's offer of grace when in fact they could not respond? How could such a thing possibly be true of the God of the Bible? It is my firm conviction that all who have never been capable of making a decision to receive Christ as Savior are safe in His arms.

Any attempt to answer the question concerning the salvation of those who can't believe must take into account the fact that these are never called upon by God to believe. It is always to those capable of believing that the challenge is issued. God invites those to Himself who can in fact respond to His invitation. Would it not be mockery for God to call upon His creatures to do, and to hold them responsible for doing, what they could not do?

THE NEED

The Bible makes no distinction between some who need God's salvation and others who do not need it. All are equally lost and therefore all alike need to be saved accordingly. Everybody is born wrong when he enters the world. Each one needs to be born again, born from above. Jesus made that very clear to Nicodemus. He said to that ruler of the Jews, "Unless one is born again, he cannot see the kingdom of God . . . you must be born again" (John 3:3, 7).

A person does not become unregenerate and therefore in need of the new birth at a certain age or when he reaches decision-making status. According to Scripture, all enter the world as sinners even before an act of sin is committed; that is in fact why they commit acts of sin—because they are sinners. (We established this earlier in Section I of this volume and need not repeat the arguments here.)

God's estimate of those outside of His Son is true, but not only of mature, normal, and sin-hardened adults. That accurate portrait is true of every single member of the human race. All, including those who can't believe, are lost (Luke 19:10), perishing (John 3:16), condemned (John 3:18), and under God's wrath and without life (John 3:36).

The problem of the salvation of those who can't meet God's one condition of salvation (can't believe) is not solved by lessening their guilt. Such a view cannot be supported by Scripture.

CHRIST'S UNIVERSAL PROVISION

Christ died for those condemned in Adam—all of them, not just adults or those capable of knowing they are condemned and therefore capable of making a decision either for or against Christ. We have developed the truth that Christ's death was unlimited in its scope in Section II. This means the Savior died as a substitute for every member of Adam's lost race.

The Bible makes it equally clear that the Savior's death by itself saves no one. The Cross's benefits must be appropriated by faith. In other words, the universal provision of redemption does not mean universal salvation. Christ died for all, but not all will be saved. The provision Christ made is universal in its scope; it was made for all but it is effective only for those to whom it is applied. Whosoever will may be saved. Many do not will and many others cannot will to be saved.

Our answer to the question of the eternal destiny of those who can't believe must be in harmony with the universal provision of salvation the Savior made at Calvary.

THE BIBLICAL TEACHING

Let us review. Every human being is born in sin. All have sinned and fall short of the glory of God (Rom. 3:23). The Lord Jesus Christ made provision for the salvation of all in His substitutionary death. Every member of Adam's race is saveable. There is only one way of salvation. The sinner can only be justified or declared righteous before God through the finished work of Christ. His death in the stead of every man is the basis of salvation. It is the only ground upon which God can forgive sin. Christ must be received as personal Savior, and when He is, His completed work of salvation is applied to the believer.

But what happens to all those who cannot meet this one condition of salvation? I believe firmly that all such receive eternal life. When they die they go to heaven. No one will spend eternity in the eternal punishment of hell who was not able to believe, to meet God's one condition of salvation. This conviction will now be defended, first from several biblical considerations and then from the study of several specific passages of Scripture.

General Teaching

Several facts of Scripture not only relate to the question of salvation for those who can't believe, but in fact support the contention that all who can't believe will not be eternally doomed. Some of these provide stronger argument than others. Taken together—and they must be to get the whole picture—they constitute formidable evidence. No particular significance is attached to the order in which they are presented here.

Children in the Bible

Many, many times the words "children" and "child" appear in the Bible. From many of these references it can be easily demonstrated that little ones have a definite place in the great heart of God and in His sovereign plan.

Not once in all the references to infants is there so much as a hint that they will ever be damned to eternal perdition after death. In many contexts where the words are used we would not expect a statement about their eternal destiny. Yet there are instances, such as when God ordered the destruction of all the Amalekites, including infants (1 Sam. 15:3), when it would have been appropriate to speak of their damnation. But not once, even when reference is made to the death of children, is there so much as a hint that any would suffer eternal separation from God (see for example Ex. 12:29–30 and Matt. 2:16).

The Person of God

A number of the descriptive characteristics of God found in the Bible lend strong support to the thesis of this chapter.

The Attributes of God

The characteristics or attributes of God tell us much more than that He simply performs in certain ways. God's attributes describe His person, not merely His behavior.

Without imposing human ideas on these divine characteristics it would seem incongruous with the very nature of God if any who can't believe die and go to hell. Consider certain of His attributes with this in mind.

God's wisdom

God has made no mistakes and He never will make one. In wisdom He has chosen and implemented the plan of redemption which will bring the most glory to Himself. God's Son is the Savior who died for all. Wisely, God has prescribed one way of salvation and only one. But those who can't believe do not refuse God's offer. They do not reject

Christ as Savior or God's revelation in nature and human conscience. In infinite wisdom God cares for them. Since rejection of the Savior is the final reason why men go to hell, those who do not reject Him because they are not able to make a conscious decision enter heaven on the basis of the finished work of Christ.

God's love

"God is love" is the clear revelation of Scripture (1 John 4:16). A more tremendous utterance cannot be found in all the Bible. It seems totally out of harmony with this truth to believe God would send to the lake of fire any who had not reached the competency enabling them to decide for the Savior. Does not God's love avail for that same company of people until such a time as it is rejected and spurned? God's infinite love for all is illustrated and supported when we see how, in love, He secures the salvation of those who can't believe.

God's mercy and grace

The psalmist wrote, ". . . the Lord is merciful and gracious, slow to anger, and abounding in mercy" (Ps. 103:8). Mercy and grace must be viewed as two sides of one truth. God's mercy means deserved penalty and punishment are withheld. The grace of God refers to His giving favor to those who do not deserve it. Both God's mercy and His grace were shown at Calvary toward all—those who can and do believe as well as those who can never believe. The punishment for sin which every member of the human race deserved was borne by Christ. What we deserved He received. He cannot be more merciful. What He does for man in salvation is based upon the mercy He displayed and revealed at Calvary. There, through the death of His Son, God made it possible to show favor, to save all, even though not one deserves it. How could it be said that God was merciful and

185

gracious toward those who can't believe if in fact any of that group perished?

God's goodness

"The Lord is good" (Nah. 1:7). Does God do good things? Does He do only good things? To both of these questions the answer must be an unqualified yes. But could that honestly be said in response to either one of the questions if He damned forever even one who could not meet the requirement for salvation which He Himself set forth?

The Bible does not teach the damnation of those who can't believe. It does teach the goodness of God. It is inconsistent with His goodness to believe any who die who can't believe are doomed.

God's justice

"The Lord," said Zephaniah the prophet, "will do no unrighteousness" (Zeph. 3:5). David the psalmist expressed the same truth regarding God's justice when he said, ". . . the Lord executes righteousness and justice for all who are oppressed" (Ps. 103:6).

Since God is just He deals equitably and according to truth with all His creatures. He is never unfair. But if He demanded of any of His creatures something which they could not do, would He be unjust? Since God has made it clear in His Word that those who reject His Son as Savior will be damned, how would He be just in refusing into His presence those who were never able to receive or reject His salvation? The Son of God came, declaring God's righteousness "that He might be just and the justifier of the one who has faith in Jesus" (Rom. 3:26). But there are many who can't believe. What will happen to these? Based upon God's justice and the satisfaction of His offended righteousness because of the work of His Son, we believe He is the justifier of those who can't believe just as certainly as He is of those who do believe.

God's holiness

"The Lord our God is holy" (Ps. 99:9). "God is light and in Him there is no darkness at all" (1 John 1:5).

What about the absolute holiness of God in relation to salvation for those who can't believe? Since God is holy and since those who can't believe are born in sin, does it not follow that they cannot be saved? No, it does not.

It would certainly be true that those who can't believe could not receive eternal life if Christ had not died for them and paid for their sin. He paid the full price demanded by God because of His offended righteousness for all—those who can't believe as well as those who can believe. The final and ultimate reason for eternal separation from the presence of God is the rejection of His Son as Savior. There is no other way to explain the many passages of Scripture which present faith as the one condition of salvation.

God's wrath

The Bible talks about the wrath of God. It is not a popular or appealing topic today, even among those who believe in it.

God's wrath is not a loss of self-control, an outburst of irrational behavior, as it often is with humans. We can understand the wrath of God by contrasting it with His love. God's love is the expression of an emotional attitude. His wrath is just as much the expression of His emotional attitude. The contrast between the two is that the former results in His favor (grace) toward the sinner. The latter results in His just punishment of the sinner. God's wrath is displayed toward those who spurn His love.

Those who experience God's wrath deserve it. They enter into it because they refuse God's way of escape. That is the repeated testimony of Scripture. But those who can't believe have not refused God's grace.

Salvation from God's terrible wrath is found in Christ

alone. It is the blood of Christ which appeases God's wrath (Rom. 5:9). Christ's work of propitiation, His sacrifice which satisfied God the Father, averts His wrath. Only upon His enemies is God's wrath poured out (Nah. 1:2). Those who can't believe are not God's enemies. Provisionally, they have been reconciled to God through Christ (Rom. 5:10).

The eternal torment of hell is a manifestation of God's wrath. Those who experience the wrath of God in hell do so because they rejected His love in Christ and thus deserve the consequences of their sin. Those who can't believe can't disbelieve either. Their original sin is covered by Christ. They are therefore not guilty of the sin which God says results in condemnation.

God can receive into His presence all those who did not receive His Son by faith because they *could not* do so. Without violating His righteous demands in any way, these are accepted into His presence. After all, His righteous demands were fully met at Calvary. The debt has been paid. Those who can and do believe do not contribute anything more toward the payment of the debt of sin by their faith. God's requirement of faith from man is not part of the payment toward his debt. The debt of sin is only charged against those who reject the payment God the Son has made and God the Father has accepted. All those who can't believe owe no more to God.

Christ's life and death

During His earthly ministry the Lord Jesus gave much attention to children. Since Christ was so interested in so many who could not believe, and since He did so much for them during His life, we have reason to believe He loves all such and grants them eternal life when they die.

The substitutionary death of Christ also provides support for believing that those who can't believe are saved at the time of their death. Jesus did die for all. Surely those who can't believe were not excluded from His gracious provision. If those who can't believe are not beneficiaries of God's salvation, Christ died for them in vain.

Someone might say, but what about those who reject Christ's salvation? Of what value or to what avail was His death for them? The answer is, Christ's death is the basis for their condemnation. Scripture clearly teaches that one who believes not is condemned for that very reason: "he has not believed in the name of the only begotten Son of God" (John 3:18). God's wrath is upon those who believe not: "He who believes in the Son has everlasting life; and he who does not believe in the Son shall not see life, but the wrath of God abides on him" (John 3:36). Only if those who can't believe are saved does the finished work of Christ have any relation whatever to them.

The basis of judgment for the lost

The apostle John saw in his vision "a great white throne" (Rev. 20:11). God was seated on the throne. The dead who appeared before the throne were the unsaved dead since the saved dead were raised earlier (v. 5). All the unsaved dead of all the ages were brought to appear before the Almighty God. Each one was judged by "the things which were written in the books" (v. 12). They were each judged "according to their works" (v. 12). All who appeared for this judgment were "cast into the lake of fire" because their names were not written in the Book of Life (v. 15). The reason their names were not in the Book of Life was because they had not believed. They had not received the Lord Jesus as personal Savior from sin. Their works demonstrated their lost condition.

All who appear before this Great White Throne will be judged according to their works. Before any are assigned to the lake of fire they will stand before God at this judgment. Those who died without ever being able to believe will not be there. They have no works: they have not done either good or evil. The basis of judgment will be according to what those who appear there have done. Equally as clear, all Christ rejectors will appear there. Since those who died before they could believe have no works, we may be sure that they will not appear before the Great White Throne. And since all the unsaved will appear there, we may also be sure that those who cannot believe are not unsaved. If they are not among the unregenerate and will not appear before God at this time, we conclude happily that they are among the redeemed.

The merit of faith

No serious student of Scripture doubts the necessity of personal faith for salvation on the part of those who can exercise it. The Holy Spirit has a vital part in bringing the sinner to see his need of the Savior and in enabling him to receive Him as his own. In fact, apart from the work of the Holy Spirit, no one would ever believe the Gospel and receive Christ as Savior. God the Holy Spirit moves upon the stubborn will of man, enabling him to respond in faith to God's offer of salvation. Jesus spoke of this divine work upon the human heart when He said, "No one can come to Me unless the Father who sent Me draws him" (John 6:44).

The Father draws sinners to Himself as the Spirit uses the Word of God to convict of sin, and eventually to bring to life, those who believe (John 3:5; 1 Peter 1:23). But this ministry of the third Person of the Godhead is not operative upon those who are not able to understand the Word and to respond to the claims of Christ.

Since faith contributes nothing to the complete salvation provided by Christ, its absence in those who cannot exercise it does not hinder the sovereign God from accomplishing in them all that He does in those who can and do believe. All who can believe must do so to receive eternal life. All who can't believe receive the same eternal life provided by Christ for them since they are not able either to receive or reject it. Freely, God gives life everlasting to all in both groups. Freely, He justifies (Rom. 3:24). Since He can justify freely those who believe, He can do the same for those who can't believe.

Scripture

Now it is time to look at the specific passages of Scripture which bear upon the question. Admittedly, not much Scripture deals directly with the subject. But those passages which do bolster my view. Not one verse of Scripture which relates in any way to the question at hand can be used to suggest the view that any of those who die without being able to respond to the Savior are doomed to eternity in hell. What information God has been pleased to give us provides great and gracious promise of eternal salvation for all who can't believe.

David

> So he said, "While the child was still alive, I fasted and wept; for I said, 'Who can tell whether the Lord will be gracious to me, that the child may live.' But now he is dead; why should I fast? Can I bring him back again? I shall go to him, but he shall not return to me" (2 Sam. 12:22–23).

David, the man after God's own heart, had sinned grievously. He was guilty of adultery and homicide. According to the law he deserved death. But he acknowledged honestly his sin, confessed it, and did not harden his heart against the Lord. The just penalty was not executed against him.

Because of David's sin the enemies of the people of God who were also the enemies of God blasphemed Israel's God. Shame and reproach were brought upon God and His people. A person's sin always seems to have a way of affecting many others. In some way God's honor and justice had to be displayed before His enemies. That is why "the Lord struck the child that Uriah's wife bore to David, and it became very ill" (2 Sam. 12:15).

David was brought to his senses by the Word of God through Nathan. After he was alone, David poured out his heart to God and prayed that the child would be restored. But his request was not granted. On the seventh day the child died (2 Sam. 12:18). The servants debated what to do. They gathered to plan their strategy. David saw them and heard them whispering and supposed rightly that the child had died. He then stopped fasting and praying. He washed and anointed himself and worshiped the Lord (vv. 19–20). The servants could not understand this sudden change of behavior. They asked him about it. David's reply constitutes one of the great texts of Scripture in support of the salvation of those not capable of believing (2 Sam. 12:22–23).

Life after death was a certainty for David. That he would in the future again be with his son was his firm belief. The psalmist never doubted that for a moment. David belonged to Jehovah and he had no doubt that he would spend eternity with Him. But neither did he have any doubt that his infant son, taken in death before he could decide for or against his father's God, would be there also.

Some argue that David's declaration merely meant he would one day join his son in death. As the child had died so would the father in due time. Such a view does not account for the anticipated reunion and fellowship with his son which is strongly implied in the statement and in the context. David's act of worship in the house of the Lord is hardly explained either, if the death of his son simply reminded David of his own certain death in the future.

Neither does this weak explanation account for the contrasting attitude which David had when his son Absalom died. After he became a man, Absalom rebelled against God and sinned terribly. He even attempted to seize his father's kingdom. He was killed in battle. When David heard of his son's death he was grief-stricken. He wept bitterly. In fact he even wished he could have died instead of his son (2 Sam. 18:33). David was not certain of Absalom's salvation and therefore of his future. But of the infant son who died he was sure. So sure was David of the child's eternal home that he knew he would go to be with him. This assurance caused him to turn from grief to worshipful prayer.

Still others who believe David was acknowledging the presence of his child in heaven argue that the child was there because he was a child of the covenant. Those who embrace this view believe only infants who have regenerate parents and who have received infant baptism (the New Testament sign of the covenant) will go to heaven when they die. Such a view lacks solid scriptural base, however.

Jesus and children

At that time the disciples came to Jesus, saying "Who then is greatest in the kingdom of heaven?" And Jesus called a little child to Him, set him in the midst of them, and said, "Assuredly, I say to you, unless you are converted and become as little children, you will by no means enter the kingdom of heaven. Therefore whoever humbles himself as this little child is the greatest in the kingdom of heaven. And whoever receives one little child like this in My name receives Me. But whoever causes one of these little ones who believes in Me to sin, it would be better for him if a millstone were hung around his neck, and he were drowned in the depth of the sea. Woe to the world because of the offenses! For offenses must come, but woe to that man by whom the offense comes! And if your hand or foot causes you to sin, cut it off and cast it from you. It is better for you to enter into life lame or maimed, rather than having two hands or two feet, than to be cast into the everlasting fire. And if your eye causes you to sin, pluck it out and cast it from you. It is better for you to enter into life with one eye, rather than having two eyes, than to be cast into hell fire. Take heed that you do not despise one of these little ones, for I say to you that in heaven their angels always see the face of my Father who is in heaven. For the Son of Man has come to save that which was lost. What do you think? If a man has a hundred sheep, and one of them goes astray, does he not leave the ninety-nine and go to the mountains to seek the one that is straying? And if he should find it, assuredly, I say to you, he rejoices more over that sheep than over the ninety-nine that did not go astray. Even so it is not the will of your Father who is in heaven that one of these little ones should perish (Matt. 18:1–14).

Jesus and His disciples returned to Capernaum where He performed a miracle, making it possible to pay the temple tax (Matt. 17:24–27). The very same day He also settled a dispute among His disciples. They argued on the road from Galilee to Capernaum about who among them would be greatest in the kingdom (Matt. 18:1; see also Mark 9:33–50; Luke 9:46–50).

To illustrate the need for simple trust and utter dependence Jesus used a little child. Mark tells us He even took the little one up in His arms (Mark 9:36). This fact helps us to understand the approximate age of the child. It was not a tiny infant but was certainly a very young child or else He would not have taken him in His arms. He not only put the child on His lap, He caressed him. That was a tender scene indeed. Without pride and resistance the child allowed the Savior to do with him as He pleased. Those who would enter the kingdom, Jesus said, must have the same attitude toward and dependence upon Him. In fact no one will ever enter the kingdom who does not become as a little child, said the Savior.

Who will be greatest in the kingdom of heaven? He who humbles Himself and has a childlike spirit of trust. He it is who is the greatest (Matt. 18:4). All who welcome a little child such as Jesus held in His arms will welcome Him (Matt. 18:5).

Without dispute Jesus put a high value upon little children. One's view of their eternal destiny must certainly take that into account. He had the "little child" in His arms as He spoke to the disciples. All that He said on this occasion must therefore be understood in that light. The tender and receptive spirit young children have toward Jesus is viewed as equivalent to faith in Him from them. Both Matthew and Mark tell us that Jesus said these little ones "believe in Me" (Matt. 18:6; Mark 9:42). It is doubtful that the "little ones" referred to were old enough to make a conscious decision for Christ as their personal Savior. Could it be because the little ones did not oppose the Savior, but instead allowed Him to do as He pleased with them that He viewed their lack of rejection as a reception of Him and belief in Him? That seems to have been the case.

Some believe Jesus' word about receiving "one such little one" does not literally refer to actual children. If that were true, His warnings about offending "one of these little ones which believe in Me" (Matt. 18:6) and despising "one of these little ones" (Matt. 18:10) referred not to little children such as the one He was holding in His arms but to those with a childlike spirit, children of the kingdom. The same would be true of the declaration that it is not the will of the Father in heaven "that one of these little ones should perish" (Matt. 18:14). This kind of view does not place enough significance upon either the physical act of Jesus or what He said with reference to that act.

It seems better to see Jesus as having in mind both actual children, like the one in His arms, and believers, children of the kingdom who become as children in their faith and trust. In other words, Jesus was talking about both literal and spiritual children. He in fact equated them in the things He discussed. The reason "these little ones" are not to be made to sin (Matt. 18:6) or to be looked down on (Matt. 18:10) is because they so represent Jesus that to mistreat them was like mistreating Him.

Angels

The reason why "one of these little ones" should not be despised is that "their angels always see the face of My Father who is in heaven" (Matt. 18:10), said Jesus. Some believe each child and each Christian has a specific angel assigned to them. Others believe holy angels perform a general ministry on behalf of God's children. What is important about this text of Scripture with respect to our subject is its clear statement that under divine guidance holy angels perform a ministry on behalf of "these little ones." They represent them before God. This truth lends strong support to the fact of their salvation. If both literal young children and children of the kingdom are in view, what is true of the one group is also true of the other one.

There is still another way to understand what Christ meant by the angels of the little ones. He may have meant by "their angels" spirits of the little children who pass from this life. The word "angel" seems to be used that way in Acts 12:15. Peter was delivered miraculously from prison and appeared at the house of John Mark's mother. A prayer meeting was in process. Rhoda, the maid, answered the knock on the door and to her complete surprise found Peter standing there. When she told those who prayed that their prayer had been answered, they could not believe her. They said it could not be Peter but that it must be his angel. By this they must have meant "it is his departed spirit." Since no other Scripture teaches about so-called guardian angels beyond these two, some believe the Acts 12:15 usage of angels throws light upon Christ's reference to the "angels" of the little ones.

Just as a good shepherd is concerned for all his sheep and does all in his power to rescue even one which goes astray, so God is vitally concerned with all His own (Matt. 18:12–13). The shepherd does not want to lose any of his sheep. Jesus said it is that way with His heavenly Father: "Even so it is not the will of your Father who is in heaven that one of these little ones should perish" (Matt. 18:14). Just as the shepherd in Jesus' illustration could not let His wandering sheep perish, so the eternal God in heaven would not will that one of His little ones should perish. When Jesus said this He was still talking about little children like the one in His arms. Any idea of reprobation for any one of the little children is excluded. Putting it positively, Jesus' statement means none of the little ones ever perish. There is salvation for all who die before they can decide for Christ.

Children and the kingdom

> Then they brought young children to Him, that He might touch them; but the disciples rebuked those who brought them. But when Jesus saw it, He was greatly displeased and said to them, "Let the little children come to Me, and do not forbid them; for of such is the kingdom of God. Assuredly, I say to you, whoever does not receive the kingdom of God as a little child will by no means enter it." And He took them up in His arms, put His hands on them, and blessed them (Mark 10:13–16).

Jesus became very upset with His disciples when they tried to keep parents from bringing their babies and little children to Him (see also Matt. 19:13–15; Luke 18:15–17). It was a common thing for Jewish parents to bring their children to a great teacher so he would bless them. When the teacher placed his hands upon them it symbolized his desire to bless them.

You would think the disciples would have learned by this time. They had already heard Jesus say how necessary it was to have a childlike spirit in order to have a place in His kingdom and be great in it (Matt. 18:1–14). Maybe they were sincere and figured the little ones would annoy Jesus; so they wanted to keep them from Him. Or it could be too that they were selfish and did not want the children, whom they considered unimportant, to steal the attention they wanted for themselves. Whatever the reason, this passage and its parallels in Matthew and Luke teach us again of Jesus' view of infants and young children. He loved them dearly and did not want His disciples or anyone else to get in their way and hinder them from being brought and from coming on their own to Him. Again He said, "of such is the kingdom of God. . . . whoever does not receive the kingdom of God as a little child will by no means enter it" (Mark 10:14–15). This provides great insight into Jesus' view of the eternal destiny of those who can't believe.

In summary of our study of specific Scripture, several important things stand out. No Scripture speaks of those who could not believe being in hell. The passages bearing directly on the subject of the eternal state of those who can't believe support the view that they will be with the Lord forever. The Savior's love for infants and children in general, and His repeated ministry toward them and for them along with the other general biblical considerations, also buttress the belief that all who can't believe enter the presence of God when they die.

CHAPTER 17 DISCUSSION QUESTIONS

1. Do you think babies and other mentally inadequate individuals are saved? Why or why not?

2. Have you lost someone close to you who was an infant or otherwise mentally inadequate? How do you feel about their final relationship to Christ? Did you feel like David when his infant son died?

3. How does a study of God's character help us to understand His provision for those who cannot believe?

4. How would you respond to someone who said, "Abortion isn't so bad. After all, those babies all go to heaven,

and if they were born into inadequate, unbelieving homes, they would probably grow up to reject the Gospel"?

5. How does God respond to those who should know better, who are accountable, but who never make a decision for Christ?

18

WHAT ABOUT LORDSHIP SALVATION?

IMPORTANCE OF THE ISSUE

At the present time "Lordship Salvation" is probably the most disputed concept about the Savior and His salvation among evangelicals. The question is not, "Is Jesus Christ Lord?" He is the sovereign God whether or not sinners or saints claim Him as such. Nor is the question, "Should believers enthrone Christ as Lord of their lives?" Of course they should. That is easy enough to defend from Scripture.

The question is, rather, "Must the unsaved promise to make Christ Lord of every area of their lives, in addition to trusting Him as their substitute for sin, to be saved?" Some highly respected and successful evangelicals—pastors, theologians, authors—are answering this question in the affirmative. If they are right, then how does that affect the long-standing and popular teaching presumably based upon Scripture, that salvation is absolutely free to the sinner? Traditionally salvation has been understood from Scripture to be a gift. The gift of salvation must be received, but it is apart from any human work or contribution of any kind. Sinners are saved by grace through faith alone. These views—the absolutely free gift view and the lordship view—cannot both be right. They are mutually exclusive. The Bible teaches one or the other or neither, but it cannot teach both without contradicting itself. The present conflict is not one merely of semantics. The differences are real and the consequences far-reaching.

Within evangelical circles today there are two basic views regarding Christ's Lordship. There is, on the one hand, what we will refer to here as the lordship view. Its advocates believe Christ must be made Lord of the sinner's life at the time he trusts Him as Savior or there will be no salvation. On the other hand, there is what we will call the faith alone view. Its advocates believe the matter of the lordship of Christ over one's life is an issue for believers and is not a part of the Gospel—to add commitment of life to God's free salvation is to add human works.

This debate strikes at the very heart of the orthodox Christian faith. It is not simply a fight over words and technicalities. The theological and practical ramifications are indeed far-reaching.

WHAT IS MEANT BY LORDSHIP SALVATION?

Advocates of the lordship view say that the essence of saving faith includes "unqualified compliance," "absolute humility," "unconditional surrender," and "absolute submission."[1] Another has asked, concerning the kind of Gospel we Christians spread, "Will it leave them supposing that all they have to do is trust Christ as a sin-bearer, not realizing that they must also deny themselves and enthrone Him as their Lord (the error which we might call only believism)?"[2]

John F. MacArthur, Jr. has written a definitive book defending the above sentiments but does not like the term "Lordship Salvation." He says it was "coined by those who want to eliminate the idea of submission to Christ from the call to saving faith, and it implies that Jesus' lordship is a false addition to the Gospel."[3]

For purposes of this study, Lordship Salvation refers to that belief which says the sinner who wants to be saved must not only trust Christ as his substitute for sin, but must also surrender every area of his life to the complete control of Christ. In other words, the sinner must enthrone Him as absolute Lord of his life or he cannot be saved. Here is what is meant by Lordship Salvation from one who holds the view: "The lordship view expressly states the necessity of acknowledging Christ as the Lord and Master of one's life in the act of receiving Him as Savior."[4]

The Lordship Salvation Issue

Those who embrace lordship salvation—or as another has defined it, "so-called lordship/discipleship/mastery salvation,"[5]—believe there is a new gospel being preached these days. By new gospel they mean "cheap grace" and "easy believism." "It encourages people to claim Jesus as Savior yet defer until later the commitment to obey Him as Lord. It promises salvation from hell but not necessarily freedom from iniquity."[6]

Serious minded evangelicals are all concerned with the lack of visible fruit by many who have "made decisions for Christ." There is a tendency on the part of some who are so enthusiastic to share their faith in Christ that they present the Gospel in such a way that only a mental assent to historical facts is called for. Many "converts" show no signs of having passed from death unto life.

A lordship salvation advocate has stated clearly why he believes the view is so urgently needed today.

> Products of modern evangelism are often sad examples of Christianity. They make a profession of faith and then continue to live like the world. "Decisions for Christ" mean very little. Only a small proportion of those who "make decisions" evidence the grace of God in a transformed life. . . . All of this is related to the use of a message in evangelism that is unbiblical.[7]

Is the solution to this problem, however, to be found by adding to the Gospel? Salvation is either by God's grace or by human effort, commitment, or work. It cannot be by both, anymore than law and grace were both means of salvation in Paul's day. A promise to live for God and obey His Word is doing something more than receiving God's salvation, and to that degree, it is a human work no matter how vociferously it is said not to be. In defense of faith alone, and contrary to lordship salvation advocates' claims, receiving God's precious gift of grace does not make it cheap or easy.

The Origin of Lordship Teaching

The forerunner of current debate erupted in the late 1950s and early 1960s. Two well-known evangelicals, Everett F. Harrison and John R. W. Stott debated the issue in *Eternity* magazine in September, 1959. Harrison was the first professor of New Testament at Fuller Theological Seminary and Stott was at the time rector of All Souls Church in London. Harrison took the position that while the acknowledgment of Jesus as Lord is essential to salvation the demand that "one must make Jesus his lord as well as his Savior to be truly redeemed" is to confuse salvation with the legitimate obligations of the Christian life. Stott, on the other hand, insisted that one must "surrender to the lordship of Christ" to be saved. "Lordship salvation" then, is the claim that to be saved one must not only believe and acknowledge that Jesus is Lord but also submit to His lordship.[8]

The lordship salvation view did not begin in the 1950s. In reality the view is as old as covenant reformed theology, with which it is very compatible, although not all who embrace a nondispensational theology subscribe to lordship salvation, and some dispensationalists embrace it.

Chantry was right when he said lordship salvation "is largely associated with Reformed theology (and rightly so)."[9] Supportive of this is the fact that the most recent full-scale defense of lordship salvation from one who claims to be a dispensationalist cites dozens of Reformed writers such as O. T. Allis, Berkhof, Boice, C. Hodge, J. I. Packer, Pink, and Warfield to support his view.

SCRIPTURES USED IN SUPPORT

Christ is called Lord (Greek, *Kurios*) many times in the New Testament. One Lordship advocate argued, "Christ is so frequently called *kurios* in the New Testament—747 times in the King James Version—that there must be some special significance behind the employment of this particular term."[10] Appeal is made to pre-New Testament usage and specific New Testament usage. Statistics are often cited for Greek version Old Testament (Septuagint) and New Testament usages with support from lexicographers (dictionary compilers).[11]

Those who hold to faith only salvation have no problem with this data. It is hard to imagine anyone wishing to be known as evangelical who would ever want to question that Jesus Christ is Lord. That has never been the issue with them.

The issue is whether or not God requires the sinner to promise Him that he will make the Lord Christ sovereign master, the Lord over his entire life all the rest of his life, before He will save him? Lordship salvation includes this requirement as part of believing "on the Lord Jesus Christ to be saved" (Acts 16:31).

When Scripture calls Jesus "Lord" it ascribes full and absolute deity to Him.[12] He is sovereign.[13] No one can have Christ as substitute for his sin who does not accept Him as such. Unless He is God the Sovereign One, He could not have atoned for sin. Jesus Himself made this very plain when He told His fiercest religious critics, "If you do not believe that I am He, you will die in your sins" (John 8:24). But accepting Jesus for who He claimed to be—the Lord God who died as man's substitute—is not the same as promising Him complete surrender and dedication of one's entire life.

The latter involves human effort or work and the former does not.

There are several New Testament passages used by Lordship Salvation teachers to defend their view.

Acts 16:30–31

> And he brought them out and said, "Sirs, what must I do to be saved?" So they said, "Believe on the Lord Jesus Christ, and you will be saved, you and your household."

Popular speaker and pastor John MacArthur says this passage and Romans 10:9 are "the two clearest statements on the way of salvation in all of Scripture" and that they "both emphasize Jesus' lordship." He concludes a very brief discussion of them with these words: "No promise of salvation is ever extended to those who refuse to accede to Christ's lordship. Thus there is no salvation except 'Lordship Salvation.'"[14]

In the same volume he says later: "The centrality of Jesus' lordship to the Gospel is clear from the way Scripture presents the terms of salvation." He then quotes several passages, Acts 16:31 among them, and makes this claim: "All of these passages include indisputably the lordship of Christ as part of the Gospel to be believed for salvation."[15]

It is important to keep in mind that MacArthur sees much more than deity and sovereignty in the term "Lord" as applied to Christ for salvation. He insists it means the sinner must promise to serve Christ and allow Him to be Master over every area of his life, all of his life.

Is that really what Paul and Silas told the Philippian jailer in response to his question—"What must I do to be saved?" (Acts 16:30–31). Putting myself in that jailer's shoes, I can't imagine that I would have understood what lordship salvation people extrapolate from the answer. Their view seems to be based on how they think Paul answered the jailer. They have been saying, "Believe on the LORD Jesus Christ" which means submitting every area of your life from now on to Him.

205

This is a serious and unjustifiable error. It involves a well-known linguistic fallacy sometimes called the "illegitimate totality transfer." In this sort of mistake, an idea drawn out of other words, or out of the general context, is wrongly read back into a particular word as a part of its meaning. This is what happened here. The word "Lord" is used by Paul and Silas to identify the Person in whom the jailer should put his faith, but in no way does it affect the meaning of the word "believe" . . . to suggest that some kind of personal surrender of the will is a part of the saving transaction in Acts 16:31 is to violently thrust into the text ideas which it does not contain.

Indeed we may go further. There is no such thing as "*making* Jesus lord of our lives." The Scriptures are clear that He *already is* Lord not only of Christians but of all unsaved people as well.[16]

The term *Lord* in Acts 16:31—or anywhere else it is used of Christ—does not mean Master over one's life. Rather it is a descriptive title of who He is—the sovereign God. It is one of many character-revealing names ascribed to Him, not a condition for salvation. The saving the jailer asked about was conditioned upon his believing (the verb). He had to believe Jesus was who He claimed to be—the sovereign Son of God who died as his substitute.

Romans 10:9–10

If you confess with your mouth the Lord Jesus and believe in your heart that God has raised Him from the dead, you will be saved. For with the heart one believes to righteousness, and with the mouth confession is made to salvation.

Earlier we referred to Romans 10:9–10 in connection with public confession as a condition for salvation. The passage is also a prooftext for lordship Salvation:

Romans 10:9–10 is probably one of the most common focal points in the lordship issue . . . again it can be assumed that *kurios* means God in the sense of the sovereign ruler. The lordship view sees in this phrase a recognition or an "exact agreeing" with God *(homologeo)*, that Jesus is one's lord or master.[17]

Appeal is made to a Greek grammar argument concerning the anathorous construction in the text. The Greek definite article does not appear before "Lord." Such a condition "places stress upon the qualitive aspect of the noun rather than its mere identity."[18]

All of this is true and applies to Romans 10:9–10. But how this in any way supports the lordship view and militates against salvation by faith alone is by no means clear. This great gospel text simply but powerfully proclaims Jesus Christ as the Savior who is also the sovereign God.

One Greek scholar stated what confessing Jesus as Lord means: "To recognize divine sovereignty in One who is truly man, or in other words, to recognize the union of the Divine and human in one person."[19]

The confession of Jesus as Lord referred to in Romans 10:9–10 is identical to that stated by the apostle elsewhere (cf. 1 Cor. 12:3; Phil. 2:11).

> No Jew would do this who had not really trusted Christ, for *kurios* in the LXX is used of God. No Gentile would do it who had not ceased worshiping the emperor as *kurios*. The word *kurios* was and is the touchstone of faith.[20]

What was said earlier in response to the use of Acts 16:30–31 to defend lordship salvation applies equally well to Romans 10:9–10: Christ cannot be received as substitute for sin unless He is received as the Sovereign God, but He can be received as God without being received as substitute. When this is done, salvation does not result.

James 2:14–26

> What does it profit, my brethren, if someone says he has faith but does not have works? Can faith save him? If a brother or sister is naked and destitute of daily food, and one of you says to them, "Depart in peace, be warmed and filled," but you do not give them the things which are needed for the body, what does it profit? Thus also faith by itself, if it does not

have works, is dead. But someone will say, "You have faith, and I have works." Show me your faith without your works, and I will show you my faith by my works. You believe that there is one God. You do well. Even the demons believe—and tremble! But do you want to know, O foolish man, that faith without works is dead? Was not Abraham our father justified by works when he offered up Isaac his son on the altar? Do you see that faith was working together with his works, and by works faith was made perfect? And the Scripture was fulfilled which says, "Abraham believed God, and it was accounted to him for righteousness." And he was called the friend of God. You see then that a man is justified by works, and not by faith alone. Likewise was not Rahab the harlot also justified by works when she received the messengers and sent them out another way? For as the body without the spirit is dead, so faith without works is dead also.

There is nothing in this passage about lordship. But it is appealed to for support of the fact that not all faith is re-demptive. "James describes spurious faith as pure hypoc-risy, mere cognitive ascent, devoid of any verifying works—no different from the demons' belief."[21]

The majority of evangelical Christians who understand what salvation by grace through faith alone means would fully agree.[22] James showed how showing partiality is an of-fense against the royal law of love (2:1–13). True love results in showing mercy and compassion upon the needy. James continues in 2:14–26 to stress the need for a practical expres-sion of Christianity. He does this by arguing that true faith really will express itself in good works. They may not always be seen by others at all times, but life cannot be hidden for-ever. "So likely it can truly be said that every believer will bear fruit somewhere (in earth and/or heaven) sometime (es-pecially and/or irregularly during life), somehow (publicly and/or privately)."[23]

Earlier James talked about a true and a false religion (James 1:26–27). Now in 2:14–26 he talks about true and false faith. The key to this latter passage are the words "say" or "says." Here is a person who claims to have faith and he may even think in his own mind he has it, but what issues from his life is not consistent with the testimony of his lips.

In context, the phrase "can faith save him" means can the kind of faith which produces nothing and profits no one—save a person? The truly implied answer is no, it cannot. On that there is widespread agreement on the part of evangelicals, including those who do not embrace lordship salvation. For those who do accept lordship salvation to use this text as an argument against the entire opposing view is to misapply it completely.

PROBLEMS WITH LORDSHIP SALVATION

The View Invests *Lord* with New Meaning

Lord, applied to Jesus, means He is God[24] and therefore the sovereign One.[25] Evangelicals on both sides of the lordship issue agree—no one can have Christ as a substitute for sin and become a child of God who does not acknowledge Him as such.

Lordship salvation people go a step further and say the sinner must turn his entire future life over to Jesus as Lord before he can receive forgiveness of sin. Nowhere in Scripture is making Jesus lord of one's life a requirement to receive salvation from the Savior.

Conflict with New Testament Examples

The New Testament contains many examples of people who were, without question, believers but who did not have Christ as Lord of their lives. Many lapsed in their faith and commitment to the Savior. Lordship salvation advocates acknowledge these and insist their view takes into account sin in the life of believers and does not demand perfection from God's people.[26]

But why *doesn't* perfection follow since *complete* surrender of all of one's life is required for salvation? The view does not allow for any life area not surrendered to participate in salvation. What logically should follow is no deviation throughout life if the salvation is to be retained. The lordship view fails to answer the real question of how much is to be surrendered for how long? What happens if Christ is not allowed to be Lord after salvation?

Lordship salvation is inconsistent with the New Testament reality of the believer's struggle with the old nature. If total surrender is required *for* salvation, is it not also required *to keep* that salvation?

Conflict with Security and Assurance

Those who promote Lordship Salvation suggest there is no middle ground. Either a person is a genuine believer and as living a life of unreserved obedience or he cannot be sure he is saved. As one writer put it, "to know assurance you have to see a pattern of holiness . . . therefore, if you are not denying ungodliness you cannot be certain you are really saved."[27]

Everett Harrison echoed the above sentiments in these words:

When faith is genuine, it will lead to a desire to know the Lord's will for the life. The acceptance of His control will not be refused. This is not the issue in salvation and it is both unfair and confusing to the sinner to introduce the issue of what he is to do for Christ before God's grace can be made operative in his life and lead him from darkness to light.[28]

As we shall discuss further in the next chapter, the Bible repeatedly assures us that our eternally secure relationship to Jesus depends, not on our own, often failing, trustworthiness, but on the trustworthiness of God Almighty. See verses such as John 10:28–30, where Jesus promises to give us "eternal life," and that we "shall never perish"; and Hebrews 12:2, where Jesus is called "the author and finisher of our faith."

Discipleship for Non-believers?

By insisting that the sinner not only receive Christ as his substitute for sin but also his sovereign Lord over every area of his life, the view places responsibility on the unbeliever that really belongs to the believer.[29]

Zuck pinpointed the problems with the lordship view of discipleship in this analysis:

> To most lordship advocates a disciple already means one who is totally committed to the Lord. But this view that "believers" and "disciples" are *always* synonymous overlooks the fact that in Scripture the word "disciples" is used of (1) curiosity seekers who later left Jesus and obviously were not genuinely saved (John 6:66); (2) true followers of Christ (Acts 11:26); (3) and the Twelve—including Judas (Matt. 10:1). In the Lordship Salvation view a person who is not a disciple of the Lord (in the sense of being a fully committed Christian) is not saved. Obviously this can bring confusion and doubt.[30]

Faith Plus Works Salvation

Salvation is hardly a gift if the recipient must promise to surrender every area of his life as long as he lives to get it. Doesn't that involve doing something to at least partially deserve the "gift"? The Bible does not add surrender or obedience to the one condition of faith for salvation.

Harrison states as one of his objections to lordship salvation the "subtle form of legalism."

> We reject the teaching that we can be saved by works. The Word of God is emphatic on this (Eph. 2:9; Titus 3:5). Why then bring works in by the side door by asserting that unless we do whatever is necessary to the acknowledging of the lordship of Christ in our lives, we are not saved?[31]

Justification Confused with Sanctification

Justification is the work of God by which He declares the believing sinner righteous before Him. This takes place at the same time as the new birth and has to do with the believer's position before God. The sinner is declared righteous because he is robed in the righteousness of Christ.

Sanctification is how the regenerate believer lives his Christian life. It is presented in Scripture in a threefold sense—positional, progressive, and perfect. The believer daily sets himself apart from sin and becomes more Christlike. This is growth in grace and is the progressive stage of sanctification. This is when discipleship and Christ's lordship are experienced, not as a condition for salvation.

The lordship view does not clarify the distinction between progressive sanctification and justification, or between discipleship and sonship. It mixes the condition with the consequences. It confuses *becoming* a Christian with *being* a Christian.

> True, a person who is justified by God's grace is sanctified positionally, set apart to God at the moment of salvation. But that is when the Holy Spirit *begins* His work of ongoing sanctification, not *finishes* it. One follows the other. Discipleship starts at rebirth and should continue on after it.
>
> Regeneration pertains to one's relationship to Christ as Savior from sin. Sanctification on the other hand pertains to one's relationship to Christ as his Lord and Master. In the new birth a person is made a new creation in Christ. In sanctification he grows in that relationship.[32]

Repentance Confused with Its Fruit

Repentance in Scripture has to do with a change of mind. Evangelicals agree no one can be saved who does not change his mind about himself and his need, his sin which separates him from God, and about Christ as the only Savior. What many don't agree on is the lordship salvation view that all the sinner's sins now and for the rest of his life must be forsaken before he can become a child of God. Nowhere is such a requirement placed upon sinners.

Once a sinner has changed his mind about his lost condition and Christ as the only Savior of sinners, then the genuine fruit of that repentance is growth in grace and the enthronement of Christ in the life. But the fruit must not be confused with the root which makes the fruit possible.

LORDSHIP BONDAGE

I do not believe a person receives eternal life by simply giving mental assent to a set of historical facts. Facts have never regenerated anybody. Neither has faith, for that matter. God by His Spirit regenerates. He brings life to sinners who are totally dead spiritually. He does this in response to and at the same time that the condition He prescribes for salvation is met—faith in His Son as substitute for sin.

God cares whether or not His children make Christ the Lord of their lives. But lordship or progressive sanctification can be committed to and experienced only by believers.

The lordship view adds to the Gospel of the grace of God what Scripture does not. This does not mean the motives of the people involved are not pure or that attempts are not made to avoid this dilemma. Brethren in Christ embrace the lordship view but that is no guarantee that what they hold is not another gospel. The gospel of God's saving grace must not be adulterated, not even by evangelicals.

CHAPTER 18 DISCUSSION QUESTIONS

1. What are two of the strongest criticisms of lordship salvation?

2. Is Jesus Christ Lord of your life? If you are a born again Christian, what steps do you need to take to develop the fruits of your justification?

3. What kinds of things do you think hold people back from maturing as Christians?

4. What are some additional requirements some people add to the basis of faith in order to obtain salvation through Jesus Christ?

5. Why do you think the idea of lordship salvation is so appealing?

19

THINGS WHICH ACCOMPANY SALVATION

A small child, Jessica McClure, wandered from her home and fell in an abandoned well in Lubbock, Texas. Her parents tried desperately to get her out. The whole community soon knew about the tragedy and got involved. Before long news of the tragic accident was on national television. Jessica became a household word. The rescue efforts were watched everywhere. Just before little Jessica's life was snuffed out, she was pulled safely from the well. The world rejoiced in her great deliverance.

Every member of Adam's race is entrapped in sin and condemnation. No one can deliver himself from sin's fetters. No effort on the part of other people, no matter how noble, can deliver anyone from his lost and hopeless condition. But then Jesus came. He alone is the Savior of sinners. He delivers all who by faith hold His hand, trust Him alone as Savior, and allow Him to deliver them.

Deliverance, that is what salvation means as used in the Bible. To be saved from sin means to be delivered from its eternal condemnation. The believer has been delivered from sin's penalty, can be delivered from sin's power in his life, and will be delivered from the presence of sin in the future.

The Three Tenses of Salvation

Penalty
Acts 16:30, 31
Rom. 8:1
PAST

Power
Rom. 6:1-13

PRESENT

Presence
I Jn. 3:1,2

FUTURE

THE HUMAN PREDICAMENT

Before a person can appreciate God's "so great a salvation" (Heb. 2:3) and all that it includes and involves, he must understand that from which he has been delivered.

Scripture is clear in its description of those outside of Christ. All who are not rightly related to God through Christ are said to be lost (Luke 15:4–7), dead in "trespasses and sins" (Eph. 2:1), "having no hope and without God in the world" (Eph. 2:12). None, Paul says, even seek after God or do good. There simply are none who are righteous outside of Christ (Rom. 3:10–12). Statements like the above speak clearly about the unregenerate's lack of any righteousness before God. Scripture also speaks of man's corrupt sinful nature. This is the source of all man's sinful thoughts, words, and deeds.

As we learned in Section I, every human being acquires from his parents and has from birth a capacity and tendency to sin. We call this the sin nature. Adam and Eve, our first parents, got their sin nature when they sinned by eating of the forbidden fruit. They passed that sin nature on to their children and they to theirs and so on down to us. Parents propagate in their own likeness. Because of the sin nature it is impossible for those who have not been born again to do anything to merit favor with God. Everything man does in his unsaved state stems from a "deceitful" and "desperately wicked" heart (Jer. 17:9).

Even after salvation the old sinful nature continues to plague the believer. Its *power* has been defeated in salvation, but its *presence* in us is still very real. The believer must seek constantly to suppress the old desires within. There is an inner struggle within the believer. Paul experienced it (Rom. 7) and so does every child of God. There is victory, however, through our Lord Jesus Christ. The believer has been blessed with a new nature. He is a new creature in Christ

Jesus. The Holy Spirit has taken up His residence in the believer. Victory is therefore available through the strength He provides.

Those who have not experienced the grace of God in salvation are "all under sin" (Rom. 3:9; Gal. 3:22). This tells us there is a divine indictment against all. In these texts God gives His concluding observation regarding man's lost estate. There is *none* righteous and *all* are under sin.

THE CHARACTER OF GRACE IN SALVATION

The character of grace in salvation is called the "riches of grace in Christ Jesus" by Lewis Sperry Chafer.[1] First, all these marvelous works of grace are totally unrelated to human merit. They are all from God. They cannot be earned. To make any contribution whatsoever for them or toward them is to remove them from the sphere of gifts. Human promise or endeavor cannot even preserve them. The Savior's merit, His accomplishments, provide the basis for the bestowment of every divine blessing here and now as well as the believer's rewards in the future. The two—riches of grace given at the time of the believer's salvation, and future rewards—must be kept separate, however.

Second, all the riches of grace are the possession of each and every believer. From the weakest and youngest saint to the strongest and oldest, all who belong to the Savior are blessed with the same spiritual blessings in Christ Jesus. Growth in grace, important as it is, does not make these blessings from God to the believing sinner more true.

Third, gifts of grace do not become effective or complete with the passing of time. No amount of human effort or promise can improve them. They are all complete as they come from the hand of God.

The believer's life can and must experience improvement. We are to grow in grace. The Bible exhorts the saved to go on to maturity. But individual development in no way alters one's position of sonship. A son or a daughter cannot be more of a child of his or her parents than he or she is at birth. So it is in the family of God. While fellowship can be strengthened and improved, the relationship cannot be. For example one cannot be more justified than he is at the time of salvation. He can, though, learn to know what is involved in justification and he can learn to live like one who is justified.

Fourth, the gifts of grace are eternal. The riches of God's grace could not be other than eternal since they come from God's hand. They must therefore be as eternal as He is. Depending as they do on the eternally finished work of the Savior, they too will be forever. Failure in the Christian walk affects the believer's fellowship with God but it does not affect his position "in the heavenlies."

Fifth, the gifts of grace are not experiential in nature. This means they are not initiated, validated, or maintained by our emotions. There is no uniform feeling experienced by all who are members of the family of God. And yet these gifts are genuine. They relate primarily to the believer's position before God and have to do with his standing, not necessarily his state at a particular time in life.

The Exemplary List

What follows is not a complete list of the things which "accompany salvation" (Heb. 6:9). No chronological order is intended by the order presented here. Keep in mind what has been said above as these divine realities are studied.

Regeneration

"Regeneration or new birth is an inner recreating of fallen human nature by the gracious sovereign action of the Holy Spirit (John 3:5–8)."[2] This work of God brings life to the be-

219

lieving sinner. Divine life is imparted when the sinner trusts the Savior as substitute for his sin.

Some insist that regeneration precedes faith. They do so because they believe if it does not, total depravity is denied. In this view faith does not result in regeneration, but springs from it. Repentance and faith are not considered as human capabilities prior to regeneration.[3]

Such reasoning fits the five-point Calvinistic system. The question is, however, what does the Bible teach about the relationship of faith to regeneration? There is no text which declares that faith results from regeneration, that regeneration comes before faith. It is always stated the other way. Humans are called on to exercise faith, to believe, to trust, in the Savior and His finished work to receive eternal life. Never are they told to believe because they have already received new life.

The universal offer of the Gospel, the call to sinners to believe and receive eternal life, is not in conflict with total depravity. The Bible teaches both. At the same time that the Spirit works efficaciously, the sinner is enabled to believe, meeting God's requirement for salvation and receiving eternal life.

> "The normal pattern for regeneration" is that it occurs at the moment of saving faith. No appeal is ever addressed to men that they should believe because they are already regenerated. It is rather that they should believe and receive eternal life. Christians are definitely told that before they accepted Christ they were "dead in trespasses and sin" (Eph. 2:1, A.V.).[4]

Scripture uses three figures to describe the eternal life imparted to spiritually dead sinners in regeneration.[5] The new birth or being "born again" (John 3:7) describes it. God is said to bring us forth by the exercise of His will (James 1:18).

Regeneration is also viewed as spiritual resurrection. Believers are "alive from the dead" (Rom. 6:13). God the Father makes believing sinners "alive together with Christ" (Eph. 2:5).

The figure of creation or recreation is also used to describe the Holy Spirit's work of the regeneration of sinners (Eph. 2:10; 4:24; 2 Cor. 5:17).

Regeneration results in membership in the family of God. The only way to become a member of God's family is by being born into it (John 1:12; 3:7; 1 Peter 1:23). This becomes a reality the moment Christ is received as personal Savior. Entering the family of God is no more a gradual process than is entering our earthly families. We must be born into both at a definite point in time.

Justification

"Justification is God's action pronouncing sinners righteous in His sight. It is a matter of our being forgiven and declared to have fulfilled all that God's law requires of us."[6]

When the sinner trusts the Savior he is clothed with His righteousness. God declares the sinner righteous (Rom. 5:1). This is God's work of grace on behalf of repentant believing sinners (Rom. 3:24). God's call precedes justification. The end result is the sinner's glorification, when he will be made like Christ (Rom. 8:30; 1 John 3:1–2).[7]

God can declare a believing sinner righteous because of his position in Christ (Eph. 2:13). To be "in Christ" is to be identified with Him in His death and resurrection. The Savior's victory at the cross and open tomb is the believer's. Christ's righteousness is imputed to those who trust Him alone as the substitute for their sin (2 Cor. 5:21; Rom. 5:17).

The result of justification is both positive and negative. Since judgment against the sinner is canceled, the believing sinner is no longer condemned. On the positive side, the sinner who trusts the Savior is also declared righteous. He has a whole new standing before God.

The Bible speaks of the believer's adoption into the family

of God (Rom. 8:15; Gal. 4:5). The believer is not only pardoned; he also has a positive standing with God. In the New Testament the term *adoption* into the family of God means to be placed as an adult son in God's family with all the rights, privileges, and responsibilities of sonship.

The sinner who trusts the Savior has citizenship in heaven at once even though he is still on earth (Phil. 3:20; Eph. 2:19). Every child of God is, from the moment of faith on, a member with all the other saints in the household of God (Eph. 2:19; 3:15).

Santicfication

To be sanctified means to be set apart by the Lord. There are three aspects of the believer's sanctification. First, each believer is set apart at salvation as far as his position before God is concerned (1 Cor. 1:30; 6:11). Second, it is the will of God that each Christian continuously set himself apart to holy living (John 17:16; 2 Cor. 7:1). Third, there is a final and complete setting apart of each believer when Christ comes again (1 Thess. 3:12–13). Only the first aspect of positional sanctification takes place at the time of salvation. This phase of sanctification becomes one of the things accompanying salvation. It is not the same as regeneration, though it is simultaneous with it.

The sanctifying work of God means that each believer is made acceptable in the Beloved (Eph. 1:6). "For by one offering He has perfected forever those who are being sanctified" (Heb. 10:14). Seated in Christ in the heavenlies, the believing sinner is secure. He is as close to the Father as is Jesus Christ the Son.

Forgiveness of sins

The Lord Jesus Christ bore the condemnation of man's sins. Therefore those sins no longer condemn the sinner who trusts the sin bearer. There is no more condemnation

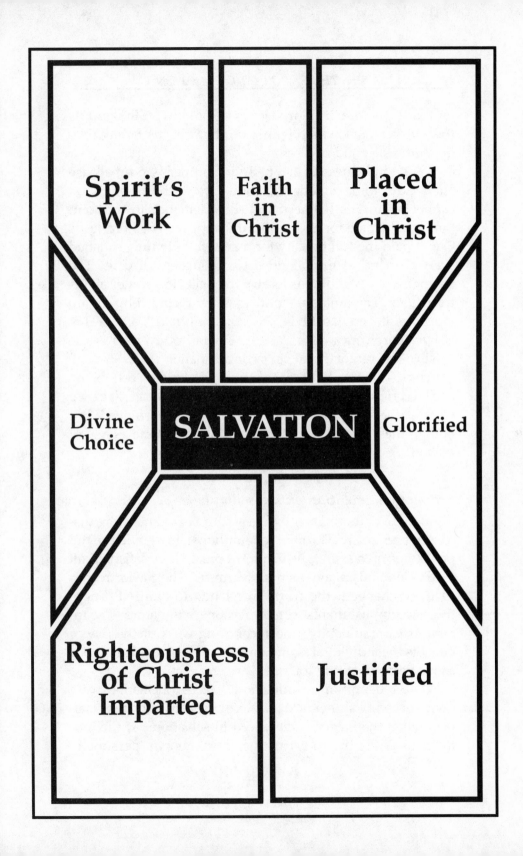

for those who are "in Christ Jesus" (Rom. 8:1). Sin disrupts the believer's fellowship with God, but not his family relationship as a child of God.

God's forgiveness of the believing sinner is not because He decides to be lenient and show pity to the sinner. God cannot retain His holiness and show leniency toward sin. Sin must be paid for and its penalty applied. The Lord Jesus Christ paid the full penalty for man's sin. He fully satisfied every demand of the offended righteousness of God. The Savior God can and does forgive the believing sinner all his trespasses. The guilt and condemnation incurred by sin are forever removed (Col. 1:14; 2:13; 3:13; Eph. 1:7; 4:32). That is what forgiveness is all about. Divine forgiveness is the erasing, the removing of sin's condemnation.

Justification has to do with a positive divine work, being declared righteous. Divine forgiveness is more of a negative work—deserved penalties and judgments are removed. But both of these divine works occur at the same time as regeneration.

Redemption, propitiation, reconciliation. . . . .

All three of these great divine accomplishments were discussed previously. Through redemption, Christ paid the full penalty of man's sin. His death propitiated, or satisfied, all God's demands against sin and sinners. The Savior reconciled, or changed, the world in relation to Himself. These three accomplishments were provisionary in nature. The redemptive, propitiating, and reconciling work of the Savior benefits the individual sinner only when he trusts the Savior as his own substitute for sin.

While redemption, propitiation, and reconciliation were divine accomplishments at the cross, they are only personalized when the Savior is embraced in salvation. At the moment of faith, the one trusting the Savior is personally redeemed, and reconciled to God. This is a divine undertaking totally unrelated to any human work. It is all of God's marvelous grace.

Members of the holy and royal priesthood

One of the striking differences between God's program with the nation Israel and the church is over the matter of priesthood. The nation of Israel had a priesthood; that is, there were those select individuals within the nation who served as priests. The church, on the other hand, does not have a priesthood within it. Rather it is a kingdom of priests (Rev. 1:6). Every member of the body of Christ, every believer, is a priest unto God. From the time of the Protestant Reformation to the present time the priesthood of all believers has been a cardinal and distinguishing doctrine of the historic Christian faith.

The primary work of a priest involves making sacrifice. But Christ's sacrifice on the cross ended the need for all sacrifice for sin. However, the believer's body is to be presented as "a living, holy sacrifice" (Rom. 12:1). Also the praise of the believer's lips and the doing of good works are called sacrifices which are pleasing to God (Heb. 13:15–16).

The priesthood of which every child of God is a member is a "holy priesthood" (1 Peter 2:5), a royal priesthood (1 Peter 2:9). Each believer is a priest to God and has full assurance of future reign with Christ (Rev. 5:10; 2 Tim. 2:12). When does one become a priest? Believing sinners become priests when they are born again, when they are justified, when their sins are forgiven, when they are redeemed and reconciled to God.

All these results occur when the sinner does nothing more or less than trust the Savior and His substitutionary work on his behalf.

SALVATION

Before

After

Before	After
Dead in sin	Regenerated
Unrighteous	Justified - declared righteous
No peace	Peace
No access	Access
No hope	Hope
Ungodly	Accepted in Christ
Sinners	Saints
Under Divine Wrath	Saved from wrath
Enemies	Reconciled to God
Lost	Saved

CHAPTER 19 DISCUSSION QUESTIONS

1. How would you explain man's hopelessness apart from Christ to a non-Christian friend?

2. What are some areas of your own life where your old nature has a tendency to dominate? What are steps you can take to allow the Holy Spirit to work in you in those areas?

3. List the "things which accompany salvation." Which ones are especially important in your own life?

4. How do justification and sanctification relate to each other? Give an example from your own life of how sanctification has improved your relationship with God.

5. Describe yourself before you became a Christian. How did you change after you became a Christian?

20

GOD'S SECURITY AND MAN'S ASSURANCE

Security and assurance go together. Even the person behind bars is assured of his security as he stares at the windowless walls of his dark cell and hears the footsteps of the guard outside.

God's security and man's assurance are companion truths when it comes to the believer's salvation. They may be viewed as two sides of the same coin. Security is what God provides for the believing sinner. It is an aspect of His great gift of salvation. Assurance is the certainty the believer has when he accepts God's security.

It is possible, of course, to be secure but not experience assurance. This is the case with many believers. But God's security does not depend upon the believer's reception or rejection of it. The believer's assurance, on the other hand, does depend upon acceptance of God's security.

In this chapter we want to develop the biblical teaching of both security and assurance. Each of these crucial doctrines will be treated separately and then conclusions drawn from this study.

GOD'S SECURITY OF THE BELIEVER

Some refer to this doctrine as the perseverance of the saints. The term "security" refers to God, who provides it.[1]

Perseverance places more stress on man's side of the relationship.

> The doctrine of the perseverance of the saints does not maintain that those who *profess* the Christian faith are certain of heaven. It is *saints*—those who are set apart by the Spirit—who *persevere* to the end. It is *believers*—those who are given true living faith in Christ—who are *secure* and safe in Him. Many who profess to believe fall away, but they do not fall from grace for they were never in grace. True believers do fall into temptations and they commit grievous sins but these sins do not cause them to lose their salvation or separate them from Christ.[2]

God does *secure* His own. They will *persevere* to the end. Both of these are true.

Secure because of God's Promise

> What then shall we say to these things? If God is for us, who can be against us? He who did not spare His own Son, but delivered Him up for us all, how shall He not with Him also freely give us all things? Who will bring a charge against God's elect? It is God who justifies. Who is he who condemns? It is Christ who died, and furthermore is also risen, who is even at the right hand of God, who also makes intercession for us. Who shall separate us from the love of Christ? Shall tribulation, or distress, or persecution, or famine, or nakedness, or peril, or sword? As it is written: "For Your sake we are killed all day long; we are accounted as sheep for the slaughter." Yet in all these things we are more than conquerors through Him who loved us. First I am persuaded that neither death nor life, nor angels nor principalities nor powers, nor things present nor things to come, nor height nor depth, nor any other created thing, shall be able to separate us from the love of God which is in Christ Jesus our Lord (Rom. 8:31–39).

Bruce's analysis of this passage is forceful:

> Could anything be a stronger encouragement to faith than the contemplation of God's saving purpose for His people,

moving forward to its appointed consummation? Since God is their strong salvation, what force can prevail against them? Since His love was freely manifested in the sacrifice of His own Son on their behalf, what good thing will He withhold from them? Paul for a moment envisages the situation in terms of a court of law where the believer stands to be judged. But who will dare to come forward as prosecutor? God Himself, the Judge of all, has pronounced His acquittal and justification; who can call His sentence in question? The prosecutor may not venture to appear, but the Counsel for the defense is present and active; "it is Christ Jesus that died, yea rather, that is risen again, who is even at the right hand of God, who also maketh intercession for us." And nothing can come between His love and His people. Not all the trials and afflictions which they had experienced or might yet experience.[3]

There are three solid platforms on which the security of the child of God rests: the promise of God, the presence of God, and the power of God.

Paul concluded writing about the great doctrines of sin, God's righteousness, and God's grace in salvation. In the immediate context he set forth truths concerning the unscrutable mysteries of God in foreknowledge, predestination, calling, justification, and glorification. In the chapters which follow (9—11) he demonstrated the faithfulness of God to His people Israel in the past and in the future. As the apostle concluded the great treatise, he showed how all these doctrinal truths relate to everyday life.

Five questions and their answers appear in this text (Rom. 8:31-39). They all relate to the security of the child of God.

The questions (Rom. 8:31–36)

These verses also contain explanations which make the answer obvious. The concluding answer, however, is given in verses 37-39.

The first question introduces the other ones by connecting them with the context. "What then shall we say to these things?" By "these things" Paul was referring especially to the things he had discussed in verses 28–30. Those verses were simply an explanation of the reason for suffering as a believer as stated in verse 17. Therefore, in reality this first question ties what precedes it with those questions which follow it.

The second question is, "If God is for us, who can be against us?" The English translation seems to imply that maybe God is not for us after all. This is a false implication. The original language used here means that in view of the fact that God is for us, who could possibly harm us?

Perhaps the personal "who" is used in this and the remaining questions because the believer's foe is personal; we face a personal devil and his evil hosts (Eph. 6:11–13). Then too, the experience of the apostle and his own conflicts may account for the emphasis here. The Holy Spirit used all his experiences for the glory of God. The extent of God's love demonstrated at Calvary proves beyond any question that He who gave all to save us will not hesitate to provide all that is needed to keep us safe (8:31).

Question number three is stated in verse 33, "Who shall bring a charge against God's elect?" Again it is personal, "who?" A legal term is used here meaning "to bring a charge against." The reference to "elect" takes us back to the one spoken of in Romans 8:28–30. The added word of explanation is, "God is the one who justifies." The implication is unmistakable. How could men, demons, or Satan call to account those declared righteous by the mighty Creator of the universe?

Verse 34 presents the fourth interrogation. "Who is he who condemns?" The inference from this question is clear. Surely the one who intercedes for the believer cannot at the same time condemn him.

Stifler in his commentary on Romans summarized the fourfold protection of Christ in this way:

As no one can open the case against and bring a charge before the court, so no one can condemn, for Christ is a fourfold
protection. Are there offenses? "He died" for them. Is there a
need of life? He is "risen again" and we are "saved by His life"
(v. 10). Do we need representation and influence at the court?
He is in the chief place of authority—"even at the right hand of
God." Do we in hours of transgression and weakness need an
advocate (1 John 2:1)? He "ever liveth to make intercession for
us" (John 17).[4]

Finally the last question, "Who shall separate us from the
love of Christ?" (v. 35). Under every adverse circumstance,
Christ's love for His own prevails. Nothing can affect His
love for us. Through His love victory is achieved. It is natural
to ask why troubles and misery come to the believer in view
of God's promised love. Human experiences often disprove
His love. We must find our confidence in His love and in His
Word, not in our circumstances. God's only begotten Son
endured the agony of Calvary and the Father did not cease to
love Him during those awful hours. When God allows His
own to suffer for Him, His love for them is strongest. Verse
36 suggests that God's people have always suffered for the
cause of God and righteousness.

The answer (Rom. 8:37–39)

Concluding and summarizing the whole matter of security,
Paul gave his final answer in these remaining verses. The
apostle declared what at first appeared to be an im-
possibility—"we are more than conquerors through Him who
loved us" (v. 37). Only the one who cannot be conquered can
be more than a conqueror. In the original, the phrase "more
than conquerors" is made up of two words. The first means
to carry off the victory, come off victorious. The other word is
a preposition meaning "above." Putting the two meanings together, the meaning is to gain a surpassing victory. This
means that all this victory is "through Him who loved us."

This clearly refers to God's love for us demonstrated at the cross. Though God does love His own during their trials here, Paul was speaking of that act of love displayed in giving His son.

"For I am persuaded" means that Paul had an unalterable conviction of soul. Literally it would read, "I stand persuaded." These two last verses (38–39) support the previous verse and elaborate upon it. No power or created being—man or angel—can separate the child of God from the Father's love in Christ. No conceivable adversary in the entire universe is left out of this list.

Secure because of God's Presence

My sheep hear My voice, and I know them, and they follow Me. And I give them eternal life, and they shall never perish; neither shall anyone snatch them out of My hand. My Father, who has given them to Me, is greater than all; and no one is able to snatch them out of My Father's hand. I and My Father are one (John 10:27–30).

The meaning of this passage hinges upon a proper understanding of the Shepherd, the sheep, any man, and the Father. Christ's teaching concerning His own death brought a sharp division among the people (John 10:19). As a result, some said He was possessed of demons while others accepted Him and His message (John 10:20–21). The unbelieving Jews questioned Him further, "If You are the Christ, tell us plainly" (v. 24). Christ's reply was that they did not believe Him because they were not of His sheep. His sheep hear the voice of the Shepherd and the Shepherd guards them eternally.

The position of the sheep (John 10:27–28)

The position of the sheep in relation to the Shepherd is one of nearness and intimacy. True to the figure, the sheep

John 10:27,28

The Shepherd...
1. calls the sheep
2. knows His own
3. gives eternal life

The Sheep...
1. hear the Shepherd
2. follow the Shepherd
3. receive eternal life

are completely dependent upon the Shepherd. He is the giver; they are always the receivers.

The protection of the Shepherd (John 10:29–30)

The sheep are said to be in the Shepherd's hand (v. 28) and also in the Father's hand (v. 29). What security! The eternal presence of the Father and the Son guarantees the eternal security of the believer. The life which Christ gives is "eternal." Those possessing it shall "never perish." No one shall pluck the sheep from the Shepherd's hand. The irrevocable word of the Shepherd is "no one shall be able to snatch them out of the Father's hand."

Lest someone imagine that there may be some difference between the Father and the Son as to the security and safety of the sheep, Christ added, "I and My Father are one" (v. 30). The Father gave the sheep to the Shepherd (John 6:37) and the Shepherd gave His life for the sheep (John 10:15). The sheep are secure.

Secure because of God's Power

Blessed be the God and Father of our Lord Jesus Christ, who according to His abundant mercy has begotten us again to a living hope through the resurrection of Jesus Christ from the dead, to an inheritance incorruptible and undefiled and that does not fade away, reserved in heaven for you, who are kept by the power of God through faith for salvation ready to be revealed in the last time (1 Peter 1:3–5).

Peter wrote to persecuted Christians. They were undergoing severe trials for their faith in Christ. Peter knew what that meant. He had had his own times of testing. The keeping power of Christ was very real to him.

A secure possession (1 Peter 1:3–4)

Moving from God's total plan and purpose in the salvation of sinners (vv. 1–2), Peter went on to deal with the basis

235

of the sinner's deliverance from sin. He began with an expression of praise, "Blessed be the God and Father of our Lord Jesus Christ, who according to His abundant mercy has begotten us again to a living hope through Jesus Christ from the dead" (v. 3).

When asked concerning their hope of heaven, many people respond, "I *hope* to make it." When Peter thought about his hope for everlasting life in heaven, he did not hope he would make it. He *knew* without doubt that he had a hope based upon the finished work of Christ.

God the Father is blessed or praised because, according to His abundant mercy, He gives each believer new life in Christ. Because He raised Christ from the dead, those who believe in Him will live also. Not only will he have hope of a future resurrection, but he now in this present life has a hope that is steadfast and sure. The hope of a believer is just as certain as is the fact of the resurrection of Christ. Though they were not eyewitnesses of the resurrection, believers today have the abundant testimony of the Scripture and the witness of that hope within.

The result of this hope is expressed in verse 4: "to obtain an inheritance which is imperishable and undefiled and will not fade away reserved in heaven for you."

Here the inheritance is reserved for the believer. Possession of eternal life is secure. Hope is "imperishable." It is not subject to decay, spoiling or a change from *within*. Likewise it is "undefiled" and it will not "fade away." This means it is without defect or flaw. It will stand the test of every evil force from *without*.

Such is the heavenly possession of every believer. Peter added that it is "reserved in heaven for you." "Reserved" means "closely guarded" or "preserved." There are no conditions attached to this promise, no "ifs" or "buts" about it. Personal faith in Jesus Christ as personal Savior guarantees the recipient of God's grace a secure inheritance.

A secure people (1 Peter 1:5)

An inheritance reserved for the heirs and the heirs kept for the inheritance mean double security. Concerning those possessing the inheritance described in verse 4, Peter said, "who are kept by the power of God through faith for salvation ready to be revealed in the last time" (v. 5). The word "kept" is a military term in the original. Observe how this word is used in 2 Corinthians 11:32. It is even used of God's peace in Philippians 4:7: "and the peace of God, which surpasses all understanding, will guard your hearts and your minds through Christ Jesus." Since it appears in 1 Peter 1:5 in the present tense, the emphasis is upon the continual process of being garnished or guarded. How the child of God needs this protection! What assurance it brings to know each saint has it!

The means whereby we are kept is highly significant. There is an immediate agency—the power of God. There is also an intermediate agency — individual faith. God, who exercised His mighty power to save the sinner, releases that same power toward the saint in keeping him saved. Paul's words in Romans 8:31–39 come into focus here: "if God is for us, who can be against us?"

Peter's reference to faith in 1 Peter 1:5 indicates the human responsibility in salvation. Faith does not save, neither does it keep one saved. However, no one is saved and therefore no one is secure who has not placed his faith in the finished work of Christ. When the unsaved trusts Christ alone as Savior, the regenerating power of God brings spiritual life to the spiritually dead sinner and that same divine power becomes operative in the security of the born-again one.

A first reading of 1 Peter 1:5 may give one the impression that all this divine work is merely with a view to salvation in the future without application in the immediate present. The verse states, "for salvation ready to be revealed in the last time."

It is the final aspect of salvation which Peter has in view in verse 5. He was not declaring that his readers would someday be saved from the penalty of their sin. That divine transaction took place the moment they trusted Christ as Savior. Rather, he was speaking of the fact that the God, who delivered them from the condemning penalty of sin, would see them all the way through. Paul seems to have had the same three aspects of salvation in mind. When speaking of God he said: "who delivered us from so great a death, and does deliver us; in whom we trust that He will still deliver us" (2 Cor. 1:10). The final deliverance from the presence of sin is just as sure and certain as the deliverance from the guilt and condemnation of sin which came at the moment of personal faith.

The safest and surest way to send something to someone is by registered mail. Only two people can legally receive and open such mail—the sender and the receiver. This is because all such mail has been legally and officially certified. It is guaranteed to be delivered to the specified person. Our salvation is like that. God, the Father, sent His Son to provide the salvation through His substitutionary death. The Holy Spirit brought conviction of sin and regeneration to the sinner. He has become the seal of our eternal salvation (Eph. 4:30). We have been received into the family of God. The only ones who could possibly break the seal would be the members of the Godhead. And they have given us their word they will never do this (2 Tim. 2:13).

MAN'S ASSURANCE OF SALVATION

There is nothing so frustrating as uncertainty. Fear of the unknown is perhaps the greatest fear of all. Life is filled with uncertainties and fears. But when it comes to the matter of salvation and eternity, the Christian need have no fears or uncertainties. Ours is a know-so salvation.

We must be careful not to encourage a false assurance in one who has never been born again. This study is concerned with the believer and the assurance of his salvation. Assurance does not produce salvation any more than works produce faith. However, assurance is the result of salvation and can be experienced as works are the result of faith and do follow it.

What Does Assurance Mean?

John Calvin apparently believed that assurance was of the same essence as faith which results in salvation.

> In short, no man is truly a believer, unless he be firmly persuaded, that God is a propitious and benevolent Father to him . . . unless he depends on the promises of the divine benevolence to him, and feels an undoubted expectation of salvation.[5]

Assurance has to do with the certainty that one has passed from death to life. It is the realization that having done what God has required—trusted in His Son alone as substitute for personal sin—He has given eternal life.

The people involved

An unregenerate person will not be at peace *with* God. He will also lack the peace *of* God. He lacks these because he has not accepted the promise of God to give life to those who believe (John 11:26). Such a one cannot have the assurance of sins forgiven. No doubt many individuals who have gone through some ceremony or ritual or who are depending upon some deed or deeds for salvation cannot understand why they still are not sure of their salvation. In such cases the simple answer is that those who trust in anything other than Christ for salvation are not saved. Of course they do not have assurance of eternal life; they don't have the life.

Those who have trusted Christ alone for salvation and have been born again have every reason to be at perfect rest.

We can go so far as to say that at the moment of faith they also have assurance or they simply haven't exercised faith. Scripture exhorts the child of God to make sure about God's call and choice of Him (2 Peter 1:10). Having done that, the believer must resist Satan's doubts by standing firmly upon the "thus saith the Lord."

Most Christians have probably doubted their salvation at one time or another. Even John the Baptist questioned at one point that Jesus was whom he believed Him to be (Luke 7:18–20). But doubt in itself is not sin. However, it is a sin to deliberately disbelieve or deny God.[6]

God's people alone have a saving relationship with Him. They have passed from death unto life. The fact that they have received Christ alone as Savior makes that certain. Therefore, they are the only ones who can and should have the assurance beyond any shadow of doubt that they have passed from death unto life.

Assurance and Security

Security and assurance are not the same. The securing of the believer is God's sovereign work. God always performs His work well. The child of God is secure in God's hands. On the other hand, assurance is the believer's acceptance of the security provided for Him in Christ, the Savior. It results from man's believing and resting in what God has said and done. Assurance cannot be earned; it must be received. It is not the result of the soul's conquest; it comes as the result of God's bequest—a secure salvation.

Assurance and Sanctification

At the time of salvation the believer is set apart by God as His own peculiar possession (1 Cor. 6:11). Believers are exhorted to set themselves apart daily from sin and its defilements (2 Cor. 7:1). All believers will eventually be set apart from the very presence of sin (1 Thess. 3:12–13).

240

Those who believe sanctification means sinless perfection or some other description of absolute purity naturally hold that sin in the believer's life causes loss of salvation and therefore loss of assurance. However, since sanctification does not mean sinlessness, the above is not true.

Those who have trusted Christ as Savior are set apart by God the moment they are saved. Thus they are secure, and assurance comes by accepting that position in the Savior. Again, the two truths are not identical, but they are related to each other.

Sin in the life of the believer breaks fellowship with God. This in turn brings unrest, disturbance of soul, and loss of assurance of salvation. At such times the child of God must avail himself of the truth of 1 John 1:9 so that fellowship may be restored. Under such conditions, sin destroys the believer's assurance; but his eternal welfare remains the same, since he is "in the beloved."

Why Do Believers Lack Assurance?

There are two basic reasons under which all other reasons seem to fall, false concepts and failure to believe God.[7]

False concepts

Many Christians harbor false notions in their minds regarding various aspects of salvation. These in turn make it difficult for them to have assurance of their salvation.

For example, the human requirement of faith is often misunderstood. Sometimes people speak of "saving faith." By this they imply faith for salvation is different from faith exercised for other things. But God does not require some special kind of faith for salvation different from ordinary faith. God demands all the faith the sinner has. He asks for *complete* trust and reliance upon His Son and His Word. It is not, however, the person's faith which saves. The New Testament teaches that Christ and Christ alone saves. No one can be saved without faith in the Lord Jesus Christ and His death in the sinner's place. But it is not the kind nor the amount of faith that brings life to the one dead in trespasses and sin.

There are also people who do not understand the difference between security and assurance. This was discussed before. Failing to understand these truths is often the reason Christians lack the assurance of their salvation.

Well-meaning but confused Christians who share the Gospel are sometimes responsible for people not having assurance. When emphasis is placed upon an emotional experience as an indicator of salvation, doubts soon arise. The new Christian worries that when he no longer "feels" the same as when he first received Christ, he is no longer saved or never was saved.

Frequently, public confession in church is made a condition for salvation. Romans 10:9–10 is misused to support this position. The confession referred to here could as well be acknowledgment to an individual or a small group or even to God. Verse 10 is the explanation of exactly what brings salvation or righteousness: it is not the confession. Rather it is "with the heart one believes to righteousness."

Public acknowledgment of Christ as one's Savior is a good thing, but it is not a condition for salvation. It is the testimony of one who has been saved.

Failure to believe God

Unbelief is an awful sin. The fact is, many Christians do not have a deep-settled assurance of salvation because they do not take God at His Word. What an insult to God this is! When one doesn't believe the promises of God regarding eternal salvation, he is calling God a liar.

Believing God's Word for deliverance from sin's condemnation is one thing. Believing His Word concerning eternal salvation is another. It is, however, inconsistent to believe Him for the one and refuse to trust Him for the other. The same person is the Savior in both cases. The same power is manifested and needed for both. And the very same promises relate to salvation as relate to the security of the saved. Blessed assurance follows from trusting God in both instances.

People have assurance at the time they are saved. They are sure they have passed from death to life. It is later that Satan comes with his questions and doubts. In times like these the troubled person must return to the promises of God's Word.

How May Believers Gain Assurance?

Genuine assurance of the forgiveness of sins can be gained through three basic means: the Word of God, the witness of the Spirit of God, and the walk of the child of God.

The Word of God

The same miracle-working word which regenerates also imparts assurance to the heart that believes. Indeed the two things are both simultaneous and inseparable.

Or to put it another way when a person believes, that person has assurance of life eternal. How could it be otherwise? Think, for example, of the words of Jesus, "Most assuredly I say to you, he who hears My word and believes in Me believes in Him who sent Me has everlasting life, and shall not come into judgment, but has passed from death into life" (John 5:24).

This is extremely clear, the believer, says our Lord, has eternal life. Moreover he will not come into judgment. In fact he has already passed out of death into life. And to believe His word is to believe these things too.

Thus it is utterly impossible for us to give credence to the gospel message without knowing that we are saved. For that message carries its own guarantee along with it. Therefore to doubt the guarantee of eternal life is to doubt the message itself.

In short, if I do not believe that I am saved, I do not believe the offer that God has made to me.[8]

Is it presumptuous to be assured of one's salvation? Not at all. It is only if salvation depends in any way upon human goodness or promise either for the reception of salvation or the retention of it. The point at issue here is not: Am I going to be faithful enough to keep saved? The crux of the whole matter is the faithfulness of God to His Word (2 Tim. 2:13).

Uncertainty of salvation comes from Satan and is contrary to Scripture. The Bible stresses the fact of eternal life or ever-lasting life for the child of God. Examples of Christ's promises include "All that the Father gives Me will come to Me, and the one who comes to Me I will by no means cast out" (John 6:37), and "And I give them eternal life, and they shall never perish; neither shall anyone snatch them out of My hand" (John 10:28).

The Word of God becomes the most basic and important basis for our assurance of salvation. Man's word fails; God's Word never fails. God wants His children to know they are saved. This is why He gave His Word: "These things I have written to you who believe in the name of the Son of God, that you may know that you have eternal life" (1 John 5:13).

Whenever a Christian doubts or questions his salvation, he is in effect rejecting the Word of God. This is why it is important to be sure salvation is based upon God's Word. When one's basis of salvation is found in the Scriptures, human circumstances will not affect that salvation. The Bible must be the foundation upon which our salvation now and forever is based.

Answers to simple questions can help a person who has doubts regarding his salvation. What did God say a man must do to be saved? Did you do that? Can God lie? Then what is true? On what then does your salvation depend? On what is your confidence based?

The witness of the Spirit

By using the Word of God the Holy Spirit brings assurance. He testifies to the believer that he is a child of God.

This is not mere subjectivity. Instead, it is the objective work of the Spirit of God upon the written Word of God to the heart of the child of God.

The believer becomes the temple of the Holy Spirit at the time of salvation (1 Cor. 6:19–20). Here He abides forever, ministering comfort and correction. John declares that the Spirit's presence in the child of God causes him to know he is saved. "By this we know that we abide in Him, and He in us, because He has given us of His Spirit" (1 John 4:13).

The Holy Spirit is the believer's Helper. Christ promised that on His departure He would send the believers another Helper (i.e., John 14:16, 26; 15:26; 16:7). Two different words in the Greek are both translated "another" in our English Bibles. One of these words means "another of a different kind" and the other means "another of the same kind." It is the latter word which is used in this passage from John. The Holy Spirit is one just like Christ in His essential being and purpose. The word "Helper" means "one called alongside to help." What a precious promise that is! The Spirit of God helps us in times of spiritual need. This is what the Lord Jesus did for the disciples when He was with them.

Just before He went to the cross the Savior told His disciples that the Holy Spirit would be their teacher. He is that for us too (i.e., John 14:26; 15:26, 27; 16:12–15). Here is another way by which the Holy Spirit gives assurance of salvation. He throws light on the Scriptures so the Christian can understand them. He teaches him the truth of God. Nothing brings assurance quicker than understanding the Word of God. Divine guidance is also given by the Holy Spirit. He leads the believer in righteousness (Rom. 8:4, 14). The Christian life is a walk which necessitates complete dependence upon the Holy Spirit for each step. Walking by depending on the Spirit's strength produces confidence and assurance (Gal. 5:16, 18).

The Spirit also intercedes for the believer. Paul stated it this way:

Likewise the Spirit also helps in our weaknesses. For we do not know what we should pray for as we ought, but the Spirit Himself makes intercession for us with groanings which cannot be uttered. Now He who searches the hearts knows what the mind of the Spirit is, because He makes intercession for the saints according to the will of God (Rom. 8:26–27).

This means the Holy Spirit makes our prayers intelligible to the Father. Often the need for prayer is felt, but the one praying does not know *how* to pray or even *what* specifically to pray for. Such experiences are common to many Christians. This is when the third member of the Trinity comes to the believer's assistance and witnesses to us, in us, and for us.

The walk of the believer

The order in which these suggestions concerning gaining assurance is given is important. First place must be given to the Word of God. Using that Word, the Holy Spirit bears witness with our spirit. In addition to these means of acquiring assurance, and in cooperation with them, there is the matter of the normal Christian experience.

Those who think the sinner must make Christ Lord of his life, or at least promise to do so, before he can be saved make assurance rest on the evidence of a surrendered walk. MacArthur cites this as the only way a believer can be assured of his or her salvation. "Genuine assurance comes from seeing the Holy Spirit's transforming work in one's life, not from clinging to the memory of some experience."[9]

The walk of the believer doesn't always reveal his spiritual condition. There ought to be spiritual fruit in the lives of God's children. Yet we know from the examples of several Bible characters that there can be times when a believer falls into sin.

Evidences of a transformed life must not be viewed as the means for a person to earn or add to his salvation. Rather, they are the result of new life within. They do not bring salvation; neither do they in any way improve it. They are outward evidences that a transformation has taken place on the inside.

Definite answers to prayer can be assurances that we belong to God. God does not hear and therefore does not answer the "prayer" of the unsaved unless it be a "calling" for salvation. Special direction and leading from the Lord is another evidence that one is a child of God.

Love for other Christians is an indication of the transformed life. A person who belongs to God's family will enjoy and seek out the fellowship of other children of God. There will be new desires, new habits, and new companionships. This does not mean Christians should isolate themselves from the non-Christians. If they are going to be reached for Christ, we must take the Gospel to them. But the one who is born again will find his old life unsatisfactory; he will crave fellowship with the redeemed (1 John 3:10–14).

The believer should expect the fruit of the Spirit in his life (Gal. 5:22–23). The redeemed have every right to expect that the works of the flesh will diminish in them as the fruit of the Spirit develops (Gal. 5:19–21).

Fact, faith, and feeling are all important for the child of God. The relation of these to each other and to the matter of assurance is vital. The facts of God's Word are the most important. What He has said about man's sin, Christ's work, and man's need is all determinative. Believing and then acting upon these facts, man receives Christ as Savior. The resultant emotional feeling will vary with each individual.

Our assurance must rest in the facts and our acceptance of the Savior of whom they speak. Our confidence should never rest in the passing and changing emotions we experience.

Be confident of your security in Christ. It does not depend on you, your efforts, or your feelings. It depends only on Christ, "the author and finisher of our faith" (Heb. 12:2).

FACT

FAITH

FEELING

CHAPTER 20 DISCUSSION QUESTIONS

1. Have you ever worried that you weren't saved? What helped you to trust God's promises?

2. Using your concordance, look up and write down at least four Bible passages concerning trusting God's promises.

3. What are the three important indicators God has given us to assure us of our salvation?

4. Do you think a Christian who is out of fellowship with God has assurance of his salvation?

5. If you were to talk to a Christian who was unsure of his salvation, how would you explain that he can know for sure he is saved and will remain saved by the power of God?

21
STRUGGLES WITHIN
AND WITHOUT

Up to this point in Section III we have discussed several aspects of the great salvation the Savior provided for sinners. The question before us in this chapter is how this sinner the Savior has saved is to live the rest of his life here on earth. Sinners are saved to be the praise of God's glory (Eph. 1:12). That is God's highest motive in redeeming the lost. Each sinner saved by God is to work out the salvation God has worked in him (Phil. 2:12–13).

In this chapter we will come face to face with the believer's enemies. These obstacles to growth in grace, these enemies of God's grace in salvation, are before every believer. Not only that, these enemies and the struggles they bring continue throughout the believer's life.

The believer is engaged in a spiritual warfare that begins the moment he trusts Christ for salvation. He is not exempted from spiritual struggles. Each believer is to fight the "good fight of faith" (1 Tim. 6:12). The riches of grace in Christ Jesus (discussed in chapter 19), do, however, adequately equip the believer so he can wage a good warfare. To be successful in the conflict each must know his enemies. To be forewarned is to be forearmed.

Sources of victory must also be known and appropriated by the believer. The one who trusts Christ for salvation should trust Him and His provisions for triumphant living as well. Many of God's people have a false conception of the Christian life. It is not a life of ease with flower-strewn pathways, as some suppose. God has never promised this. He has promised victory for the surrendered, obedient believer over the trials, temptations, and hardships of life.

Paul the apostle summarized and explained the war going on inside the believer in these words: "For what I am doing, I do not understand. For what I will to do, that I do not practice; but what I hate, that I do" (Rom. 7:15).

THE ENEMY WITHIN

Why was it that the great apostle to the Gentiles didn't do what he wanted to do? And the things he didn't want to do, he found himself doing? Why does the Christian still suffer conflict between good and evil? It is because the one who has trusted Christ as Savior and has passed from death unto life still possesses the same old capacity to sin with which he was born (Rom. 7:17–18). His position before God has changed, but the old tendency and capacity to sin is still there. This tendency to be at odds with God comes from the sin nature. The believer has both an old sin nature and a new nature.

Nature, as used here, does not mean personality. Believers do not have two personalties. Nature, whether referring to the old nature or the new, refers to the capacities and tendencies of each individual.

Some evangelicals believe Christians only have a new nature.[1] This teaching has two serious flaws. One, it must redefine sin as committed by the believer. Two, it fails to distinguish carefully between the believer's position before God and his practice in the world, between positional and progressive sanctification.

As noted earlier, to be sanctified means to be set apart:

251

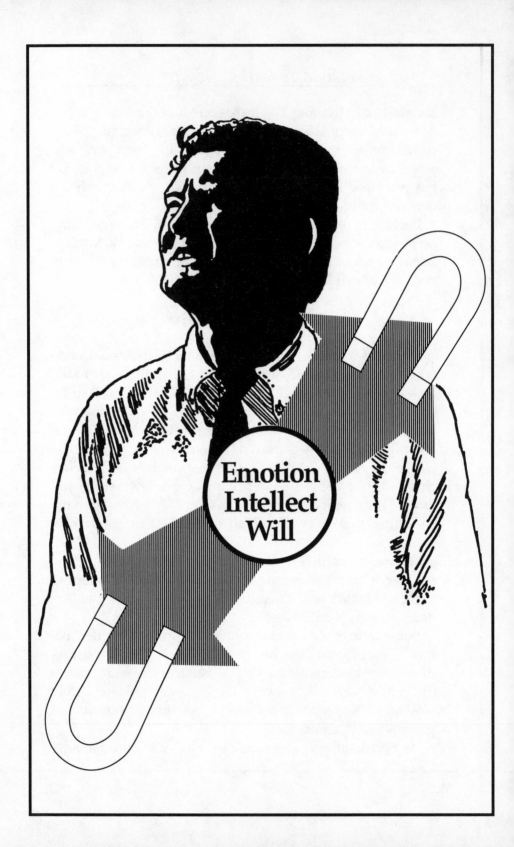

Emotion
Intellect
Will

```
                    ┌─────────────────┐
                    │ SANCTIFICATION  │
                    └─────────────────┘
                             │
                             │
   ┌────────────────┐        │        ┌────────────────┐
   │  REGENERATION  │        │        │  GLORIFICATION │
   └────────────────┘        │        └────────────────┘
           │                 │                 │
           │                 │                 │
           │          Separation to            │
           │              God                  │
           │                 │                 │
           │                 │                 │
    Impartation of           │          Realization of
     Divine Life             │          Christlikeness
                             │
                             │
                             │
                        Positional
                        Progressive
                         Perfect
```

While the etymological origin of the Hebrew root *qadas* is surrounded by obscurity, its fundamental force seems to be to set apart an object from ordinary usage for a special (religious) purpose or function, and in particular to set apart for God. In biblical Greek its equivalent is *hagiazein*, "to sanctify."[2]

As we noted before, sanctification has three aspects.[3] God's choice of His own before the foundation of the world (Eph. 1:4) is a kind of sanctification. His choice set the believer apart from those not chosen.

The believer does have an enemy within—whether it be called the old nature or something else. This is why there are struggles, conflicts between good and evil, within the child of God. Paul, for example, often did what he didn't want to do (Rom. 7:15). The one who has passed from death to life still possesses the same old abilities and tendencies to sin with which he was born. Regeneration does not remove the compulsion to sin.

The Condition

According to Paul's teaching in Romans 7 (and the general instruction of the rest of the New Testament), the flesh, or old man, remains unchanged in the believer. It is just as wicked as it ever was. It has not been altered in any way and is therefore capable of the same corrupt deeds. There is a contemporary teaching that the old nature in a saved person is different from the old nature in an unsaved person. Not so. It is a trick of the devil to get people to think this is true.

Before the Christian is victorious in his Christian life he must bring himself to acknowledge what Paul did. "I know that in me (that is, in my flesh) nothing good dwells" (Rom. 7:18). He must also come to grips with the great truth of who he is and what he has in Christ. The saved person is not in the same position of hopeless failure as is the unsaved man. Through Jesus Christ, the indwelling Holy Spirit, and the new nature, the child of God can be victorious. He can be an overcomer through Christ. However, it is only when we acknowledge our position in Him and our real need that we trust Him for refuge.

The Conflict

Torn inside between old desires to do that which we know is evil and new desires to please God, the battle rages. The internal conflict manifests itself in everyday life as the believer is tempted to sin. The source of this conflict is the old sin nature. The believer has a vital role in determining to whom he will give allegiance—the old nature or the new nature.

The moment the sinner trusts Christ there is conflict in him between the powers of darkness and those of light. Christ left no doubt in His disciples' minds of the conflict they would face when He said, "in the world you will have tribulation" (John 16:33). Literally he said, "You have tribulation now and you will continue to have it." Jesus was not saying merely that the conflict would come *from* the world, though that is certainly a source of conflict. What He was saying is that His own would experience conflict because they were in the world, the seat of Satan's stronghold. The temptations of the world system cause internal distress and conflict for those who take their stand with the Savior.

This spiritual warfare in which every child of God is engaged and which he is either winning or losing demands being clothed in the whole armor of God and the plain fact is that before salvation this conflict did not exist.

THE ENEMIES WITHOUT

The Christian's external foes cause as much struggle for him and are as persistent in opposing the things of the Lord as is the old nature within.

The World

The world is the Christian's enemy because it represents a philosophy diametrically opposed to the will and ways of

God. It is a system headed by the devil and at odds with God (2 Cor. 4:4). The world hates the believer who lives for Christ (John 17:14). The Lord told His disciples of their coming conflict with the world (i.e., John 15:18–20; 16:1–3, 32, 33; cf. 2 Tim. 3:12).

The world's hatred for the believer manifests itself in various ways. It is not always in a direct and violent way. More often it is in subtle and insidious ways. Satan's anti-God philosophy is evident in every phase of modern education, for example, which is built on an evolutionary hypothesis. Hatred makes itself known in the business world, social life, the entertainment world, and even in religion.

We should be careful not to adopt the current philosophy which seeks to make Christianity compatible with the world. Biblical Christianity does not parallel the philosophy of the world. It intersects it at every turn. The world is in opposition to the Christian view of God and the world.

Not all suffering and persecution the Christian endures is because of sin in his own life. Christ suffered at the hands of the world, yet He did no wrong. Sometimes we suffer simply because we belong to Him. The servant is not greater than his Lord. Satan is the god of this age, the prince of the power of the air, the prince of the world. The one who is in the world but not of it must expect constant opposition from him.

The Devil

Satan never appears before the Christian as he really is. He is a deceiver appearing as an angel of light. Using clever devices he tries every possible strategy to trick the child of God. He hinders the work of God (1 Thess. 2:18) and seeks to frustrate the work of God in the believer's life. He is the epitome of wickedness. The believer's downfall is his highest concern and his efforts are always corrupt and evil. Peter, who fell victim to Satan's temptations, said he "walks about like a roaring lion, seeking whom he may devour" (1 Peter

5:8). Paul said Satan's wiles or tricks could be resisted by the believer only as he put on the whole armor of God (Eph. 6:11). Paul also reminded the Ephesians that their most serious warfare was "against principalities, against powers, against the rulers of the darkness of this age" (Eph. 6:12).

But Satan is defeated. Even before His death Christ spoke with certainty of Satan's overthrow (John 12:31). The sentence of judgment was issued on him at Calvary. The execution of that sentence will take place when he is cast into the lake of fire forever. Until then he and all the demons of hell are arraigned against the people of God, seeking to do all within their power before their own ultimate destruction.

The areas of the devil's attacks on the Christian may be summarized as the lust of the flesh, the lust of the eyes, and the pride of life.

Through the lust of the flesh Satan seeks to get us to misuse our God-given physical appetites. Depending upon our weakness, he tempts us to impurity of life, overindulgence in food and drink, or improper expenditure of time and money, or any combination. Living in an age given to sin and a land of plenty the believer must guard against sin in these areas. The believer's body is the temple of the Holy Spirit (1 Cor. 6:19–20). The personal presence of the Holy Spirit should have an effect upon our everyday living.

Many sinful things are in the world around us. Through the lust of the eyes we entertain impure thoughts (Matt. 5:28). The sex-mad world in which we live makes everyone susceptible to temptation and sin. The lust of the eyes involves more than sex, however. A craving for more and more material things is also common in our affluent society. It is still sin to covet and to place undue emphasis upon things which will pass away. The philosophy of the world—eat, drink and be merry for tomorrow we die—has become so glamorized that many Christians unwittingly have adopted it.

Perhaps the believer is more susceptible to the pride of life than to either of the other two areas of Satan's attacks. Even Christians who are busy serving the Lord often fall prey to this trick of Satan. This is the "I love myself" attitude.[4] It finds expression when one thinks that no one else can do anything quite like he can. This is thinking more highly of oneself than he ought. In short it spells pride. Often this attitude is concealed under a cloak of hypocrisy. More often it becomes evident to others in words and actions. We need to remind ourselves of Paul's words, "But by the grace of God I am what I am" (1 Cor. 15:10). Apart from the grace of God and His great provision for us we would be completely overthrown by our enemies.

THE WAY OF VICTORY

Victory is possible through the work of the members of the Godhead within us. Being in love with *God the Father* brings victory over the world (1 John 2:15). Love for the world is evidence of a lack of love for the Father. Living in the light of the believer's identification with God the Son and His redemptive work produces victory over the flesh (Rom. 6:1–11; Col. 3:1–3). Finally victory over the devil comes by being controlled by the power of the Holy Spirit (Eph. 5:18).

The Word of God

"Your Word I have hidden in my heart, that I might not sin against You" was the testimony of the psalmist (Ps. 119:11). David viewed the Word of God as a vaccination against sin. But in order for it to be effective, it had to be hidden in his heart. That is, its truths had to be known, studied, believed, and appropriated. A mind occupied with spiritual things will be less susceptible to sin than one occupied with worldly concerns. Studying God's Word helps Christians to establish biblical goals and there is less appeal from sin. The

Word of God teaches the believer about his enemy, his own weakness, and the means of his victory over sin.[5]

Christ responded to the assaults of Satan by finding protection in the Word of God. Three times He responded to Satan with, "It is written," more literally, "It stands written" (Matt. 4:4, 7, 10). In each instance He quoted from the Book of Deuteronomy (Deut. 8:3; 6:16; 6:13). If the sinless Son of God found the Scriptures to be His source of victory in the hour of need, how much more should we?

Hebrews describes the Word as that which penetrates the innermost thoughts and motives of the human heart (Heb. 4:12). Its purpose is to protect one from sin by exposing the reader to his needs.

The Present Ministry of Christ

Christ's presence with the believer is as real now as when He walked the earth. He said to His discouraged disciples, "I am with you always" (Matt. 28:20), and "I will never leave you nor forsake you" (Heb. 13:5). Paul declared the same truth when he said, "Christ in you, the hope of glory" (Col. 1:27), and "Christ lives in me" (Gal. 2:20). Ministry of the indwelling Christ keeps the believer from sin.

The work of Christ in heaven is related to the believer's walk on earth. Christ is the believer's Intercessor (John 17; Heb. 7:25). This work of Christ prevents sin in the believer's life. The Savior prays for His own as He did for Peter and the other disciples. He prays that we will not fall into sin.

If we do not submit to the Savior's ministry of intercession and we fall into sin, He does not forsake us, but ministers as our Advocate (1 John 2:1). He pleads our case before the Father, not for leniency, but to affirm His own sufficiency and covering for the believer's sin.

The Indwelling of the Holy Spirit

One of Christ's great teaching themes concerned the indwelling of the Holy Spirit in the believer (John 14:16). The

Spirit's presence in the believer in this age makes his body the temple of the Holy Spirit (1 Cor. 6:19–20). Paul taught the Corinthian Christians that sin could not be condoned because of the Holy Spirit's presence within the believers.

The Spirit's presence provides a convicting ministry. He brings our sin to our attention. He teaches us the Word through His illuminating ministry and in this way keeps us from sin (1 Cor. 2:14–16). God-given abilities for service are also given by the Holy Spirit. He equips us for service (1 Cor. 12:4, 11). The Holy Spirit assists the child of God in his prayer life. He makes our prayers intelligible to the Father when we do not know how to pray as we should (Rom. 8:26).

God has done everything possible to keep believers from sinning. Struggles within and without are real. Failure is never God's fault. Victory is possible. Paul's cry must be ours, "O wretched man that I am! Who will deliver me from this body of death? I thank God—through Jesus Christ our Lord" (Rom. 7:24–25).

CHAPTER 21 DISCUSSION QUESTIONS

1. Of the three "enemies" of believers, which one causes the most trouble in your life? What are some steps you can take to combat these temptations to sin?

2. Commit yourself to regular personal Bible study as an important step in sanctification. Write your commitment below, date it, and sign it. You can commit yourself to fifteen minutes each day, or thirty minutes three times a week, or some other regular schedule.

3. Commit yourself to regular personal prayer as another important step in sanctification. Write your commitment below, date it, and sign it. You can commit yourself to several days daily, for a longer period several times each week, or a combination.

4. If a Christian came to you, discouraged about the sin in his life, how would you advise him to resist sin and grow in obedience to Christ?

5. What are three ways you know the Holy Spirit works in your life to help you avoid sin?

22

BACKSLIDING

I grew up in a home and a church where the terms "backslidden" and "backslide" were used frequently to describe people who professed faith in Christ but who had fallen into sin and were no longer interested in living as Christians. Another way to describe this condition was to say such an individual had "fallen from grace." My parents, preacher, and peers understood this to mean the one who had backslidden or fallen from grace had lost his salvation.

As used in this chapter 1 do not imply such a meaning. Rather, backsliding refers to a Christian's regression in spiritual growth and his failure to move on in Christian maturity. When the believer sins he does not fall from God's grace, but he often does revert back to his pre-salvation lifestyle—he yields to the sin nature within instead of yielding to the new nature and the ministry of the Holy Spirit in him.

In chapter 20 we dealt with the scriptural teaching of the believer's assurance of God's security. Now it is time to study the reality of sin in the Christian's experience. Backsliding involves sin.

THE REALITY OF THE CHRISTIAN'S SIN

Some within the evangelical community believe a person who has been born again and has received "the second work of grace," "the second blessing," or as others refer to it, "the baptism of the Holy Spirit," is no longer capable of sinning. Such a view represents a serious misunderstanding of the doctrine of sanctification and the baptizing work of the Holy Spirit. To be sanctified is to be set apart, not to be sinless. Everyone who trusts Christ alone as Savior is baptized by the Holy Spirit into the body of Christ (1 Cor. 12—13). The fact is, Christians do sin. It will not do to try to distinguish between sin and mistakes, as is often done. Sin is still sin. All sin is offensive to God.

Christian Practices

The Bible provides many examples of people who were born again but still sinned. Their sin was not right and God did not condone it. God hates sin in anyone's life, but sometimes even those closest to the Lord failed Him (i.e., Peter). Christ's own disciples sometimes needed to be rebuked (i.e., John 13). The prophets used by God to warn others of sin and its consequences were often guilty of sin in their own lives. Even the priests who offered sacrifices for the sin of the people had to offer first for their own sins (Heb. 5:3). Moses failed God and as a result was not permitted to enter the Promised Land. Paul prayed that God would not sideline him because of his failures (1 Cor. 9:27).

In addition to the biblical examples of those who sinned, there are many biblical exhortations to believers against sinning. The writers of Scripture constantly warned Christians of the dangers of sin in their lives. Some of the strongest exhortations against sin in the believer's life are found in passages such as Galatians 5:17–21; 6:1; Ephesians 4:22–32; 5:1–33; 6:10–20. This establishes the fact of the reality of sin in the Christian's life.

Biblical examples of Christians who sinned demonstrate the honesty of the Scriptures in reporting even the ugly side of human behavior. Beyond that they also provide a mirror to our own lives. Honesty demands that we acknowledge sin and failure in our lives. Paul's testimony is ours. "I find then a law, that evil is present with me, the one who wills to do good" (Rom. 7:21).

God's Precepts

God's Word teaches the reality of the Christian's sin, not only by setting forth examples of Christians who have sinned, but also by positive affirmation of the fact. This is what we mean by God's precepts. These can be demonstrated most forcefully from the Book of First John.

This is the book often used to defend the doctrine of sinless perfection, that is, that some Christians no longer sin (i.e., 1 John 3:4–10). The explanation of this passage and the answer to this problem must first be found in the context of 1 John 1:5—2:6. John already established the fact of the believer's sin. The present tense of the original language in 1 John 3:4-10 emphasizes continuous sinning, or the lifestyle of sinning. Many scholars believe 1 John 3:4–10 has reference to the new nature within the believer as that which cannot sin.[1]

Returning specifically to 1 John 1:6—2:1, we find that the believer not only possesses the sin nature (1:8), but he also commits acts of sin (1:10). To deny these is to accuse God of lying (1:10) and to deceive ourselves (1:8). Is it not clear from 1:6 that Christians can walk in darkness or sin? Such sin can be cleansed by the same blood of Christ which brought salvation in the first place (1:7). John exhorted his Christian readers to confess their sins. Lest they think he was condoning their sin, because he told them of available forgiveness, he told them emphatically not to sin (2:1).

THE RESULTS OF THE CHRISTIAN'S SIN

Most Christians rarely give attention to sin's effects on God. Usually Christians concentrate on the person sinning and/or the person sinned against. But sin, all sin, has serious effects on God as well. In fact, sin's effects on God ought to be our first and major concern.

Effects on God

Although Scripture promises God's forgiveness for confessed sin, this does not mean He is not affected by it. The very fact that the Christian's sin needs confessing tells us God is offended by it. To "confess" sin means to agree with God that we have sinned and that it is a terrible offense to Him. God is hurt by our stubborn persistence in sin.

Sin in the life of the Christian grieves God, the Holy Spirit. Paul's exhortation is clear, "do not grieve the Holy Spirit of God" (Eph. 4:30). This means that the third Person of the Trinity should not be hurt or offended. How can He be treated in this way? By sin—sin in the life of the believer in whom He dwells. The verses before and after this command are descriptive of the kinds of sins which grieve Him.

Grieving the Holy Spirit of God through personal sin is a serious thing. So is quenching His ministry (1 Thess. 5:19). This means to stifle His ministry on behalf of the child of God through sin. The Spirit of God is quenched when the Christian says "no" to Him. The context of this passage deals with sin in the believer, especially in relation to the return of the Lord. The Thessalonian Christians were enduring severe persecution because of their faith in Christ. This no doubt caused some to become impatient and short-tempered with each other and thus to sin by refusing to allow the Spirit to work in their lives.

Effects on the Believer

What effect does backsliding have on the one who sins? Does it really matter if we are not what we might be or what we once were in our Christian experience? God deals differently with Christians when they sin than He does with non-Christians.

The apostle John states several bad effects upon the believer when he sins. These serve as illustrations of the consistent teaching of Scripture on this matter.

Loss of fellowship with God

"That which we have seen and heard we declare to you, that you also may have fellowship with us; and truly our fellowship is with the Father and with His Son Jesus Christ" (1 John 1:3).

John's purpose in writing about Christ and sin was so Christians could have fellowship with one another and with the Father and the Son. Sin mars that fellowship. It makes one uncomfortable in God's presence. We are no longer on speaking terms with God.

Loss of direction in life

"If we say that we have fellowship with Him, and walk in darkness, we lie and do not practice the truth" (1 John 1:6).

When we sin we walk in darkness. This means we are confused and uncertain about life because of our sin. "Men who profess to combine fellowship with God with the choice of darkness as their sphere of life, actively affirm what they know to be false; and on the other hand, they neglect to carry out in deed what they claim to hold."[2]

Loss of confidence in prayer

And by this we know that we are of the truth, and shall assure our hearts before Him. For if our heart condemns us, God is greater than our heart, and knows all things. Beloved, if our heart does not condemn us, we have confidence toward God. And whatever we ask we receive from Him, because we keep His commandments and do those things that are pleasing in His sight (1 John 3:19–22).

Many prayers are not answered because the one praying is not in fellowship with God because of sin. This is the clear teaching of this passage. Isaiah, the prophet, said essentially the same thing of the children of Israel (Isa. 1:15). Sin in the life of a child of God affects man's fellowship with God.

Loss of joy

"These things I have spoken to you, that My joy may remain in you, and that your joy may be full" (John 15:11).

The inner peace of God departs when we sin. Happiness is gone. Sin produces unrest and inner struggles.

Persistence in sin brings additional penalties from God. The writer of the book of Hebrews wrote of divine discipline and scourging. "For those whom the LORD loves He chastens, and scourges every son whom He receives" (Heb. 12:6).

Saphire, the Bible commentator, said, "Chastisement is sent by fatherly love. In heaven no chastisement is needed; in hell no chastisement is possible; earth is the scene, and the children of God the subjects of chastisement."[3]

Scourging is added to the discipline of Hebrews 12:6. This word comes from an old word which means "whips." It refers to hard lessons God's children must learn. It refers to breaking of one's stubborn will. At some time or other God must deal with each of His own so that their stubborn wills become submissive to His own perfect will.

Death is the most severe form of God dealing with Christians who refuse to forsake their sin. We sometimes speak of such sin as "sin unto death." John wrote of this in his first epistle (1 John 5:13-17). There are other texts of Scripture which seem to refer to the same thing (i.e., 1 Cor. 5:5; 11:29, 30; Heb. 6; John 15:6). Nowhere in Scripture is the "sin unto death," or the sin which results in God's judgment in physical death, defined. Evidently it could be any sin which the believer refuses to confess and forsake. This judgment by physical death means that God removes the individual from the earthly scene because his life and testimony are no longer productive for Him. Moses' sin became the sin unto

268

death. God took his life and did not permit him to enter the Promised Land.

THE REMEDY FOR THE CHRISTIAN'S SIN

If sin is a reality in the Christian's experience, and if the results of that sin affect God and man, what can the believer do when he sins?

Preventive Measures

God has made every provision for His children to enable them to live lives pleasing to Him. God has made a fourfold provision to keep His own from sinning. The question is, are we availing ourselves of these divine resources?

The work of God the Son

Christ is not only the believer's source of salvation, He is also his source of sanctification. The same finished work at Calvary and the open tomb, which is the only basis for our salvation, is also the only basis for our daily walk. When the sinner trusts Christ alone, His accomplishments on the cross become the believer's. Paul described this relationship as being "baptized into His death" (Rom. 6:3) and "raised with Christ" (Col. 3:1). The believer "puts on" Jesus Christ as he engages in warfare with the devil (Rom. 13:14; Eph. 6:11–18). The Savior's present ministry at the Father's hand also helps keep the believer from sin, "He ever lives to make intercession" (Heb. 7:25). When we disregard this work and sin anyway, He does not forsake us. Then He becomes our Advocate. When the believer sins he has an "Advocate with the Father, Jesus Christ the righteous" (1 John 2:1).

The work of God the Holy Spirit

All the ministries of the Spirit of God relate to the believer's walk with God. The work of God the Holy Spirit is a divine provision to keep the believer from sin.

First, the Spirit is the divine agent who regenerates, imparts divine life (Titus 3:5), and baptizes the believing sinner into the body of Christ (1 Cor. 12:12–13). He forms a vital union between them and Christ. The same Holy Spirit indwells each believer (1 Cor. 6:19), providing all the necessary resources to live for God. These ministries of the Spirit take place simultaneous to trusting Christ as Savior. They are divine undertakings to which man contributes nothing.

There are, however, other ministries the Spirit performs only in response to the discharge of human responsibilities. God's people are exhorted to be filled or controlled by the Holy Spirit (Eph. 5:18). That is, they are to surrender themselves to His blessed control. Each believer is to "walk in the Spirit" so he will not "fulfill the lust of the flesh" (Gal. 5:16). The Spirit is not to be grieved by the child of God (Eph. 4:30). He is grieved or hurt by sin.

The work of God the Father in discipline or child training (Heb. 12:5–11)

In this passage it is God's purpose to nurture and train Christians to conform them more and more to the image of His Son (Rom. 8:29). He does not forsake His children, but uses various means to bring them to maturity. The Father's hand of discipline is another of His provisions to keep His own from sin.

The Word of God

God has also made provision through His inspired Word, the Scriptures. It is through this Word of God that He brings life to those dead in trespasses and sins (James 1:18; 1 Peter 1:23). Through the same Word He feeds His children (1 Peter 2:2), convicts them (Heb. 4:12), cleanses them (Ps. 119:9), guides them (Ps. 119:105), equips them for spiritual warfare (Eph. 6:17), and equips them for service (2 Tim. 3:16–17).

These great provisions from God must be appropriated by the believer to receive their benefits. When the child of God draws upon these resources of God, he is protected from sin. The enemies the believer faces in the devil, the world and the flesh are great. The divine provisions are greater. It is when we do not utilize these divine measures that we sin, or backslide.

Curative Measures

Confess sin

The same characteristics in God—His faithfulness to His Word and His justice or righteousness—which result in eternal punishment for the unregenerate lead to forgiveness and cleansing for the regenerate who confess their sin (1 John 1:9).

The forgiveness John referred to in this text is to be distinguished from the forgiveness the believing sinner experiences when he trusts Christ as Savior (i.e., Acts 13:38–39; Rom. 3:25). The Father's forgiveness of the erring believer has been called "parental forgiveness," the forgiveness of those already in the family of God.

The word translated "confess" in 1 John 1:9 means to agree with. Confession involves acknowledging to God that He and His Law have been violated. When sin is concealed or covered, the believer will not "prosper" (Prov. 28:13). Until David confessed his sin with Bathsheba he was miserable and out of fellowship with God (Ps. 51).

God's promise is that when sin is confessed, He will both "forgive us our sins and cleanse us from all unrighteousness" (1 John 1:9). These two works of God remind us first that the believer's sin constitutes a debt or obligation which God Himself cancels. He forgives our sin. Second, the believer's sin mars him; it makes him unclean, needing the cleansing only God can provide.

God is described as "faithful and just" (1 John 1:9).

"The first word may mean that He is faithful to His nature and character (cf. 2 Tim. 2:13)."[4]

The second word, "righteous," describes further who God is as well as what He does. "Righteousness is completely fulfilled in God both in respect to what He does and what He is. Here action and character 'as we speak' absolutely coincides . . . the forgiveness and the cleansing of those who 'confess their sins' are naturally connected with God's faithfulness and righteousness. . . . He has laid down conditions for leadership with Himself which man can satisfy and He will satisfy."[5]

According to 1 John 1:9 we are to confess specific sins. This is indicated by the plural "sins." We are to make no excuses when we seek forgiveness for our sin. Sin must be viewed as God views it. We are not to beg and plead with God for forgiveness. The statement is clear—if we confess He will forgive. This confession is first of all and primarily to God. He is the one offended by our transgression. No doubt others have been offended and all such wrongs should be righted; but our first responsibility is to God. Cleansing also comes to the one who acknowledges his sin and looks to God for forgiveness. The spiritual defilement caused by sin is washed away.

It is a sin to disbelieve God. He has promised to forgive and cleanse if we meet His requirement for confession. That should settle the matter. Satan often comes and brings doubt about the reality of God's work. The only recourse is to cling to God's promises in His Word.

There is no other cure for backsliding. Feeling sorry for sin is not enough. Trying to do better will not suffice. The simple remedy for the believer's sin is to acknowledge it immediately before God, to see it as He sees it. This brings the forgiveness and cleansing of God.

Forsake sin

When our confession is genuine, we make an honest attempt to forsake the sin. True confession involves the hatred of sin, for that is how God reacts to sin. One cannot share

FORGIVENESS OF SIN

Because
of Christ

Because
of Christ

God's point of view regarding sin without abhorring it. God commands the believer to "put off" the old man with his evil deeds (Eph. 4:22). There is to be a crucifixion of sin: "Therefore put to death your members which are on the earth" (Col. 3:5). We are not to let sin reign as a monarch in our mortal bodies (Rom. 6:12).

There is to be a continuous *fleeing* from sin, *pursuing* righteousness, and *fighting* the good fight of the faith (1 Tim. 6:11–12). To put it in a positive way this means seeking "those things which are above" (Col. 3:1). Those risen with Christ are to have this as their first order of business.

For salvation from sin the sinner believes on the Lord Jesus Christ. For forgiveness of sin the saved sinner confesses his sin, knowing that God will forgive and cleanse from sin.

To be effective, confession of sin must be as specific as requests for other things from the hand of God. We are guilty of generalizing both in the repetition of worn-out phrases in our prayer life and in confessing our sins.

When the Christian sins he backslides. Restoration to fellowship with God and progress in the Christian life comes with sincere and honest confession to God.

CHAPTER 22 DISCUSSION QUESTIONS

1. What is the worst sin you think you have committed since you became a Christian? Do you believe God can forgive you for it? What steps can you take to appropriate God's help in avoiding that sin in the future?

2. Think of a recent sin you have committed. Pray and ask the Lord to forgive you not only for the sin, but for how your sin affected Him.

3. List some of the helps God gives us for our Christian maturity and avoidance of sin.

4. Assess your present Christian life with your long-term goals. What are your specific goals in relationship to any sin habits in your life?

5. How would you counsel a Christian friend who came to you for advice, discouraged about an ongoing sin problem in his life?

23

YOU—THE GOSPEL—THE LOST

When you get great news, you naturally want to share it. Salvation is the best news of all, and God has ordained that human beings redeemed by His grace should propagate His divine message of salvation to the lost.[1]

Faith comes by hearing and hearing by the Word of God. That sacred task has been committed to humans alone. God in His infinite wisdom has included humans in carrying out His sovereign plan of salvation.

No greater honor could be afforded to people than to cooperate with God, to be laborers together with Him. Too many Christians prefer to sit in the grandstands and observe God at work. The Bible tells us that we are to get on the stage as it were, to become participants with God in the spread of the Gospel. The stress in this chapter will be upon the spiritual requirements involved in being an effective evangelism tool.

THE RESPONSIBILITY TO WITNESS FOR CHRIST

The Fact

The fact is that God's will is for each of us to be a witness for Him.

Not all Christians are fluent and free in talking about

Christ. Personalities are different and therefore not all of us will witness in the same way or to the same extent.

The Bible clearly states that each believer is a representative for Christ. "Therefore we are ambassadors for Christ, as though God were pleading through us; we implore you on Christ's behalf, be reconciled to God" (2 Cor. 5:20).

Ambassadors for human affairs are chosen especially for their tact, their dignity and their courtesy, and because they are gifted with persuasive powers. Ambassadors for Christ should show the same characteristics. They must never bludgeon people into the kingdom of God, but must speak the truth in love because it is a gospel of divine love. Paul, who was perhaps the greatest of all ambassadors for Christ, appeals to his readers "by the meekness and gentleness of Christ" (2 Cor. 10:1).[2] An ambassador is a representative of another or of others.

An ambassador is expected to be loyal to the cause he represents. Above all else he must be faithful, true, and honest. Examples of such loyalty can be found in Scripture (i.e., Dan. 3:17, 18; 6:10). Another outstanding characteristic of an ambassador is the fact that he has news to tell. It is not his prerogative to amplify, add to, or alter that news in any way. He simply delivers information from those who sent him.

Every believer is an ambassador for Christ. What a privilege and responsibility that is for every child of God! The length of time one has been saved does not affect the fact of ambassadorship. All who are saved are ambassadors (cf. Matt. 28:19–20; Acts 1:8). The question remains, what kind of ambassadors are we? How well do we represent our Savior?

The Command

Among the last words of Christ to His disciples was His commission to take the Gospel throughout the world: "Go therefore and make disciples of all the nations, baptizing them in the name of the Father and of the Son and of the Holy Spirit, teaching them to observe all things that I commanded you; and lo, I am with you always, even to the end of the age" (Matt. 28:19–20).

The "go therefore" and the "I am with you always" of these parting words must have reminded these men of similar words Christ often had spoken to them. He told them they would witness about Him because they had been with Him from the beginning (John 15:27). With words which must have alarmed them, He said that as the Father had sent Him into the world so He would send them into it (John 17:18).

The command of Christ motivated the apostle Paul to become the greatest missionary the world has ever known. The love of Christ constrained him to take the message to those who had not heard, "For the love of Christ constrains us, because we judge thus: that if One died for all, then all died" (2 Cor. 5:14). Because of God's boundless love for all men and Christ's substitutionary sacrifice on their behalf, Paul was brought to the place where he could say, "I am a debtor" (Rom. 1:14); "I am ready to preach the gospel" (Rom. 1:15); and "I am not ashamed" (Rom. 1:16).

The Examples

There are many New Testament examples of the Christian responsibility to witness. Several are recorded in John 1.

First is the witness of John the Baptist in 1:19–34. His testimony to the Jews was clear. His entire message was concerned with Christ. John's description of himself is important. He came for a witness (vv. 7–8). In accordance with that, he testified that he was a voice crying in the wilderness (v. 23).

Andrew's and Simon's experiences are recorded in John 1:35–42. They accepted John the Baptist's testimony and left him to follow Jesus. This was fruit from John's witness. Of

these two Simon Peter is more familiar. Though not very fa-
mous, every time Andrew is seen in Scripture he brings
someone to Jesus. In this way John's witness was multiplied
(John 1:42; 6:8, 9; 12:20–22). What would we know about
Peter if Andrew, his brother, had not told him about the Savior? (John 1:41)

Philip and Nathanael are discussed in John 1:43–51.
Christ confronted Philip with the challenge, "Follow Me"
(v. 43). Jesus went directly to Philip. Overflowing with en-
thusiasm, Philip then sought out Nathanael (vv. 44–45).

THE REQUIREMENTS FOR WITNESSING
FOR CHRIST

A surgeon's glove must be properly prepared and used if
the operation is to be successful. There are several things
which must be true of the surgeon's glove. First, it must be
completely empty so that the doctor's hand and fingers can
be placed all the way into it. It must be sterile. No reputable
surgeon would think of using gloves that were not prepared
in this way. Last, but by no means least, the glove must be
completely filled. The glove must fit the hand and the hand
must fit the glove. It would be most awkward, if not impossible, to perform a successful operation with gloves a few
sizes too large or too small.

The believer is like a glove used by Jesus, the Healer of
broken hearts. The three features true of the human physician's glove must also be true of each of us if we are going to
be effective witnesses for the Savior.

Emptied Lives

This involves nothing short of total surrender. This is not
the same as sinlessness. It means we have dedicated our entire being to Christ and His control. He is made the Lord; He
is acknowledged as Lord of our lives.

279

Anything which impedes progress and hinders fellowship must be subjected to His will, according to the admonition of Paul in Romans 6:11–12. Sin must not reign as the king on the thrones of our lives. Sin must be put to death constantly (Col. 3:5).

Changed Lives Are Necessary

Scripture reveals at least three ways by which the believer is cleansed of sin. First, the Word of God itself has a cleansing affect on our lives. Jesus said to His disciples, "You are already clean because of the word which I have spoken to you" (John 15:3). His word has a purifying effect on those who receive it.

Second, the blood of Jesus Christ, God's Son, cleanses us from all sin (1 John 1:7–9). John was not speaking here to the unsaved. The believer is to confess his sin and experience cleansing through the blood of Christ.

Third, the child of God is to cleanse himself, "from all filthiness of the flesh and spirit, perfecting holiness in the fear of God" (2 Cor. 7:1), and "therefore, having these promises, beloved, let us cleanse ourselves." This cannot be done apart from the Word and the cleansing blood of Christ. The Christian is to make every effort to avoid that which defiles.

Filled Lives

This is the only ministry of the Holy Spirit commanded of the believer. The other ministries are sovereignly bestowed without the believer's cooperation, but not against his will. "And do not be drunk with wine, in which is dissipation; but be filled with the Spirit" (Eph. 5:18). It is possible to be emptied of self and cleansed of sin but unaware of what it means to be filled with the Spirit. The Spirit is not given to the believer in portions. Each believer receives the entire Person of the Holy Spirit at the time of salvation. But the believer gives more of himself to the Spirit as he matures. Just

as strong drink gains control of the person drinking it, so the child of God is to be controlled by the Holy Spirit.

One who does not love people cannot be a soul winner. It is difficult to love some folks, but without love we will never succeed in witnessing for Christ. Genuine compassion also is necessary to fulfill our responsibility. This means more than mere pity. Compassion is pity moved into action. The Lord had compassion on individuals and on the multitudes. If we are to witness we must have the same.

Someone has said, "Don't ever talk to men about God until you have talked to God about men." That is more than a nice motto. Prayer should include strength, wisdom, tact, and the motivation and guidance of the Holy Spirit in our witness. He must do the work. We can only give out the good news. He must do the saving.

The ambassador of Christ must be dedicated to the Word of God. Our arguments and reasonings do not bring conviction or salvation. It is the ministry of the Holy Spirit using the Word of God that brings life.

Great patience and Spirit-directed persistence are required. Feelings must not be carried on the sleeve. The ambassador for Christ will not be welcomed and received by all. The message of sin alone is offensive to the unsaved. There is a stigma attached to the cross. We must be willing to bear the reproach involved in the message of Calvary.

THE REALITY OF WITNESSING FOR CHRIST

Here are some helpful suggestions for sharing the Gospel in a natural, persuasive manner.

Preparation for Witnessing

How much must a person know before he can witness to someone else about Christ? He must know that he himself has passed from death to life. Until this has been settled

there will be neither the burden nor the ability to communicate Christ to others. Peter in his first epistle put the order in proper sequence. He stressed *knowing* that one has been redeemed first (1 Peter 1:18). Being assured of that, one is then in a position to *grow* from the Word (1 Peter 2:2). The natural result will be the *showing* forth of God's praises (1 Peter 2:9).

Bible training is helpful, but we must not get the false impression that formal Bible training is essential to be an effective witness for Christ. The believer should study the Word regularly for his own needs as well as for answers to questions non-Christians raise. We don't have to have all the answers before we can be effective in witnessing. Focus on the crux of the matter—their relationships to Jesus Christ.

Approaches to Witnessing

Friendliness is the beginning

People will not give serious attention to your witness unless they detect genuine interest in them. They can usually tell whether the person talking to them is genuine or hypocritical.

Kindness is essential

Kindness is closely related to friendship but it is not the same thing. This involves many things not directly related to the Gospel. Deeds of kindness are seldom forgotten by folks. These must be sincere expressions of love and interest.

Tactfulness is important

Tactfulness is almost next to godliness. Jesus was always tactful in His approach to people. Ordinary common sense helps. This is where being led of the Spirit comes into the picture. People are different and God knows all about us and all about the people to whom He leads us. There is no rigid stereotype approach which fits all people.

Personal interest must be shown

To the woman at the well Jesus talked first about what was uppermost in her mind. This should be our approach. Gain the confidence of people by becoming interested in their work, families, interests, and concerns. If we show more genuine interest in our neighbors and friends' interests, we will be better witnesses to them. Of course, all our efforts must be made with full dependence upon the Lord.

Ways of Witnessing

There are two ways to witness for Christ or evangelize the lost—by life and by lips.

There are many ways our lives can be used in witnessing. Nothing attracts those outside of Christ more than a consistent, honest, and godly life. Sermons get better results when lived than when preached.

When it comes to witnessing with our lips we are often fearful. Some people are naturally shy and cannot and will not do what others may do naturally and freely. People must be treated in keeping with what they are and not what we would like them to be.

As a concluding summary of the discussion of sin, the Savior, and salvation, let us review what it is we tell the unsaved. All we say must be based on the Word of God. Three essential facts embrace the heart of the Gospel.

First, all have sinned and come short of God's glory (Rom. 3:23). This sin brings death (Rom. 6:23).

Second, Christ died for sinners (Rom. 5:18; 1 Cor. 15:3). He, the just One, died for the unjust to bring us to God (1 Peter 3:18).

Third, as many as received Christ become sons of God (John 1:12). They will never perish but have everlasting life (John 3:16). There is no other way of salvation (Acts 4:12).

Salvation is not nearly as complicated as we often think. These three simple facts should form the core of our witness.

Good news! Christ died for us and in Him we have life! Rejoice, our sin is covered by our Savior, and we are saved. Take this good news with confidence, experience it in your own life, and share it with others.

CHAPTER 23 DISCUSSION QUESTIONS

1. "Lifestyle evangelism" is a popular phrase in Christian circles. What do you think it means and how does it relate to what the Bible says about effective evangelism?

2. Do you think it is harder to form a longterm friendship commitment with a non-Christian or to go door-to-door witnessing? Which would you rather do? Which do you think would be the most effective?

3. Think about the last time you shared your Christian faith with a non-believer. What was the most frustrating part of your conversation? What was the most rewarding? What would you do differently next time?

4. Review the scriptures used in this chapter. Outline what you think a scriptural approach to evangelism includes.

5. Commit to sharing the Gospel with at least one person this week in a relaxed friendship setting.

NOTES

SECTION 1—SIN

CHAPTER 1—DEFINING SIN

1. See the following for further evidence: "Toward a New Humanist Manifesto,"*The Humanist,* January-February 1973; "Humanist Manifesto 2," *The Humanist,* September-October 1973; "The Secular Humanist Declaration Pro and Con," *Free Inquiry,* Spring, 1981.

2. See Norman L. Geisler, *Is Man the Measure?* (Grand Rapids: Baker Book House, 1983).

3. James Oliver Buswell, *A Systematic Theology of the Christian Religion* (Grand Rapids, Zondervan Publishing House, 1962), 1:263–64.

CHAPTER 2—SIN IN THE ANGELIC WORLD

1. Anthony A. Hoekema, *Created in God's Image* (Grand Rapids, MI: Eerdmans, 1986), 129.

2. Some question whether these two passages refer properly to Satan, or only to the king of Tyre. The king of Tyre, however, was a type of Satan.

3. Charles C. Ryrie, *Basic Theology* (Wheaton, IL: Victor Books, 1987), 141.

4. Ibid., 142–43. See also Charles L. Feinberg, *The Prophecy of Ezekiel* (Chicago: Moody, 1969), 158–63, for more on the identification of Satan in these verses.

5. See Millard J. Erickson, *Christian Theology* (Grand Rapids, MI: Baker Book House, 1985), 1:411–32, for an excellent discussion of the problem of evil.

6. E. J. Young in *The New Testament Critical Commentary* (Grand Rapids, MI: Eerdmans), 1:441, sets forth an opposing view.

7. Ryrie, *Basic Theology*, 144.

8. See his *Biblical Commentary on the Prophecies of Isaiah* (Edinburgh: T & T Clark, 1875), 1:312.

CHAPTER 3—THE SIN OF ADAM AND EVE

1. See Karl Barth, *Church Dogmatics IV/I*, translated by G. W. Bromiley, (Edinburgh: T & T Clark, 1761), 508 and H. M. Kuitert, *Do You Understand What You Read?*, translated by Louis B. E. Smedes (Grand Rapids: William B. Eerdmans Publishing Company, 1970), 40.

2. See writings of Gary North, Rousas John Rushdoony, David Chilton, James Jordan, and especially Gary DeMars, *The Debate Over Christian Reconstruction* (Fort Worth: Dominion Press, 1988), and an excellent critique of the movement by H. Wayne House and Thomas Ice, *Dominion Theology: Blessing or Curse* (Portland, OR: Multnomah, 1988).

3. See Robert Lightner's "Theonomy and Dispensationalism," *Bibliotheca Sacra*, January-March, 1986 through July-September, 1986.

4. Charles C. Ryrie, *Basic Theology* (Wheaton, IL: Victor Books, 1987), 202–203.

CHAPTER 4—MANKIND'S SIN

1. Lewis Sperry Chafer, *Systematic Theology* (Dallas: Dallas Theological Seminary Press, 1964), 2:296.

2. Erickson, *Christian Theology* (Grand Rapids, MI: Baker Book House, 1985) 2: 637.

3. An excellent discussion of total depravity or total inability appears in *The Five Points of Calvinism* by David N. Steele and Curtis C. Thomas (Philadelphia: Presbyterian Reformed Publishing Company, 1963), 24–30.

4. Erickson, 2:642.

5. Ibid.

6. Ibid., 2:655–658.

7. Gordon H. Clark, *Religion, Reason, and Revelation* (Philadelphia: Presbyterian Reformed, 1961), 221 ff.

8. For a helpful response to these, see Erickson, 1:414–432.

CHAPTER 5—GOD AND THE SINFUL HUMAN RACE

1. Evangelical Ministries to New Religions defines the New Age Movement as a "spiritual social and political movement to transform individuals and society through mystical enlightenment hoping to bring about a utopian era of a 'new age' of harmony and progress. While it has no central headquarters or agencies, it includes loosely affiliated individuals, activists

groups, business and professional groups, and spiritual leaders and their followers. It produces countless books, magazines, and tapes reflecting a shared-world view of vision. How that world view is expressed, what implications are drawn and what applications are made differ from group to group" ["Experts on Nontraditional Religions Try to Pin Down the New Age Movement" *Christianity Today*, 17 May 1989, 68].

2. Shirley MacLaine, *Out on a Limb* (New York: Bantam Books, 1983), 204.

3. From Benjamin Creme, *The Reappearance of Christ and the Masters of Wisdom* (North Hollywood, CA: Tara Center, 1980), 134.

4. Benjamin Creme, *The Message from Maitreya, the Christ #98* (N. Hollywood: Tara Center, 1981), 204.

SECTION II—THE SAVIOR

PART ONE—THE PERSON OF THE SAVIOR

1. My approach here must not be misunderstood to be from the perspective of the twentieth century "functional Christology." As I hope I have demonstrated thus far, I hold firmly that the New Testament teaching of Christ's nature is of equal importance with its teaching of His work. See Millard J. Erickson's *Christian Theology* (Grand Rapids: Baker Book House, 1985) 2:698–703 for further understanding of what "functional Christology" is and what its weaknesses are.

CHAPTER 6—LIFE BEFORE BIRTH

1. Of course, any such appeal to Scripture in defense of Christ's preexistence is based on the assumption of Scripture's inspiration and authority. On the other hand, John Knox and other contemporaries (see Knox, *The Humanity and Divinity of Christ*, 1967, 7–9) argue that the church has attributed divine preexistence to Jesus which He did not have. Their definition of the concept of preexistence has been summarized as "in terms of God's foreknowledge, purpose and plan that in the fulness of time a man would be born in whom He could and would uniquely reveal Himself" (Norman Anderson, *The Mystery of the Incarnation*, [Downers Grove, IL: InterVarsity Press, 1978,] 130).

2. "Father of eternity" refers to His creative authority and should not be used to confuse the personal distinction between the person of the Father and the person of the Son. (See Gleason Archer, *Encyclopedia of Bible Difficulties* [Grand Rapids: Zondervan Publishing House, 1982], 268.)

3. John F. Walvoord, *Jesus Christ Our Lord* (Chicago: Moody Press, 1969), 32.

4. See C. H. Macintosh, *Things New and Old* (Vol. 19) for refutation of Raven. See also the unpublished paper, *Eternal Sonship or Incarnational Sonship* by George Zeller. This excellent paper may be purchased from the Middletown Bible Church, 349 East Street, Middletown, CT 06457. I am indebted to Mr. Zeller's work in my presentation of this theme.

5. John MacArthur, Jr., *Hebrews* (Chicago: Moody Press), 22–23.

6. John MacArthur, Jr., *Galatians* (Chicago: Moody Press), 107–108.

7. Walvoord, *Jesus Christ*, 42.

8. Ibid., 42–44.

9. Henry Alford, *The Greek New Testament*, 3:203.

10. Walvoord, *Jesus Christ*, 44.

CHAPTER 7—THE MAN CHRIST JESUS

1. Two significant titles on the virgin birth are Robert Gromacki's *The Virgin Birth* (Nashville, TN: Thomas Nelson Publishers, 1974), and George L. Lawlor, *Almah . . . Virgin or Young Woman* (Regular Baptist Press).

2. J. Gresham Machen, *The Virgin Birth of Christ* (Grand Rapids: Baker Book House, 1930), pp. 317–379.

3. Charles L. Feinberg, "The Virgin Birth in the Old Testament," *Bibliotheca Sacra*, July-September, 1962.

4. J. Oswald Sanders, *The Incomparable Christ* (Chicago: Moody Press, 1971), p. 28.

5. John F. Walvoord, *Jesus Christ Our Lord* (Chicago: Moody, 1969), p. 96.

6. Millard J. Erickson, *Christian Theology* (Grand Rapids: Baker Book House, 1985) 2:706.

7. See Leon Morris' *Jesus Is the Christ* (Grand Rapids: William B. Eerdmans Publishing Company, 1989), 43–67 for an answer to E. Ch. Kāseman's denial of it in his *The Testament of Jesus* (London: 1968).

8. A discussion of the sinlessness of Christ and a defense of impeccability appear in John F. Walvoord, *Jesus Christ Our Lord* (Chicago: Moody, 1969), 145-52.

9. A. T. Robertson, *Word Pictures in the New Testament* (Nashville: Broadman Press, 1932), 365.

CHAPTER 8—VERY GOD OF VERY GOD

1. These are the words describing Christ in the Nicaean Creed. Denial of the deity of Christ is not new. A new expression of the denial, however, has appeared in *The Myth of God Incarnate*, edited by John Hick, and written by a group of liberal British churchmen and theologians. The authors repudiate the orthodox and biblical doctrine of Christ. Two excellent responses to the book are *The Truth of God Incarnate* edited by Michael Green (Grand

Rapids: William B. Eerdmans Publishing Company, 1977) and George Carey's *God Incarnate* (Downers Grove, IL: InterVarsity Press, 1977).

2. J. Gresham Machen, *Christianity and Liberalism* (Philadelphia: The Presbyterian Guardian, 1923), 80–116.

3. J. Oswald Sanders, *The Incomparable Christ* (Chicago: Moody, 1971), 65.

4. The Creed reads:

We believe in one God, Father Almighty, maker of all things, visible and invisible. And in one Lord Jesus Christ, the Son of God, begotten of the Father; only begotten, that is, of the substance of the Father, God of God, Light of light, very God of very God, begotten not made being of one substance with the Father: by Whom all things were made both in heaven and on earth: who for us men, and for our salvation, came down from heaven and was incarnate, and was made man; He suffered and rose again the third day; He ascended into heaven, and is coming to judge both the quick and dead [cited from Robert L. Ferm, *Readings in the History of Christian Thought* (New York: Holt, Reinhardt and Winston, 1964), 138].

5. Donald G. Bloesch, *Essentials of Evangelical Theology* (New York: Harper & Row, 1978), 1:138–39.

6. Louis Berkhof, *Systematic Theology*, 94–95.

CHAPTER 9—THE GOD-MAN

1. John F. Walvoord, *Jesus Christ Our Lord* (Chicago: Moody Press, 1969), 114.

2. James Oliver Buswell, *A Systematic Theology of the Christian Religion* (Grand Rapids: Zondervan Publishing Company, 1962), 3:55.

3. Charles C. Ryrie, *Basic Theology* (Wheaton: Victor Books, 1987), 250.

4. John A. T. Robinson, *The Human Face of God* (Philadelphia: Westminster Press, 1973), 113–14.

5. *Commentary on Philippians*, translated by John Pringle (Grand Rapids: William B. Eerdmans Publishing Company, John Calvin, 1948), 57.

6. A. H. Strong, *Systematic Theology* (Philadelphia: American Baptist Publication Society, 1907), 2:703.

7. Ibid., 2:262.

CHAPTER 10—PROPHET, PRIEST, KING

1. John F. Walvoord, *Jesus Christ Our Lord* (Chicago: Moody Press, 1969), 137.

2. Charles Hodge, *Systematic Theology* (Grand Rapids: William B. Eerdmans Publishing Company, 1968), 2:464.

3. Lewis Sperry Chafer, *Systematic Theology* (Dallas: Dallas Seminary Press, 1948), 5:61–62.

4. Charles C. Ryrie, *Basic Theology* (Wheaton: Victor Books, 1987), 259.

PART TWO—THE WORK OF THE SAVIOR

CHAPTER 11—OBEDIENCE AND SUFFERING IN LIFE

1. See Robert Lightner, "The Savior's Suffering in Life," *Bibliotheca Sacra*, January-March, 1970, from which I have adapted much of the content of this chapter.

2. L. Berkhof, *Systematic Theology* (Grand Rapids: William B. Eerdmans Publishing Company, 1968), 379.

3. Ibid., 380–81.

4. Charles Hodge, *Systematic Theology* (Grand Rapids: William B. Eerdmans Publishing Company, 1968), 2:613.

5. John Murray, *Redemption Accomplished and Applied* (Grand Rapids; William B. Eerdmans Publishing Company, 1955), 28.

6. George Smeaton, *The Doctrine of the Atonement* (Grand Rapids: Zondervan Publishing House, 1957), 110.

7. Lorraine Boettner, *The Atonement* (Nutley, NJ: Presbyterian Reformed Publishing Co.), 59.

8. Boettner, *The Atonement*, 55.

9. Berkhof, *Systematic Theology,* 380–381.

CHAPTER 12—OBEDIENCE AND SUFFERING IN DEATH

1. L. Berkhof, *Systematic Theology* (Grand Rapids: William B. Eerdmans Publishing Company, 1953), 386.

2. G. Bromley Oxnam, *A Testament of Faith* (Boston: Little, Brown and Co., 1958), 40.

3. Ibid., 39, 41.

4. Harold DeWolf, *A Case for Theology in Liberal Perspective* (Philadelphia: The Westminster Press, 1959), 77.

5. The "Lapsarian" controversy concerns the logical order of the decrees of God. Actually there is only one decree or plan of God with many parts. Scripture simply does not state the order in which God planned the various stages of His plan. In fact, it is even questionable whether God ever viewed them as separate items anyway. It would be more in keeping with the character of God to say that He conceived of each part and of the whole of His sovereign decree at one time. At any rate, theologians have attempted to arrange the logical order for the various parts of God's plan. The word "Lapsarian" comes from the Latin *lapsis* meaning "fall." When the prefix *supra* meaning "above" appears, it means placing the decree of God to elect men before His decree to allow the Fall of man. At the time of Arminius,

supralapersarism was being circulated by Dirck Coornhert (1522-1590). This extreme view has been modified by many who call themselves Calvinists today. Many Calvinists adopt the infralapersarian view instead. This view places the decree to elect some from among the sinful race after the decree to permit the Fall. Still others, however, prefer the sublapsarian view which places the decree to elect not only after the Fall, but also after the decree to provide salvation for all. Calvinists are found among all three of these positions, and these are all in opposition to the Arminian view which, though it is identical to the sublapsarian view, makes salvation depend on foreseen human virtue and faith. Though John Calvin does not directly discuss this particular issue, most of his followers believe he held to infralapsarianism and can find nothing to the contrary in his writings.

6. Philip Schaff, *The Creeds of Christendom* (New York: Harper and Son, Publishers, 1919), III.

7. This is readily apparent even in the recent defense of Arminianism: *The Grace of God, the Will of Man*, edited by Clark Pinnock (Grand Rapids: Zondervan Publishing Company, 1989).

8. "Confession," cited by William G. T. Shedd, *Calvinism: Pure and Mixed* (New York: Charles Scribners Sons, 1893), 102.

9. Richard Watson, *Theological Institutes* (New York: Carlton and Porter, n.d.), 52:61-80.

10. Ibid., p. 447.

11. Schaff, *The Creeds*, III.

12. Thomas Cloutt, ed., *The Works of John Owen* (London: J. F. Dove, 1823), 5:290-291.

13. R. B. Kuiper, *For Whom Did Christ Die?* (Grand Rapids: William B. Eerdmans Publishing Company, 1959), 73.

14. Archibald Alexander Hodge, *The Atonement* (Grand Rapids: William B. Eerdmans Publishing Company, 1953), 363.

15. Thomas Crawford, *The Doctrine of the Atonement* (Grand Rapids: Baker Book House, 1954), 21.

16. John F. Walvoord, *Jesus Christ Our Lord* (Chicago: Moody Press, 1969), 183.

17. For a full discussion of this issue see Robert Lightner, *The Death Christ Died* (Schaumburg, IL: Regular Baptist Press, 1983).

18. Lorraine Boettner, *The Reformed Doctrine of Predestination* (Philadelphia: Presbyterian and Reformed Publishing Company, 1961), 152.

CHAPTER 13—LIFE AFTER DEATH

1. J. Oswald Sanders, *The Incomparable Christ* (Chicago: Moody Press, 1952), 223.

2. See Encyclopedia Britannica, 15th ed. Propaedia, S.V. "The Cosmic Orphan."

291

3. William Layne Craig, *The Sun Rises: The Historical Evidence for the Resurrection of Jesus* (Chicago: Moody Press, 1981), 21–22.

4. Norman L. Geisler, *The Battle for the Resurrection* (Nashville: Thomas Nelson Publishers, 1989), p. 28. This book is a full-length expose and critique of the new battle within evangelicalism.

5. John F. Walvoord, *Jesus Christ our Lord* (Chicago: Moody, 1969), 202–203.

6. Robert P. Lightner, *Evangelical Theology* (Grand Rapids: Baker Book House, 1986), 90. See further Charles C. Ryrie, *The Holy Spirit* (Chicago: Moody Press, 1965), 49–51 for a discussion of these passages.

7. The Markan reference is often questioned on textual grounds.

8. Some evangelicals believe Christ ascended to heaven prior to the event recorded in Acts 1. For a discussion of this view see John F. Walvoord, *The Holy Spirit* (Findlay, OH: Dunham Publishing Co., 1958), 220–221, and also Leon Morris, *The Gospel of John* (Grand Rapids: William B. Eerdmans Publishing Company, 1971), 840–41.

9. These are presented in outline in Charles C. Ryrie's, *Basic Theology* (Wheaton, IL: Victor Books, 1987), 271–274.

10. Walvoord, *Jesus Christ*, 224–25.

11. Ryrie, *Basic Theology*, 273.

12. Ibid., 273.

SECTION III—SALVATION

CHAPTER 14   GOD'S PLAN OF SALVATION

1. Henry Clarence Thiessen, *Introductory Lectures in Systematic Theology* (Grand Rapids: William B. Eerdmans Publishing Company, 1949), 344.

2. Clark H. Pinnock, gen. ed., *The Grace of God, the Will of Man* (Grand Rapids: Zondervan Publishing Company, 1989), 228.

3. L. Berkhof, *Systematic Theology* (Grand Rapids: William B. Eerdmans Publishing Company, 1941), 114.

CHAPTER 15—THE HOLY SPIRIT'S ROLE
IN SALVATION

1. Charles Hodge, *Systematic Theology* (Grand Rapids: William B. Eerdmans Publishing Company, 1968), 2:667.

2. See Robert Lightner, *Speaking in Tongues and Divine Healing* (Schaumburg, IL: Regular Baptist Press, 1978).

3. Charles C. Ryrie, *The Holy Spirit* (Chicago: Moody Press, 1965), 81–82.

CHAPTER 16—THE HUMAN CONDITION
OF SALVATION

1. See Charles C. Ryrie, *Dispensationalism Today* (Chicago: Moody Press, 1965). Here dispensationalism is defined as "a distinguishable economy in the outworking of God's purpose," 29.

2. Lewis Sperry Chafer, *Salvation* (Wheaton: Van Kampen Press, 1917), 49.

3. J. Gresham Machen, *What Is Faith?* (Grand Rapids: William B. Eerdmans Publishing Co., 1925), 172.

4. Jack Cottrell, *Baptism, A Biblical Study* (Joplin, MO: College Press Publishing Co., 1989), 45–46, 53, 60.

5. Ibid., 40–41.

6. Ibid., 75.

7. Charles C. Ryrie, *Basic Theology* (Wheaton, IL: Victor Press, 1987), 337.

8. Zane C. Hodges, in *Absolutely Free* (Grand Rapids: Zondervan Publishing Company, 1989), 167–80, does not see repentance as the other side of the same coin as faith. Rather, he sees it as one of several ways God uses to prepare the sinner to accept the Savior's free gift of salvation.

9. For a definitive work on the relation of faith to repentance concluding with the view expressed above, see Robert Nichols Wilkin, *Repentance as a Condition for Salvation in the New Testament* (unpublished ThD dissertation, Dallas Theological Seminary, 1985).

10. A biblical reply to "Lordship Salvation" has been given by one fully qualified as a New Testament scholar and theologian—the work was referred to above—Zane C. Hodges, *Absolutely Free.* This is a definitive response to the lordship viewpoint which we will discuss in the next chapter.

11. Neil Punt, "Universalism: Will Everyone Be Saved?" *Christianity Today,* 20 March 1987, 43–44.

12. Roger Nicole, "Universalism: Will Everyone Be Saved?" *Christianity Today,* 20 March 1987, 35. He does not hold this view but explains it and refutes it.

13. Clark Pinnock, "Universalism: Will Everyone Be Saved?" *Christianity Today,* 20 March 1987, 40.

14. Ibid.

15. Ibid., 34.

16. Jon Braun, *Whatever Happened to Hell?* (Nashville: Thomas Nelson Publishers, 1979), 48.

17. Ibid., 49.

18. See Punt, 43–44 and his *Unconditional Good News* (Grand Rapids: William B. Eerdmans Publishing Company, 1980).

19. Punt, 44.

20. Punt, 43.

21. Michael Green, "Towards A Theology of Evangelism," *Crux*, March, 1981, 18:6.

22. Joseph M. Ferrante, "The Final Destiny of Those Who Have Not Heard the Gospel," *Trinity Studies*, Fall, 1971, 1:1:60–62.

23. See James I. Packer, "The Way of Salvation, Part 3," *Bibliotheca Sacra*, January 1973, 4 for illustration.

24. Nicole, 37.

25. Braun, *Whatever*, 142.

26. See William G. T. Shedd, *The Doctrine of Endless Punishment* (New York: Charles Scribner's Sons, 1886), 15–17.

27. I recommend Michael Browson and Stephen Huntoon's, *Destiny of the Heathen* (3100 Carleton Boulevard, Jackson, MI 49203) for a treatment of the five views on the question on the destiny of the unevangelized.

28. Ibid, 10–11.

CHAPTER 17—WHAT ABOUT THOSE WHO CAN'T BELIEVE?

1. See Robert Lightner, *Heaven for Those Who Can't Believe* (Schaumburg, IL: Regular Baptist Press, 1977) for a fuller treatment of this question. I have reproduced portions of this work in this section with minor changes.

2. R. A. Webb, *The Theology of Infant Salvation* (Clarksville, TN: Presbyterian Committee of Publication, 1907), 279.

CHAPTER 18—WHAT ABOUT LORDSHIP SALVATION?

1. John F. MacArthur, Jr., *The Gospel According to Jesus* (Grand Rapids: Zondervan Publishing Company, 1988), 153.

2. J. I. Packer, *Evangelism and the Sovereignty of God* (Downers Grove, IL: InterVarsity Press, 1961), 89.

3. MacArthur, 28–29 (footnote).

4. Kenneth L. Gentry, "The Great Option: A Story of the Lordship Controversy," *Baptist Reformation Review*, Spring 1976, V:1:52.

5. Charles C. Ryrie, *So Great Salvation* (Wheaton: Victor Books, 1989), 29.

6. MacArthur, 15–16.

7. Walter J. Chantry, *Today's Gospel, Authentic or Synthetic* (London: Banner of Truth Trust, 1971), 13–14.

8. Lewis Johnson, Jr., "How Faith Works," *Christianity Today*, 11 September 1989, 21.

9. Chantry, 52.

10. Ibid, 63.

11. Examples would be F. Brown, S. R. Driver, and Charles A. Bridges,

A Hebrew and English Lexicon of the Old Testament, and Gehard Kittel, *Theological Dictionary of the New Testament.*

12. Ryrie, 69–77. See also Hodges, 169–171.

13. See Darrell Bock, "Jesus as Lord in the Book of Acts and the Gospels," *Bibliotheca Sacra,* April-June, 1986.

14. MacArthur, 28.

15. Ibid, 207.

16. Zane C. Hodges, *Absolutely Free* (Grand Rapids: Zondervan Publishing Company, 1989), 169-71. To support his contention here Hodges refers to a more detailed study of "Illegitimate Totality Transfer" in James Barr, *The Semantics of Biblical Languages* (Oxford: Oxford University Press, 1961), 218–22.

17. Chantry, 66.

18. H. E. Dana and Julius R. Mantey, *A Manual Grammer of the Greek New Testament* (New York: The MacMillan Company, 1955), 149.

19. B. F. Westcott, *The Epistles of St. John* (Cambridge: MacMillan, 1892), 142.

20. Archibald Thomas Robertson, *Word Pictures in the New Testament* (Nashville: Broadman Press, 1931), 389.

21. MacArthur, 170.

22. Zane C. Hodges represents an interpretation which understands James 2:14–26 to refer to Christians whose faith is no longer vital and vibrant rather than to the false, hypocritical faith of unregenerates. (See his *Dead Faith—What Is It? A Study of James 2:14–26* [Dallas: Redencion Viva, 1987].

23. Ryrie, 46–47.

24. Ibid., see footnote 22.

25. Ibid., see footnote 23.

26. See Charles C. Ryrie, *Balancing the Christian Life* (Chicago: Moody Press, 1969, pp. 170–73 and Everett F. Harrison, "Lordship Salvation," *Eternity,* September 1959.

27. Roy B. Zuck, "Cheap Grace?" *Kindred Spirit,* Summer 1989, 6.

28. Harrison.

29. See Hodges, 67–76, 83–88 for an excellent discussion of the meaning of discipleship in the New Testament. Also see J. Dwight Pentecost, *Design for Discipleship.*

30. Zuch, 7.

31. Harison.

32. Zuch, 6.

CHAPTER 19—THINGS WHICH ACCOMPANY SALVATION

1. John F. Walvoord, ed., *Systematic Theology* (Wheaton: Victor Books, abridged ed., 1988), 2:131–48.

2. J. I. Packer, "Regeneration," *Baker's Dictionary of Theology* (Grand Rapids: Baker Book House, 1960), 440.

3. See John Murray, *Redemption Accomplished and Applied* (Grand Rapids: William B. Eerdmans Publishing Company, 1955), 95–96.

4. John F. Walvoord, *The Holy Spirit* (Findlay, OH: Dunham Publishing Co., 1958), 135.

5. Ibid., 131–32.

6. Millard J. Erickson, *Christian Theology* (Grand Rapids: Baker Book House, 1985), 3:954.

7. See for fuller discussion John Murray, pp. 132–34.

CHAPTER 20—GOD'S SECURITY AND MAN'S ASSURANCE

1. For a strong defense of the security of the believer, see Robert Glen Gromacki, *Salvation Is Forever* (Chicago: Moody Press, 1973). All of the problem passages are dealt with in this volume. For defense of the contemporary Arminian view of this subject, in other words, the denial of security, see Robert Shank, *Life in the Son* (Springfield, MO: Westcott Publications, 1960) and I. Howard Marshall, *Kept by the Power of God* (Minneapolis: Bethany Fellowship, 1975).

2. David N. Steele and Curtis C. Thomas, *The Five Points of Calvinism Defined, Defended, Documented* (Philadelphia: Presbyterian and Reformed Publishing Co., 1963), 56.

3. F. F. Bruce, *The Epistle of Paul to the Romans* (Grand Rapids: William B. Eerdmans Publishing Company, 1975), 178–79.

4. James M. Stifler, *The Epistle to the Romans* (New York: Fleming H. Revell, 1897), 158–59.

5. John Allen, trans., *Institutes of the Christian Religion* (Philadelphia: Presbyterian Board of Christian Education, 1936), 3:2:16.

6. I recommend Gary R. Habermas' book *Dealing with Doubt* (Chicago: Moody Press, 1990).

7. In *So Great Salvation* (Wheaton: Victor Books, 1989), 142–43 Charles C. Ryrie summarizes three reasons why believers lack assurance.

8. Zane C. Hodges, *Absolutely Free* (Grand Rapids: Zondervan Publishing Company, 1989), 50.

9. John MacArthur, *The Gospel According to Jesus* (Grand Rapids: Zondervan Publishing Company, 1988), 23.

CHAPTER 21—STRUGGLES WITHIN AND WITHOUT

1. See David C. Needham's *Birthright* (Portland: Multnomah Press, 1979) for a full-length defense of this view. MacArthur and other lordship

enthusiasts also hold the same view. MacArthur wrote, "I believe it is a serious misunderstanding to think of the believer as having both an old and new nature. Believers do not have dual personalities . . . there is no such thing as an old nature in the believer" (John MacArthur, *Freedom from Sin—Romans 6—7* [Chicago: Moody Press], 31-32). For refutation of the above, see Lewis Sperry Chafer, *He That Is Spiritual* and Renald E. Showers, *The New Nature* (Neptune, NJ: Loizeaux Brothers, 1986).

2. Philip E. Hughes, Baker's Dictionary of Theology, 470.

3. I heartily recommend *Five Views on Sanctification* (Grand Rapids: Zondervan, 1989).

4. See excellent discussion on the Christian and self-love in Norman L. Geisler's *Ethics: Alternatives and Issues* (Grand Rapids: Zondervan, 1978), 139-157.

5. I highly recommend the regular memorization of Scripture. The Bible Memory Association, Box 12000, Ringgold, LA 71068-2000 has an excellent program for all ages.

CHAPTER 22—BACKSLIDING

1. This passage (1 John 3:4-9) has been interpreted variously. The question is, what does John mean when he says one who abides in Christ sins and one who sins has not known God? R. W. Stott, in *The Epistles of John* (Grand Rapids: William B. Eerdmans Publishing Company, 1974), 131-32, summarizes the most popular answers to this question: (1) The sins refer to specific and notoriously wicked sins; (2) What is sin to the believer is not sin to God since He sees the believer through Christ; (3) The old nature continues to sin but not the new nature within the believer; (4) John was here describing the ideal and not reality; (5) Willful and deliberate sin is in view; (6) Habitual and persistent sin is in view.

The translators of the New American Standard Bible embraced this latter view as can be seen from the emphasis placed upon the "practice" of sin in their translation of the passage.

2. Brooke Foss Westcott, *The Epistles of St. John* (Grand Rapids: William B. Eerdmans Publishing Company, 1952), 19.

3. Adolph Saphire, *The Epistle to the Hebrews* (New York: Loizeaux Brothers, 1946), 663.

4. John R. W. Stott, *The Epistles of John* (Grand Rapids: William B. Eerdmans Publishing Company, 1974), 77.

5. Westcott, 24-25.

CHAPTER 23—YOU—THE GOSPEL—THE LOST

1. Three helpful books on this subject are *Evangelism and the Sovereignty of God*, by J. I. Packer (Chicago: InterVarsity Press), *The Theology of Evange-*

lism by Ernest Pickering (Schaumburg, IL: Regular Baptist Press); and *Life-Style Evangelism* by Joseph C. Aldrich (Portland: Multnomah Press).

2. R. V. G. Tasker, (Grand Rapids: William B. Eerdmans Publishing Company, 1974), 90.

Scripture Index

OLD TESTAMENT

NEW TESTAMENT

SUBJECT INDEX

PERSON INDEX

Abelard 105
Aldrich, Joseph C. 298
Alford, Henry 56, 288
Allis, O. T. 204
Anderson, Norman 287
Anselm 105
Archer, Gleason 287
Arminius, Jacob 107
Barr, James 295
Barth, Karl 286
Berkhof, Louis 70, 93, 95, 289, 290, 292
Bloesch, Donald 289
Bock, Darrell 295
Boettner, Loraine 94, 290, 291
Boice, James Montgomery 204
Braun, Jon 172, 293, 294
Bridges, Charles A. 294
Brown, F. 294
Browson, Michael 294
Bruce, F. F. 229, 296
Buswell, James Oliver 19, 74, 285, 289
Calvin, John 78, 239, 260, 289, 326
Campbell, McLeod 105
Chafer, Lewis Sperry 33, 82, 285, 289, 293, 297
Chantry, Walter 203, 294, 295
Chilton, David 286
Clark, Gordon 286

Clement of Alexandria 68
Clement of Rome 68
Cottrell, Jack 166, 293
Craig, William 129, 292
Crawford, Thomas 291
Creme, Benjamin 287
Dana, H. E. 245
Demars, Gary 286
DeWolf, Harold 290
Driver, S. R. 294
Eiseley, Loren 129
Erickson, Millard J. 34, 38, 285, 286, 287, 288, 296
Feinberg, Charles L. 285, 288
Ferrante, Joseph M. 294
Geisler, Norman 130, 285, 292, 297
Gentry, Kenneth 294
Green, Michael 288, 294
Gromacki, Robert 288, 296
Grotius 105
Harrison, Everett 203, 295
Hick, John 288
Hodge, A. A. 112, 291
Hodge, Charles 93, 151, 204, 289, 290, 292
Hodges, Zane C. 293, 295, 296
Hoekema, Anthony A. 285
House, Wayne 286
Hughes, Philip Edgecomb 297
Ice, Thomas 286

313

ANNOTATED BIBLIOGRAPHY

The following book list has been divided into three categories. These three—Beginner's Level, Intermediate Level, and the Advanced Level—will enable you to find the particular help you need.

SIN

Beginner's Level

Boice, James Montgomery. *Foundations of the Christian Faith* (appropriate sections). Downers Grove, IL: InterVarsity Press, 1986.

A basic study of the fall of the race and its results.

Geisler, Norman L. *Is Man the Measure? An Evaluation of Contemporary Humanism.* Grand Rapids, MI: Baker Book House, 1983.

The various kinds of humanism are examined and evaluated from philosophical, scientific, ethical, and biblical perspectives.

Ryrie, Charles C. *Basic Theology* (appropriate sections). Wheaton, IL: Victor Books, 1987.

In outline fashion the major areas of the doctrine are set forth from a biblical perspective.

Intermediate Level

Erickson, Millard J. *Christian Theology.* Vol. 2 (appropriate sections). Grand Rapids, MI: Baker Book House, 1984.

The author discusses the nature, source, results, magnitude, and social dimension of sin.

Hoekema, Anthony A. *Created in God's Image*. Grand Rapids, MI: Eerdmans, 1986.

The important doctrine of the image of God in man—its meaning and significance—is discussed.

Walvoord, John F. (ed.). *Lewis Sperry Chafer's Systematic Theology*. Abridged edition. Vol. 1 (appropriate sections). Wheaton, IL: Victor Books, 1988.

From a dispensational perspective, the author presents the biblical doctrine of sin.

Advanced Level

Clark, Gordon H. *Behaviorism and Christianity*. Jefferson, MD: The Trinity Foundation, 1982.

The secular and the Christian positions are contrasted.

Geisler, Norman L. *The Roots of Evil*. Grand Rapids, MI: Zondervan, 1978.

A philosophical and biblical analysis of the origin, nature, and purpose of evil.

THE SAVIOR

Beginner's Level

Gunn, James. *Christ the Fullness of the Godhead*. Neptune, NJ: Loizeaux Brothers, 1983.

This work emphasizes the deity and humanity of Christ.

Ryrie, Charles C. *Basic Theology* (appropriate sections). Wheaton, IL: Victor Books, 1987.

All the major aspects of the person and work of Christ are included and defended from Scripture.

Sanders, J. Oswald. *The Incomparable Christ*. Chicago, IL: Moody, 1971.

A well-illustrated treatment of Christ's person and work.

Intermediate Level

Borland, James A. *Christ in the Old Testament*. Chicago, IL: Moody, 1978.

All relevant Scriptures related to Christ in the Old Testament are included.

Lightner, Robert P. *The Death Christ Died*. Schaumburg, IL: Regular Baptist Press, 1983.

A scriptural defense for the unlimited extent of the atonement.

Snyder, John. *Reincarnation vs. Resurrection*. Chicago, IL: Moody, 1984.

A contemporary problem explored and evaluated.

Advanced Level

Anderson, Charles C. *Critical Quests of Jesus*. Grand Rapids, MI: Eerdmans, 1969.

An evaluation of all the liberal historical quests for Jesus.

Warfield, Benjamin Breckinridge. *The Person and Work of Christ*. Philadelphia, PA: Presbyterian and Reformed, 1950.

A classic defense of the Christ of Scripture.

SALVATION

Beginner's Level

Buis, Harry. *The Doctrine of Eternal Punishment*. Philadelphia, PA: Presbyterian and Reformed, 1957.

Traces the biblical teaching through Old and New Testaments and historical and contemporary thought.

Gromacki, Robert Glenn. *Salvation Is Forever*. Chicago, IL: Moody, 1973.

Addresses not only the positive biblical evidence but also the problem passages.

Hodges, Zane C. *Absolutely Free*. Grand Rapids, MI: Zondervan, 1989.

This is an excellent response to MacArthur's *The Gospel According to Jesus*.

Ryrie, Charles C. *So Great a Salvation*. Wheaton, IL: Victor Books.

Distinguishes between the one condition of salvation and making Christ Lord of one's life.

Intermediate Level

Horne, Charles M. *Salvation*. Chicago, IL: Moody Press, 1971.

Written from the 5-point Calvinistic perspective.

Ironside, H. A. *Except Ye Repent*. Grand Rapids, MI: Zondervan, 1972.

Traces the doctrine in Scripture and sets forth its consistent meaning.

MacArthur, John F. *The Gospel According to Jesus*. Grand Rapids, MI: Zondervan, 1988.

Sets forth the thesis that to be saved the sinner must trust Christ as his substitute for sin and enthrone Him as Lord of his life.

Packer, J. I. *Evangelism and the Sovereignty of God*. Chicago, IL: InterVarsity Press, 1961.

Relates the two doctrines to each other from a strong Calvinistic position.

Advanced Level

Morris, Leon. *The Apostolic Preaching of the Cross*. Grand Rapids, MI: Eerdmans, 1980.

Explores the New Testament meaning of critical issues related to the death of Christ.

Scott, John R. W. *The Cross of Christ*. Chicago, IL: InterVarsity Press, 1986.

Relates the Cross to salvation and living the Christian life.